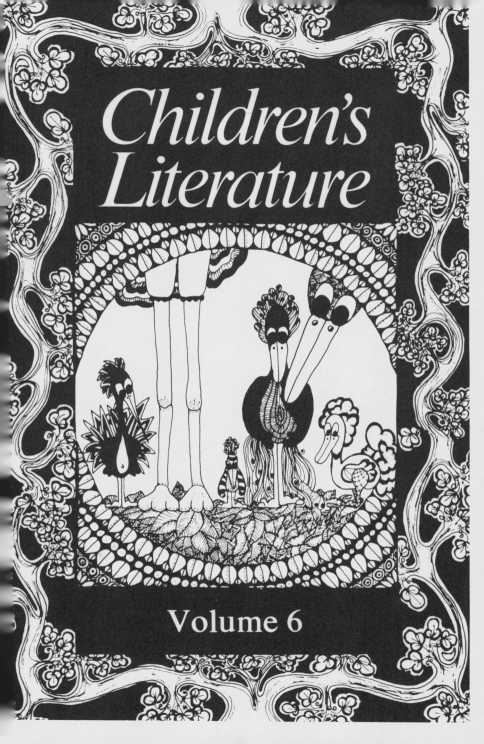

Children's Literature

Volume 6

Children's Literature

Volume 6

Children's literature: the great
excluded

Volume 6

Annual of
The Modern Language Association
Group on Children's Literature and
The Children's Literature
Association

Temple University Press
Philadelphia

"Children's Literature"

EDITOR-IN-CHIEF:
  FRANCELIA BUTLER
COEDITORS:
  LEONARD R. MENDELSOHN and
  WILLIAM E. SHEIDLEY

BOOK REVIEW EDITOR:
  MERADITH TILBURY McMUNN

ADVISORY BOARD: Marilyn Apseloff; Bennett Brockman, Chairman; Martin
  Gardner, Narayan Kutty, Alison Lurie, William T. Moynihan, Peter F.
  Neumeyer, William Rosen, Glenn E. Sadler
CONSULTING EDITORS: Rachel Fordyce, Jan Bakker, Ross Miller, Thomas J.
  Roberts
SPECIAL CONSULTANTS: Charity Chang and Edward G. Fisher
CONSULTANTS FOR THE CHILDREN'S LITERATURE ASSOCIATION:
  Alethea Helbig and Jon C. Stott
MANAGING EDITOR: Peter S. Anderson
EDITORIAL ASSISTANTS: Carol Boardman, Sharon Hann-Johnson, Howard
  Mayer

Editorial Correspondence should be addressed to:
  The Editors, *Children's Literature*
  Department of English
  Concordia University
  Sir George Williams Campus
  Montreal, Quebec H3G 1M8
  Canada
                    or
  The Editors, *Children's Literature*
  Department of English
  University of Connecticut
  Storrs, Connecticut 06268

Manuscripts submitted should conform to the second edition of the *MLA Sty
Sheet.* An original and one copy are requested. Manuscripts should be
accompanied by a self-addressed envelope and postage.

International Standard Book Number: 0-87722-104-9 cloth; 0-87722-105-7 paper
Library of Congress Catalog Number: 75-21550
Cover illustration by Elizabeth Arnold

Contents

Copy 2

The Editor's High Chair

Articles

Reviews

Varia

Children's Literature

Volume 6

The Editor's High Chair

With the publication of Alex Haley's *Roots,* all ethnic groups are beginning to search out their own roots. As a result, there is a great and growing interest in that universal root literature shared by children and adults: the folktale. Important meetings such as that of Children's Books International IV at the Boston Public Library in 1978 are planned to investigate the folktale.

Actually, however, the role of the folktale as the literature of the future began with the Brothers Grimm in the nineteenth century. Literary figures, including the critic, G.K. Chesterton, added impetus to the growth of the literature. In the early twentieth century, his seminal essay, "The Ethics of Elfland," was influential enough so that it was later included in an anthology of great essays edited by the philosopher-mathematician, Alfred North Whitehead. Chesterton pointed out how fairy (folk) tales open our eyes: "They make rivers run with wine only to make us remember, for one wild moment, that they run with water."

Other important writers have fostered the continued growth of respect for folktales. In "On Fairy-Stories," J.R.R. Tolkien has compared folktales to the soup at the back of an old stove: "The Pot of Soup, the Cauldron of Story, has always been boiling, and to it have continually been added new bits, dainty and undainty."

Psychologists of various schools have also furthered the growth of interest in folklore. Bruno Bettelheim's best selling work, *The Uses of Enchantment,* urges the wholesome quality of the tales. In his essay, "A Note on Story," (*Children's Literature*, Volume 3), James Hillman of the Jung Institute, Zurich, describes how, as a depth psychologist in Zurich for thirty years, he has used folktales to help adults get the jig-saw puzzles of their minds together. Folktales are therapeutic for all ages.

At the present time, "adult and child have come to be set against each other," according to Hillman. If this is the case, then it would seem to follow that it would be good to set up national story-telling centers, where students could be trained to tell stories to the major ethnic groups. The storytellers could go out into the towns and cities, into neighborhoods, gather children and adults, and tell them some of the most loved folk stories of that particular group—Greek, Jewish, white or black.

In the Centers, besides the trainers of storytellers, there could be scientists and scholars in various disciplines—clinical psychologists, psychiatric social workers, cultural anthropologists—who would prepare questionnaires which could be taken into the neighborhoods, and when completed, would give a more comprehensive picture of neighborhood needs and problems.

It may be argued that the ancient art of storytelling is not practicable in a television-oriented world. But such eminent child psychologists as Dr. Jerome Singer at Yale have indicated they believe that families can be retrained to listen if they are convinced of the wholesomeness of Story for all concerned. Not only the listeners but the tellers would benefit, for the practice would give work to many hundreds of young and old people who (hopefully) would be paid partly by the town, partly by the government. Instead of remaining passive, old people could tell stories. (That they can write poetry has already been demonstrated by that imaginative and people-loving writer, Kenneth Koch, in *I Never Told Anybody Teaching Poetry in a Nursing Home*. New York: Random House, 1977.)

Some persons concerned with sex role stereotypes and violence in folktales have failed to see that folklore contains all of life, the good and the bad, and helps us to achieve a psychic balance. But important scholars of children's literature, including Virginia Haviland and Anne Pellowski, have long appreciated the wisdom of the tales, which they have collected and disseminated. Universities have recognized the significance of the study of folklore and have established Institutes, such as that at Indiana University, and have produced such valuable works as the Stith Thompson *Motif-Index,* which is used internationally.

This issue of *Children's Literature* begins with an interview with one of the great friends of the folktale, the famous Yiddish novelist, I. B. Singer, an ardent believer in the future of the folktale as a shared literary experience for children and adults. A previously neglected fairy tale by Samuel Johnson is also printed in this issue, with an accompanying essay by its editor, Ruth MacDonald. The fairy tale and the essential nature of fantasy are investigated in separate articles by Jane Filstrup and James Heisig. Three articles consider prominent illustrators—Arthur Rackham,

William Blake, Maurice Sendak, and William Kurelek—while a fourth is concerned with perhaps the most famous if the most controversial applicant of the illustrator's art, Disney, and his enduring duck. National literatures receive scrutiny with discussions of two British classics, *Peter Pan* and *Treasure Island,* and with an assessment of Gorky's role in disseminating children's classics in Soviet Russia. The historical dimension is supplied by a consideration of Drayton's *Nymphidia* and by the journal's ongoing forum on the concept of childhood in the Middle Ages, conducted in this issue by the eminent medievalist, C. H. Talbot. Francelia Butler writes on the literary experience of children in a nineteenth-century commune. There are as well the review articles (as opposed to book reviews), which survey and analyze current developments in the immense world of children's books. Finally, there is Constance Gremore's helpful comprehensive index to the first five volumes of *Children's Literature.*

—Francelia Butler

Articles

Isaac Bashevis Singer on Writing for Children*

Emanuel Goldsmith, author of *Architects of Yiddishism at the Beginning of the Twentieth Century,* has described Isaac Bashevis Singer as "one of the most remarkable authors who has ever lived . . . wiry, inescapable style, an intensely personal, inimitable vision, a Machiavellian wit, but above all else, it is the bracing, revivifying character of his insights that makes him important."

Mr. Singer is a born story teller beloved both by children and adults because of the warm humor and wisdom of heart embodied in his writing.

Question (Q). Most folktales and fairytales were originally intended for adults. Through the years they have been abandoned to the children. What kinds of behavior do these tales try to teach and what is the effect of these teachings on children?

I. B. Singer (A). I don't believe that most of the fairytales and stories were created to teach people anything, and this is a good thing, because once a story is made to teach, one can foresee what it is going to say. Fairytales I admire most. You read a story and then when the story is ended you ask yourself what does it teach? What is it saying? You are bewildered by their pointlessness, but they are beautiful anyhow and I think that children love these kinds of stories.

For example, my father used to tell me stories—religious kinds of stories—about a man who was a good man on this earth and then he died and went to Paradise. These kinds of stories used to bore me, because I knew already that the good people go to Paradise and the bad people are roasted in Hell. But sometimes my mother told me stories which were so pointless that you really could learn nothing from them. Let's say that a bear swallows three children or something like this and then they cut open his belly and the children go free. A story like this had no meaning, but it had beauty. In children's literature the writers of course can tell a story with a moral, but they should be careful not to be too much on the didactic side. The stories should have beauty in themselves.

*Questions asked of Mr. Singer by students of Children's Literature at Von der Mehden Auditorium, The University of Connecticut, April 3, 1977.

The great works of literature actually teach us nothing. What does *Madame Bovary* teach us? That a woman that was unfaithful to her husband commits suicide? We know that not all women who betray their husbands commit suicide or are killed. Many of them live to an old age. When Tolstoy wrote *Anna Karenina*, the story was the same. Anna also betrayed her husband and she also committed suicide. We learn actually from *Anna Karenina* nothing, for whatever we had to learn we could already have learned from *Madame Bovary*. But the story is beautiful anyhow. I think it is a great tragedy that modern writers have become so interested in messages that they forget that there are stories which are wonderful without a message; that the message isn't everything. I once said that if all the messages would disappear and only the Ten Commandments would be left, you would have enough messages for the next 10,000 years. It is not the message which is so important but the story itself. But many writers live today in a kind of amnesia. They forget that a story has an independent life. It can exist without a message, although a message is sometimes good for it, but only sometimes.

Q. Were you a writer or storyteller as a child? Who told stories to you when you were a child?

A. Well, first of all my father and mother were both excellent storytellers. They told us stories. I heard stories all the time. In addition I used to read what they used to call storybooks in Yiddish. These were little books which cost a penny apiece. I used to buy them. I said once that if I would have a million rubles—I would buy all these storybooks. Actually there were not enough storybooks to buy them for a million rubles; there were only maybe a few score. I read the stories of the famous Rabbi Nakhman of Bratzlav, a famous rabbi who was not only a great saint and a great Jewish scholar, but also a great poet, one of the most puzzling personalities who has ever lived. And he told stories which his disciple wrote down and these stories influenced me immensely. I would say that although he was a rabbi and a saint there was no message in his stories. His disciple said that those who know the Cabala will find out what the message is. Since I was not a great Cabalist then and I am not yet today, I love the stories by themselves. I never found any message in them, but they are most fantastic and wonderful. I am astonished that these stories are not yet made as literature for children. I intend, if it's possible, to write a kind of digest of them. I still love stories and readers always call me up, since my telephone is listed in the telephone book, and if they tell me they have a story to tell me, I say immediately, "Come up! I want to hear it." I still think that the story is the very essence of literature. When writers forget the art of storytelling, they forget literature. It's a great tragedy that writers have forgotten their main aim, that they have to tell stories.

Q. Will you please explain the origin of Yiddish folktales and do you take all your children's stories from Yiddish folktales?

A. I don't take all my stories from Yiddish folktales because I invent stories myself. After all, these folktales were invented by someone; the people did not tell them all. There was always a man who talked out the story and then it became a part of folklore. I would say I use both methods. If I find some that are beautiful folktales, especially those which were told to me by my mother and father, I would use them. And if not, I say to myself, "I am a part of the folk myself. Why can't I invent stories?" And, of course, I have invented a number of stories. Sometimes I hear a little story, a spark of a story, and then I make from the spark a fire. At least this is what I try to do. My mind is full of stories and to me the human history is actually an aggregation of millions of little stories. If a day passes in my life without a story, I am disappointed. But thank God, one way or another, the Almighty is always sending stories to me. As far as the origin of the stories, their origin is the human imagination. What else?

Q. In your lecture here a year ago, you stated that "Symbolism is not good for children because although by nature a child is a mystic, he is also by nature a realist." In what ways is a child a mystic and a realist, and how conscious are you of simplifying the symbolism for children for the sake of clarity as you put it?

A. As a rule every good story is symbolic and if it doesn't have a symbol, you can try to find a symbol or invent a symbol. Children have a great feeling for mysticism. They believe in the supernatural; they believe in God; they believe in angels; they believe in devils. They don't question you if you tell them a story which is connected with the supernatural. But children don't like nonsense. There are some writers who think that if they write a story which doesn't make any sense, just because it makes no sense it is full of symbols. Symbolism is often a wall behind which unable writers hide in order to make themselves important. I have seen many writ-

ers who think that a child can take nonsense, and it isn't true. A
child will believe in the supernatural, but even in a supernatural
story, the child wants logic and consistency. I once read a story
where a man said that three little stones fell into a kettle and out
came three little monkeys. The child just does not believe in these
things. Although I am very much against Russia, I think that they
are right about one thing: that writing nonsense and telling children
things that are completely unbelievable is not good for the child's
mind. Because although the child has less experience than the
adult, the child has already a sense of logic and knows what makes
sense and what doesn't make sense. Distortion of reality is not
really symbolism. Distortion of reality is bad writing. Many of
these little books which make no sense at all are doing damage to
children's literature. First of all, a lot of people set out to write,
because if you are not bound by any logic and by any consistency,
everybody can be a writer. The child, good and independent reader
that he is, is also a severe critic. The wonderful thing about children is that you cannot hypnotize a child to read a story because
the author was a great man. You can tell him it was written by
Shakespeare or by the Almighty himself, but the child does not
care about authority. If the child doesn't like a story, the child will
reject it immediately. The same thing is true about reviews. No
child will read a story because it got good reviews. Children, thank
God, don't read reviews. Of course, children don't care at all about
advertising. If the story was advertised on the whole page of *The
New York Times* it will not change the child's mind about the story.
I wish that our adult readers would be as independent in this respect as the children are. And because they are great readers and
independent readers and because they are not hypnotized by all
this mish-mash, one should be very careful with them. One should
never give them nonsense and say that this is symbolic. The great
symbols don't come from nonsense but from sense. The stories
from the Bible and the Book of Genesis are full of sense and at the
same time highly symbolic.

Q. When asked why your stories for children always have happy
endings you have been quoted as saying, "If I have to torture
someone, I would rather torture an adult than a child." In what
other specific ways do you alter your writing for children?

A. I try to give a happy ending to a story for a child because I
know how sensitive a child is. If you tell a child that a murderer or

a thief was never punished and never caught, the child feels that there is no justice in the world altogether. And I don't like children to come to this conclusion, at least not too soon.

Q. Many of your children's stories include traditional folk material from Jewish culture. Would you call yourself more of a storyteller or a story creator?

A. First of all the reason why they all come from Jewish tradition is that I believe literature must have an address. You cannot write a story just about people. When you tell a story to a child, "There was somewhere a king," the child would like to know where the king was. In Ireland, in Babylonia? The same thing is true about adult literature. Literature, more than any other art, must have an address. The more the story is connected with a group, the more specific it is, the better it is. Let's say we write a letter to Russia. First, you say it's to Russia. Then you have to say, what city? What part of Russia? What is the number of the house and so on and so on until you come to the specific person, and when you mail it, it will come right there to the intended person. The same thing in a way is true about literature. The more specific it is the more influence it has on a reader.

Q. Critic Marilyn Jurich argues that the nature of Yiddish folk humor is to urge acceptance. She says, "Change for the poor, oppressed, cannot be realized, not by the ordinary man. To urge change is to meet despair or destruction. Only deliverance is from God and the only joy is in experiencing God's presence in whatever peace is attainable." Do you feel this urging of acceptance is a characteristic of your writing for children?

A. I would say that all generalizations, especially about literature, are false. Of course, there may be such stories also, but to say that all Jewish stories are of this kind is false to me. By the way, I don't really understand exactly what she means by "accept." Of course, if we write a story we want it to be accepted. What is the meaning of the word "acceptance"? She wants the poor people to be accepted by the rich? You explain it to me; Do you know what this critic is saying?

Q. Well, I think that she is saying by acceptance to accept that which is given to you, if it is suffering, to accept suffering. If it be fortune, to accept fortune.

A. I don't really try to teach my readers that they should accept all the troubles in the world. In other words, if there was a Hitler, they should accept Hitler. Actually the Jew has not accepted the badness of the world. It is a Christian idea that we should accept everything. I would say that a Jew, although he believes that everything is sent by God, he is also a man of great protest. Of rebellion. Fighting evil. And because of this to say that the Jewish story is of acceptance is kind of a generalization, which does not really jibe with our reality. We have never accepted neither Hitler nor Haman, none of the enemies of humanity. The opposite. We fought them. It is true that in the Hitler holocaust, the Jew who fought Hitler, was like a fly fighting a lion. But just the same it is not in our nature to be passive when the evil powers come out.

Q. What do you think about the study and criticism of children's literature in the universities?

A. I know that the universities teach writers who want to write for children and it's a wonderful thing; and I am very happy to see so many people here interested in this. But I really don't know enough about the universities to come to any generalization. I would say that wherever I go, people are interested. Children's literature is not anymore a stepchild of literature. It's becoming a very legal kind of literature. Of course, children's literature is still very young. One hundred years ago it almost did not exist. It did not exist among the Jewish people in my time. We didn't have such a thing as literature for children. I think that children's literature has a great future because it is still telling a story. In this respect it has never become ultra-modern.

Q. Some children's book experts believe in a prescribed vocabulary for children at various age levels. Your stories, even for the very young, contain much vocabulary that some might call too advanced for young children. How conscious are you of your vocabulary when writing for children?

A. I would say that if you don't remember all the time that a child is a child and you treat him as an adult, there is a good chance that the child will act like an adult; if not one hundred percent at least fifty percent or sixty percent. Because of this I am not very careful about using words which people think that the child will not understand. Of course, since I write in Yiddish sometimes these words in Yiddish may be more simple than they come out in English but I will say a child will not throw away a book because there are a few words that he does not understand. The opposite— the child will be intrigued and will look into a dictionary or it will ask the mother or the teacher what the word means. A child will throw away a book only if there is no story, if it doesn't make sense and is boring. Amongst the adults there is lately a theory that a good book has to be boring; that the greater a bore, the better writer he is; some writers even boast about it—how boring they are. The great masters tried their best to be easy and to be understood. Any child can read *Anna Karenina* or even *Madame Bovary* if it has a feeling for love and sex. So I am not afraid of difficult words.

Let's not forget about one hundred years ago, eighty years ago or even fifty years ago, whole generations were brought up on poetry. They were brought up on Pushkin and Byron. A book of poetry was in every house. Many young women and young men learned poetry by heart. But what happened to poetry now-a-days? It has become so erudite, so confused and so obscure, that people just stopped enjoying it. So now the biggest publishing company publishes a book of poetry in 800 copies and 500 are given away to reviewers and other poets. The poet of today began to speak to other poets. He speaks to nobody else. There is a great danger that this may happen to adult literature altogether. It will become so profound and so erudite that it will be like a crossword puzzle, only for pedantic minds who like to do these puzzles. I am often afraid that this may happen to children's literature. I know that it cannot happen, because the child will say, "No," in a big voice.

Q. In your discussion last year of the conditions necessary for you to write, you spoke of three things. You must have a plot, you must have a passion to write, and you must feel that you are the only one that can write that particular story. What special thing do you think that you have that you share with children?

A. I would say that I see to it that the stories which I tell the children no other writer would have told them. This does not mean that they are better than other stories. When you read a story by Andersen, you will know that this is not a Grimm story. It is an Andersen story. When you read a story by Chekov, you say this is not a Maupassant story, but a Chekov story. The real writer manages to put his seal on his work. He tells you a story which others cannot tell. Only if I see that this story has my "seal," it is sort of, say, my story, I will tell it. And this is the reason I will not just write stories about abstract things which any other writer might be able to do. A Russian story must be Russian and a French story must be French. You may be an internationalist, you may be cosmopolitan, you may think that all the nations are clannish and we should unite. But when it comes to literature, you cannot really move away from the group and its culture.

When I write a story, whether it's adult or for children, I have to say, "This is my story."

Children in the Middle Ages

C. H. Talbot

In a short paper, it is impossible to discuss all the ideas about childhood in the medieval period which various writers have put forward. But one that needs remarking upon at the outset is that which propounds the theory that in the Middle Ages "no distinction was made between the different levels of childhood." Anyone who is at all conversant with the biographies of the saints; with the lives of abbots, monks, and nuns; or with the chronicles of monasteries and cathedral churches written between the eighth and twelfth centuries will realize that such a theory is untenable. If one accepts that according to medieval ideas there were only two stages in life before reaching adulthood, namely *infantia* and *pueritia,* and that these two stages covered the years from birth until the age of fifteen, it would seem that "childhood" in the modern sense differed little, if at all, from the medieval concept and that its developing stages were clearly understood. Early texts are smothered with phrases like "when he had gone beyond the years of infancy and reached the time of childhood"; "when he had outgrown the age of infancy and reached the age of reason (*aetatem intelligibilem*)"; "when his years of infancy were over and he was about seven"; and so on. In the life of Cuthbert there is a phrase that is even more precise: "when he was in the first year of his childhood, that is, in his eighth year," and in that of Bertulph: "when he was a boy about eight years of age." It would be tedious to repeat such evidence, piling one example on another. People in the Middle Ages were quite aware of the differing needs in children as they grew in stature, strength, and intelligence. And they were careful to observe the different patterns of behavior as the baby was swaddled, weaned, given to nurses, handed over to tutors, and finally allowed to fend for himself. In the same way, childhood was sharply defined from puberty; the days of discipline and tutelage from the time of adulthood and freedom. The texts are legion, but these few examples should suffice: "When I emerged from the state of childhood and began to enjoy the freedom of doing what I liked," says one; "when he had reached the age of puberty and grew to a man's strength," says another; "when he had attained the age of puberty, when it is usual to enter on the ways of the world''; and finally ''when he had thrown off the usual schoolboy's yoke and was free to go his own way.''

As to the idea that medieval people did not recognize the psychological differences between children and adults, one has only to read the descriptions, given by Bartholomaeus Anglicus in the thirteenth century, first of boys and then of girls:

> Boys have tender bodies, but they are flexible, very light and easy in movement. Their minds are docile, without a care or an anxiety in the world, and because they lead a sheltered life, the only things they appreciate are those that make them laugh. Their only fear is that of being beaten with a cane. They would much rather have an apple than a bar of gold. As they have no sense of shame they have no hesitation in disclosing their private parts, and whether they are praised or blamed they care not. They are quickly aroused to anger, but just as quickly placated. Because their flesh is tender they are easily hurt and they find hard work difficult. They are extremely unstable. They have a tremendous appetite for food, and because they eat too much they tend to suffer from various ailments. They are known to inherit disease from their diseased parents, as anyone can see from the case of lepers and those who suffer from gout. Boys can be distinguished from adults by the sound of their voices and the expression of their face.

To this description Bartholomaeus adds that of Aristotle:

> Little boys often display bad habits and behaviour. They think only of the present and have no thought for the future. They delight in all kinds of games and tomfoolery, and refuse to take any account of money and other useful things. Indeed, the most important things in life seem to have little worth in their eyes. They always want what is bad for them. They prefer the company of boys of their own age to that of grown-ups. They will cry and wail over the loss of an apple or pear more than over the loss of their inheritance. They never remember anything good that is done for them and they want whatever they set their eyes on, demanding it either by shouting or violent movements of their hands. They love gabbling and talking with boys of their own age, but avoid the company of their elders. They are quite incapable of keeping a secret, and no matter what they see or hear, they repeat it immediately, so that everyone knows about it. They are quick to laughter and quick to tears, continually shouting, chattering and laughing. Even when they are asleep or

dozing they cannot keep quiet. As soon as they are washed and cleaned they get dirty again, and whilst they are being washed by their mother or having their hair combed, they struggle with all their might to get away. They think only of their bellies and never know when they have had enough, so that they are always wanting to eat and drink. No sooner have they got out of bed in the morning than they immediately start to eat again.

Without going into the physical differences between boys and girls, which Bartholomew naturally enumerates, the following characteristics apply to girls:

> Their voices are higher, they speak with great facility and volubility; they walk with short, mincing steps; they easily show bad temper, are impertinent, remorseless in their hate, full of envy, impatient of work, craft, bitter-tongued and easily led into passion and lust.

Aristotle's ideas are not much different, except that he adds the fault of "being too prone to lying."

That these descriptions of children are not mere academic exercises can be shown from those passages in numerous books where the ideal child is depicted as not always joking and laughing and getting into trouble, as not a glutton for food, and so on. Take this example from the life of St. Guthlac:

> When he had passed the infant stage and began to talk like a small boy, he was absolutely no trouble either to his parents, his nurses or to groups of little children of his own age. He never took part in the pranks of the boys, he did not listen to the gossiping of the old married women, he showed no interest in the silly stories bandied about by the common folk, he took no notice of the frivolous and lying tongues of hangers-on, took no part in the senseless bawling of the farm-labourers, and did not try to imitate the cries of various birds and animals as boys of his age usually do.

What one can infer from this is that the rest of the children in the village, allowed a free rein, were up to every kind of mischief that their boisterous spirits led them to. They gave vent to every expression and activity which their untamed and untutored natures urged on them. Whether this differed in any marked respect from what happens in childhood now is a rhetorical question.

The age of seven was the time when childish exuberance was

first put under restraint. Then came the moment when the boy was put under a tutor or sent to school and when the girl, either at home or in a convent, prepared herself for duties in later life. But very often a child began to learn his or her letters long before that age was reached, and we read of children of five years of age, of three even, who started their schooling almost as soon as they could speak. Bardo, born in Opershoven in 981, was sent to a woman named Benedicta as soon as he was weaned "and while he lay in her bosom she taught him all she knew, so that in a short time, almost like playing, he learned the whole psalter." The same approach may be elicited from St. Jerome's letter of advice to Gaudentius on the education of his small daughter, Pacatula:

> Let her get to know quite early the forms of the letters, joining up syllables, learning the names of things and then combining words. And to encourage her to repeat the words in her shrill little voice offer her cakes and sweetmeats, titbits, beautiful flowers, sparkling stones or enchanting dolls as a prize if she makes progress. And in the meantime let her separate threads with her fingers and tear pieces of cloth, so that she will learn not to tear it later on. And after she has finished her work let her play games, cling to her mother's neck, and be kissed by all around her. Let it be a pleasure for her to learn what is imposed on her, so that it may seem not hard work but a game. But when the little maid with her milk teeth *has reached the age of seven* and begins to blush, let her learn how to keep quiet, to think before she speaks and to memorize the psalter.

Jerome then proceeds to outline the further stages in her upbringing.

It will not have escaped the attention of the reader that in this particular case the teaching of the child was carried out within the circle of the family. This was by no means an exception. From the ninth century onwards there are increasingly frequent instances of small children being educated by their own parents, especially where the children were destined for a lay career, and this points not only to a tender affection for children, to a desire for imbuing them with a love for learning, but also to the liberal education of the parents themselves. Of Luidger, later bishop of Münster, who died in 809, the following details are recorded:

> As soon as he could walk and talk he began to collect the rind and bark of trees (the material we use for lights), and everything

of the sort that he could find. And while the other children were playing, he used to make himself little books out of the things he had gathered. When he could find any fluid, he imitated those who write, and he used to carry them to his nurse to take care of, as if they were useful books. When anyone said to him: "What have you been doing today?" he would answer that he had spent the whole day making books, or writing, or reading. And when he was asked further: "Who taught you," he would reply "God taught me."

Apart from the story being charming, it indicates that the child was familiar with books, with reading and writing. Had he not seen these activities exercised in his home, he could not have known anything about books or pens or reading and writing.

In the life of John of Gorze we read that his father, who was nearly ninety years of age when John was born, could not bear to let him out of his sight, and so the boy was educated at home during his tender years. Odo of Cluny, speaking of his own father, said: "He knew by heart all the histories of the ancients and the *Novellae* of Justinian (the code of law). At his table during meals there was always reading of the gospel." Everhard, count of Friuli, whose will was dated A.D. 867, divided all his books among his several children, leaving the most precious of them, a complete Bible, to his eldest son.

The majority of children, as has been said, began their formal education at the age of seven. Most of them would have learned the alphabet by that time and would have been able to link the letters together to form words and even to read. But there were some who had not progressed this far, and they had to start at the beginning. It may well be, as some writers affirm, that children learn their letters by constant repeating after the teacher, but there is evidence to show that they also learned them by writing them down. One little fellow (his name escapes me at the moment) whose daily task was to write down on his *tabella* the letters he had learned each day so that the teacher could check on his progress was found to have three times more letters than he should have. When he went to bed at night his *tabella* had the proper number, but by the time he woke up for school the letters were in triplicate. Only the angels could have achieved such a feat! This was also the way that elder people, desiring in later life to achieve some measure of literacy, taught themselves. Charlemagne, who never attained any proficiency at writing but was an avid reader, kept such a *tabella* under his pillow so that if he did not sleep well, he could refresh his memory during the night. Another literary aspirant, whose vocation was guarding cattle in the fields, asked a passing monk to teach him the alphabet, but since the monk had neither parchment nor *tabella* on which to write it, he inscribed the letters on the man's belt. The cowherd, thus equipped, soon learned to read and make up words.   Perhaps, at this point, it might be expedient to explain exactly what a *tabella* was. It appears in many cases to have been a slate framed in wood and furnished with a handle such as one sees on a hair brush. (There is an illustration of this in the Katherinen Gradual, where the child, who is holding one in his left hand, is being dragged by his mother reluctantly to school.) But there was another kind consisting of a wooden tablet covered with wax. Parchment was much too expensive for use by untutored pupils endeavoring to form their first letters. Even for accomplished scholars, the use of the wax tablet as the basis of their first draft was usual. Drafts of letters, financial accounts, records of ecclesiastical synods or councils— anything, in fact, of a nature which required correction, emendation, or polishing—were consigned to wax tablets. William of Newburgh, writing his commentary on the Song of Songs, complained that he could find no one to transcribe his wax tablets to parchment. The poet Baudry de Bourgeuil was grateful for a gift of such tablets, eight in all, which were fastened together with twine to form a small book and covered with green wax, whose color was more gentle on the eye. If this was the case with the writing of important texts, it was all the more so with the first gropings of children with the ABCs.

As for actual learning, it was, except for the few, a painful task to which adjustment was not made too easily. Shakespeare's description of the schoolboy as "creeping like snail/Unwillingly to school" was as applicable in the Middle Ages as it is now. The teacher or *paedagogus* was by definition a man of severe countenance and rigorous discipline. It was easy for Ratherius of Verona to say: "You are a master and should strive to be loved rather than feared," but with a clutch of forward pupils more attracted to play than lessons, it was difficult to put into practice. Some pupils, as Ratherius admitted, were incredibly stupid. One boy, the son of a rich merchant, could not repeat the alphabet after three years' coaching. Some were recalcitrant and others plain lazy, but here and there a few could be found who were quick-witted and studious, able to absorb more than the teacher could give them. Tolerance, therefore, was the quality of a good master. Alas, such masters were rare. The rod was unstintingly applied—so much the more easily as the child's frock, when lifted up, usually revealed bare buttocks, unprotected by underpants and such like frivolities. A box on the ear or a bang on the head with a book was even simpler and equally effective. One young pupil, slow to learn his lines, was struck so frequently over the ear with a psalter that he remained deaf in one ear for life. Some of the boys undoubtedly deserved such punishment, such as the one described by Guibert of Nogent, a handsome boy of rich parents, who hated discipline, who was a born liar and a thief, who continually absented himself from school and spent his days skulking in the vineyards. Guibert himself on the other hand was a diligent scholar, but rather slow and dull. His teacher was an old man who had taken up literary studies only late in life and who was not sufficiently competent to explain problems with that simplicity which is demanded by the mind of a child. When Guibert failed to learn what the old man was incapable of teaching, he was beaten unmercifully. After one such calamitous day of unlearned lessons and undeserved stripes, he was asked by his mother as he crept to her knees whether he had been beaten that day. Upon his unwillingness to implicate the old man, his shirt was taken off to reveal the black-and-blue weals inflicted on his back by re-peated canings. His mother was outraged that so tender a child should have been subjected to such savage beatings and with her eyes filled with tears declared: "Never again will you go to school: you shall never more suffer such pain just to learn letters." But Guibert, who took these beatings as a matter of course, affirmed his determination to continue his schooling even if it should kill him.

It was to lessen the vulnerability of children to such occasions of punishment that Ratherius wrote a book for Rostagnus, the son of a wealthy friend, when he was sent to study grammar at the monastery of Lobbes. He entitled the book *Sparadorsum* because its purpose was to explain the rudiments of learning in so simple a fashion that a small child could easily understand it and so "spare his back" from the usual thrashings.

But not all boys were so fortunate. We have the instance of a small boy in London, easily led astray at that tender age by the example of his playmates, who went off to play games and completely forgot about his lessons and the warnings of his schoolmaster. When the next day dawned and the time came for him to show what homework he had done, he was stricken with fear because he could not remember a single line of his lessons and could think of no excuse. So he ran away from school and eventually found himself in the Church of St. Paul, where he began anxiously to pray at the tomb of St. Erkenwald. The master meanwhile, noticing his absence from the class and realizing that he was playing truant, went in search of him and found him gabbling away at his prayers for deliverance. The master, who had already made up his mind to give the boy as many stripes as the mistakes he made in his lessons, told him to stand up, recite his lines, and repeat, without the help of a book, the content of the lesson. To the consternation of the teacher the boy rattled it off from memory without a single mistake.

That little girls did not fare any better than their male counterparts can be inferred from a number of texts. One of the most vivid instances is that of St. Mildred. She was sent abroad by her mother to be educated in a French convent not far from the sea. For some reason not specified, but perhaps because she defied the mistress, the irate abbess treated her roughly and pulled out her hair. The poor child, unable to send tidings to her mother overseas, waited until some English travelers visited the abbey, and then, enclosing strands of her bloodied hair in a manual of prayers, she begged them to deliver it to her parents on their return home. The response was swift and decisive. A ship was put to sea, manned with armed men, and Mildred was snatched away and brought home.

Though beatings were common, they were not always looked upon as necessary or even desirable. A certain abbot, who was discussing with St. Anselm the education of small boys, said to him: "What shall I do with them? We never stop beating them and yet they seem to get worse instead of better." "What are they like when they grow up?" said Anselm. "Dull and no better than animals," answered the abbot. "You must be feeding them on an extraordinary diet," said Anselm, "to transform rational creatures into animals." "We try every way we can" said the other "to restrain them and make them better, but all to no purpose." "Tell me, Father abbot," said Anselm:

If you planted a tree in an orchard and then closed it in on all sides so that it could not stretch out its branches, what kind of a tree would you have after a few years? Would it not be useless, with branches all twisted and intertwined? And whose fault would it be except yours, who have restricted it too much? This is exactly what you are doing with your small boys. They are planted in the orchard of the school in order to grow and bear fruit, but you terrify them so much with your threats and stripes, that they have no freedom at all. And so, since they are crushed down without discretion, they turn their minds to thinking up ways of avoiding correction, and of acting deceitfully and obstinately. Because you show them no affection, no compassion, no goodwill or gentleness, they get the impression that all your actions towards them are rooted in hatred and envy. And as they grow older, so the feelings of rancour and suspicion increase, because human nature is prone to evil ways. Have you ever seen a goldsmith working? Does he create a most beautiful human figure out of silver and gold simply by continually hitting it? I think not. Sometimes he gently presses and taps it, at other times he smoothes and moulds it into shape. So should you act. Well-baked bread is good and useful for him who can digest it, but if you give it to a suckling child it will choke rather than feed him. In the same way that a small child needs milk, so does it need mildness, kindness, compassion, cheerful encouragement, living support and many other things of the same kind.

When talking of schools and discipline, we must not carry away the idea that all was misery and severity. St. Aelred had this to say to his sister, who was a recluse:

Do not allow little girls to come to your cell. There are some recluses who spend their time teaching little girls, so that their hermitage is turned into a school. She sits at the window and and they sit down outside. As she gazes on each one of them and watches their childish antics, she first gets angry, then laughs, then threatens. At one moment she is caressing, at another she is beating them. After that she beckons nearer the one that has just been punished and strokes her face, clasping her round the neck and embracing her, calling her daughter one minute and darling the next.

Aelred did not agree with this kind of behavior because it distracted the recluse from her true vocation, but it is obvious from his words that affection for children and gentle treatment, as well as rough, was not unusual.

In this connection it should be pointed out that the high mortality among children during the Middle Ages did not entail, as some would have us believe, a hardening of attitudes towards the young. Biographical narratives of medieval times record numerous examples of mothers dying from grief at the loss of a child, of others falling into deep melancholy and mental unbalance when bereft, of uncontrollable sadness leading to loss of interest in life and even to suicide. The lives of the saints are full of stories of mothers bringing their sick and dying children to be restored to health and life, whilst a court poet, Paul the Deacon, lamenting the death of the baby Hildegard, could write: "So small a maid to leave so great a sorrow."

It is also a fallacy to believe that all children who died in medieval times were the victims of disease, of malnutrition, of neglect, or of some other social disaster. In most cases small children died from accidents caused by their own playfulness, curiosity, willfulness, or ignorance. Time and time again we read of children falling down wells, being drowned in streams or marshes, being scalded by boiling water, breaking limbs whilst playing, being thrown from a horse, cutting themselves with knives, swallowing rings and necklaces, and so on. In all cases the parents were distraught and could not be consoled until the child was sound and well again. Two examples will suffice. A little boy, accompanied by his younger sister, was aimlessly roaming about in the manor of Ingham when by chance he fell down an unused well. The bottom was full of thick mud and he was sucked down so deep into it that neither his body nor his clothes could be seen. The little girl began to cry and called out that her brother was buried in the well. Upon hearing her, the mother began to wail piteously and, sobbing, picked up a rake and ran to the well where she scraped feverishly in the mud trying to catch some part of his clothing. At length the rake caught his clothes and she was able to drag the boy out, but whether he was alive or dead could not be seen. They carried him home, washed him, rubbed him, laid him in front of the fire, and waited for him to show some signs of life. But he did not move. After prayers were said for his recovery he suddenly began to breathe, opened his eyes, unloosed his clutched fists, slowly regained strength, and within a short time was walking, laughing, and babbling as small boys usually do.

Another little boy, not yet three years old, was one day playing with a knife at Cuckfield, when he fell down. The knife pierced his chest to a depth of nearly three inches and remained fixed in his body. The accident happened about three o'clock in the afternoon and no one could staunch the blood which flowed continually until the time of vespers. The mother was frantic with grief, while the father, heavy with sorrow, resigned himself to the death of the child. Recognizing in the child's pallor and the rigidity of the limbs the signs of death, the mother began to lament, "My child is dead, my child is dead" and was inconsolable but made a vow to go on pilgrimage to the tomb of St. Edmund should the child recover. Almost immediately the child stirred, looked at his mother, and said, "No, mother, I am not dead, I am still alive." Within a short time, to everyone's relief and joy, he recovered.

These and hundreds of other instances are evidence enough that parents in the Middle Ages were not indifferent to the loss of their children. Nor were they lacking in affection and compassion for those of their children who were born deformed. It is too painful to repeat the descriptions of such malformed creatures, who invariably struck observers with horror and disgust, but the devotion with which they were tended by their parents, often of very limited means, is wholly admirable.

The story of Hermann the cripple must be familiar to every one concerned with the Middle Ages, but it bears repetition for the light it throws on this aspect of regard for children.

From his earliest years he was afflicted by a kind of paralysis which crippled all his limbs. . . . The joints of his body were so monstrously loosened that if he were placed in any position he could not move at all and was quite incapable of turning on his side without help. When he was placed in a chair, in which he was usually carried about, he could not sit upright and could not bend over to do anything at all. His mouth, his tongue and his lips were so contorted that he could hardly express any intelligible sounds, though he tried to do so in a kind of drawling babbling fashion. Yet he was always gay and smiling, always trying to talk to those who would listen to him and very keen on taking his part in discussions. If he had anything new to express, he used to scribble it down with his weak and crippled fingers.

He had been brought to the monastery by his parents when he was very small and it was there, surrounded by compassionate and un-

derstanding companions, that he grew to manhood, receiving and
giving great affection. He eventually became an accomplished
scholar, poet, musician, and scientist, one of the first to make and
then to explain the intricacies of the astrolabe.

School was not one unending task of learning lessons. There
were holidays when children were free from restraint and when
they could give full vent to their childish whims. We read of them
going down together with the master to the seashore, scrambling
over the sands, and getting washed out to sea by the rising tide. We
read of the pranks they played on the feast day of the Holy
Innocents and of their attempts, not unlike the "rags" of today to
capture some important person and hold him to ransom. At San
Gall, as luck would have it, they grabbed hold of the abbot himself
and, hedging him about, pushed him towards the master's chair
and set him down. Gazing on them in smiling amusement, not
unmixed with an air of severity, he said, "So you have made me
your master for today? Very well: I will exercize the master's privilege. Strip!" A sense of doom descended on the giggling assembly
and laughter turned to gloom. Then one precocious youngster
piped up and reminded the abbot that corporal punishment could
always be bought off by an impromptu Latin verse. So a reprieve
was granted, and when two of the boys had dashed off rhyming
couplets, the abbot embraced them, granted three extra days' holiday for the whole school, and paid for a feast besides.

There were also theatrical performances to amuse the children.
Gerhoh of Augsburg relates that when he was master of the
scholars there he was not only present at such performances but
presided over them. No doubt the plays of Roswitha filled a gap on
holidays also. Strictly moral though her dramatic situations were,
farce was not excluded, and the scene where the governor
Dulcitius emerges smutty-faced from his amorous embracing of
pots and pans, which he has mistaken for religious virgins, must
have raised a ripple of laughter.

Apart from these entertainments, which were artificial, there
were plenty of games of all kinds to relieve the monotony of school
life: running, leaping, wrestling, swimming, ball games, and many
other exercises in which strength, agility, stamina, and competi-
tiveness were tested. Rough play was normal and a certain amount
of teasing, especially of sensitive children, was not unknown.
When Adalbert of Prague was going home from school one day, his

companions pushed a girl who was passing into the mud. Then for a joke, they threw Adalbert on top of her. The other scholars coming up behind them ran up to see what was happening—laughing and guffawing and making coarse jokes until the boy was reduced to tears.

When it is asked, what kind of books did the children read at school, it must be conceded that practically all of them were of a didactic nature. Grammar, syntax, arithmetic, and other boring subjects cannot be transformed into enthralling stories. But it would be a mistake to think that because there was nothing on the same plane as *Winnie the Pooh,* nothing to claim the attention of a child existed. The fables of Aesop and Phaedrus were available, as they are now, and they were illustrated. The *Aeneid* of Vergil was a widely read book in which even the youngest could find pleasure, for it contained elements of everything that could play upon the emotions and excite the imagination. Children shed tears over the fate of Dido, they felt pity and terror at the destruction of Troy, and they were roused to enthusiasm over the games—when teams of rowers competed for the coveted trophy and when, after the boxing match, the young bull was felled by one tremendous blow from the cestus-bearing victor. We know all this from the admission of scholars who, later in life when their tastes had altered, begrudged the time they had spent on the "figments and lies" of the poets.

And if it be thought that children would not have sufficient grasp of Latin to enjoy poets like Vergil, it should be recalled that many teachers would not allow any language except Latin to be spoken in their class. When students at the age of fourteen went to the universities, they were forbidden to speak any other tongue but French and Latin under pain of fine. In this connection it is not without relevance that Grotius brought out an edition of Martianus Capella's *Marriage of Philology and Mercury,* one of the basic texts in medieval schools, at the age of fourteen. But apart from Vergil there were other poets who held a fascination for young minds, and by the twelfth century other fruitful sources of imaginative literature were in the hands of students. Aelred himself recalls how he and his companions wept over the story of Arthur.

But what of the boys who were not sent to school to learn letters and who were destined for a secular career? From scattered remarks one receives the impression that they were brought up by

their parents to develop their bodies rather than their brains, or at
best, to become acquainted with the running of an estate and the
administrative tasks connected with it. But we also have positive
evidence, particularly from Italian towns, that boys were taught to
exercise martial pursuits from an early age. At Pavia there was a
mock battle in the main square of the town on every Sunday between the beginning of January and Ash Wednesday. The city was
divided into two parts, north and south, and both parts were separated into parishes, each with its own "regiment." The boys fought
with wooden weapons, sometimes two by two but more often
parish against parish. They were armed with wooden shields and
wore helmets made of wickerwork, padded inside to soften the
blows. Over the face they wore interlaced iron guards. Helmets
were decorated with a device showing to which parish they belonged. Attached to the helmets were tails of horsehair, so that if
the boys fell or were beaten to the ground, their companions could
pull them to their feet. This martial display was still common in the
fourteenth century. But at Brescia, where, perhaps, such games
had got out of hand, they were forbidden in 1313 for all boys except those under ten years of age.

We have been speaking so far about that small section of the
populace which had the means and the leisure to enjoy a literary
education. The books written by this minority and addressed to a
minority cannot possibly mirror the outlook or the conditions of
the common folk. The romances on which so much emphasis has
been laid, with their doughty knights and their glamorous ladies, reflect the life of the court and the attitudes of mind that went with it,
and they are about as characteristic of the community as monastic
customs or the rules for recluses. They provide a very slanted view
of medieval society. To say, as does Ariès, that the family in the
Middle Ages was simply an institution for the transmission of a
name and an estate is a gross distortion. It may have a seed of truth
if applied exclusively to the upper classes. But what of the vast
majority, who had neither name nor estate? Until quite late, at
least in England (and we can include the Celtic fringe), a man was
known by the name of his father—Jack's son, John's son,
William's son, Fitzgerald, Fitzpatrick, Fitzmaurice, and so on, or
he was distinguished from others by the addition of his
birthplace—John of Salisbury, etc. Later his name would be provided by his craft—Baker, Smith, Cook, Mercer, Draper, Farmer,

and so on. In cases like this there was always a strong family tie, for the simple reason that the family was an economic unit. The family worked together to provide the members with as good a livelihood as their combined efforts could achieve. The fact that children from an early age began to adapt themselves to the serious task of living within that family did not imply a lack of feeling or affection for them on the part of their parents. Children willingly undertook to share in domestic duties, enjoying the small responsibility that was laid on them and eager to release their parents for work on more arduous tasks. Nor did it entail a loss of "childhood." To lead the cows to pasture, to watch the sheep in the meadows, to bring back the horses or oxen from ploughing, to feed the chickens or collect the eggs—all these activities, admittedly, are worlds apart from reading fairy stories. One concerns the world of reality, the other of "make-believe." But to infer that there is not as much delight in the one as there is in the other is wholly to misunderstand what a child really likes. The only parallel that remains with us today by which an understanding of medieval conditions can be gained is that of a predominantly agricultural or craft community. These communities can be seen in action not merely in Eastern countries but in many parts of Europe as well. To witness the happy look on the face of a little girl of three driving two huge bullocks back to their stalls with no more than a wisp of willow; to watch a small boy of ten enthusiastically helping his father to repair a motor engine; to meet four boys between the ages of nine and fourteen engraving intricate patterns on Persian metal work, these and other instances do much to remove the impression that children are happy only when they are fooling about. Children's intelligence, initiative, love of responsibility, and joy in exercising skill are much underrated. Nothing irks children as much as being treated like children. They wish, as far as is possible, to be the equals of their elders: they look forward to the day when they will be independent. Medieval people recognized this and encouraged it. Surgeons like Lanfrank wrote books on surgery for their young sons: Bertapaglia allowed his son of eleven to assist him at surgical operations; Chaucer composed his treatise on the Astrolabe for "little Lewis"; and merchants of every kind encouraged their boys to help with the accounts. There was no coercion in this. A child will naturally try to imitate what he sees his elders doing, often against the express wishes of his parents or teachers.

Otloh of Ratisbon, speaking of his early days, says:

> When I was still a little child I was sent to school where I
> quickly learned my letters, and long before the time when I
> should have learned to write and without any command from my
> master I began to practise writing. But I did this in a furtive way
> and without anyone showing me how to do it. As a result I got
> into the habit of holding my pen the wrong way. I became so
> accustomed to this that my teachers were unable to correct me
> afterwards and I found it quite impossible to alter. Many who
> noticed this said that I would never be able to write well, but by
> the grace of God it turned out otherwise.

He became one of the most prolific scribes of his age.

It is only in this sense that the assertion "the child became the
natural companion of the adult" has any truth. In all the monastic
customs, in all the regulations for schools and much else, a strict
separation of child from adult was enforced. They read and studied
in a separate part of the cloister, they slept in separate dormitories,
concessions were made to their age which would not be counte-
nanced in grown-up people. The Middle Ages was well aware of
the difference between child and adult, but the great difference between our own attitude and that of the medievals is that they recognized when the age of childhood came to an end. They did
not try to enforce an artificial childhood on girls and
youths who had reached the stage of puberty. They had no
sentimental ideas about treating as schoolboys those youths whose
change of voice, ebullient strength and spirit, impatience of parental authority, and assertive independence showed them to be ripe
for the world of men. If nature had fitted them for the responsi-
bilities of parenthood, nothing but disaster could follow from an
attempt to keep them wrapped up in swaddling clothes. To say that
the seventeenth century changed all this is not a reason for con-
gratulation but indictment. And the outbreaks of violence from
youth resentful of the negation of their rights as adults is confirmation of it. Too late and too tardily, legislators are beginning to re-
vise their views on what constitutes an adult. Within the past few
years the age at which a person is considered adult has been low-
ered from twenty-one to eighteen, to sixteen, and already the age
of fourteen is under consideration.

A complex question of childhood in the Middle Ages cannot be
resolved in a brief article. But not all has been said on this matter
and further assessment is desirable.

REFERENCES

The sources of the material contained in this article are from numerous medieval texts. The principal ones are given below.

Bartholomaeus Anglicus, *De rerum proprietatibus*.
Chrodegang of Metz, *Patrologia latina*, 89.
D'Achery et Mabillon, *Acta Sanctorum Ord. S. Benedicti*, 7 vols.
Guibert de Nogent, *Patrologia latina*, 156.
C. Horstman, *Nova Legenda Angliae*, 2 vols.
Lanfranc, *Patrologia latina*, 150.
Mabillon, *Annales Monastici*, Paris, 6 vols., pp. 1703–1739.
Pertz, *Monumenta Germaniae Scriptores*, II.
Ratherius of Verona, *Patrologia latina*, 136.
Rerum Italicarum Scriptores, XI, i.
Udalrici, *Consuetudines*, *Patrologia latina*, 149.
Wroswitha, *Patrologia latina*, 137.

Michael Drayton's Nymphidia

A Renaissance Children's Classic?

Warren W. Wooden

The major difficulty encountered in discussing children's nonacademic reading during the Renaissance is that little, if any, children's literature as such (books, as F. J. H. Darton puts it, "which would openly allow a child to enjoy himself with no thought of duty nor fear of wrong"[1]) was published prior to the eighteenth century. Yet long before they became a distinct object of the book trade, English children read avidly of whatever literature was available to them, and in the process they made some adult books—*Pilgrim's Progress, Robinson Crusoe, Gulliver's Travels* are all familiar instances—their own. But of the various kinds of ostensibly adult literature to which children have been drawn, the fairy tale has endured as the most popular.

Early evidence of this affinity is sparse but tantalizing. In *The Tatler* (No. 95: 1709) Richard Steele describes a visit to the home of his eight-year-old godson. The boy had abandoned Aesop to immerse himself in medieval and Renaissance chivalric romances. As for the boy's little sister, Steele writes that "the mother told me, 'that . . . Betty . . . deals chiefly in fairies and sprights.' "[2] What had the little girl, who according to her mother was a better scholar than her brother, been reading of fairy lore? One critic speculates that "it seems likely that these fairies and sprites were of native origin."[3] Another suggests, "she may possibly have come upon *Nymphidia* or Spenser or browsed among the poets."[4]

Michael Drayton's *Nymphidia* (published in 1627) has been justly called "the finest of all seventeenth-century fantasies."[5] Critical consensus no longer considers the prolific Drayton a major Renaissance poet.[6] It is nevertheless true, as his modern editor remarks, that "*Nymphidia* has won wider and more continued popularity than any other poem of Drayton's."[7] I suggest that much of the sustained popularity of Drayton's fairy poem lies in its particular appeal to children, and I propose to analyze the elements in the poem which contribute to this appeal.

Like his Warwickshire countryman William Shakespeare, Drayton was originally a country boy, widely read but without university training, who made his mark in London as a poet of talent and versatility. And again like his friend Shakespeare, Drayton appears to have written for the widest possible popular audience. Thus in the early seventeenth century, while Donne and the metaphysical poets wrote for and circulated manuscripts among an avant-garde intellectual coterie and Jonson and the Tribe of Ben wrote neoclassic verse for the cultivated and aristocratic, Drayton aimed at a far wider reading public. Consequently, he insisted on printing his verse—"attempting," one recent critic persuasively argues, "to write for a national audience," not just for the Court or for Londoners but for an audience widely dispersed all through the country.[8] Although we assume the *Nymphidia* was written with an adult audience in mind, the calculated breadth of appeal for which Drayton strove certainly contributed to the comparative accessibility of his work to children. As a fairy story treated in the mock-heroic mode, the *Nymphidia* is constructed to give pleasure to various strata of the reading public—the well educated and the casual reader, the courtier-sophisticate and the country-traditionalist. The first two stanzas of *Nymphidia* announce Drayton's intention to cultivate this wide range of appeal:

> Olde CHAUCER doth of *Topas* tell
> Mad RABLAIS of *Pantagruell,*
> A latter third of *Dowsabell,*
> with such poore trifles playing:
> Others the like have laboured at
> Some of this thing, and some of that,
> And many of they know not what,
> But that they must be saying.
>
> Another sort there bee, that will
> Be talking of the Fayries still
> Nor never can they have their fill,
> As they were wedded to them;
> No Tales of them their thirst can slake,
> So much delight therein they take,
> And some strange thing they faine would make,
> Knew they the way to doe them.[9]

The first stanza announces the mock-heroic treatment of the subject, a technique specifically literary and presupposing the reader's familiarity with both ancient and modern classics of the heroic genre. Similarly, the range of allusion speaks to a well-educated audience, for Chaucer's English was rough going for many seventeenth-century readers and Rabelais was not widely available in English. But stanza two evokes the native, oral tradition of fairies—tricksters as familiar to children as to adults. Drayton then announces at the outset that he casts with a wide sweep, suggesting a readership of varied literary backgrounds and implicitly promising something for everyone including young readers.

Among the pleasures to be shared by readers of every background, for example, are those imparted by meter, rhyme, and stanza form. It seems likely that a modern critic's observation that "poetry, unlike other forms of literature, is common ground for both children and grown-ups,"[10] would have been axiomatic in the early seventeenth century, when poetry still dominated prose as *the* medium of literary expression. *Nymphidia* is composed of eighty-eight verses of a surprisingly versatile 8-line stanza rhyming *aaabcccb*. It is a development of the 6-line tail-rhyme stanza of Chaucer's *Sir Thopas* which was similarly designed to deflect the meter of the old heroic ballads and metrical romances to humorous purposes. Drayton's b-tail rhymes are double however and generally in trimeter as opposed to the tetrameter of the a- and c-lines. As one might expect, the effect of the short-line stanza built on triplets and punctuated with feminine rhymes is lively and mercurial. The poetic form complements the impetuous capering of the fairies and contributes significantly to the poem's sense of good fun. Drayton's absolute mastery of this frolicsome stanza is nowhere so evident as in the fairy Nymphidia's spell (11. 409–432) however, when the poet subdues his stanza for an incantation which might well have sent a pleasurable thrill through a young reader. A full appreciation of the comic effect of *Nymphidia's* stanza form finally depends upon reading the poem aloud so that the triplets and feminine rhymes may receive full emphasis.

Despite Drayton's references to Chaucer and Rabelais and his indebtedness to the stanza form of *Sir Thopas*, it is the fairy poetry of Shakespeare to which *Nymphidia* is most directly indebted. As numerous critics have pointed out, the domestic difficulties of Oberon and his queen in *A Midsummer Night's Dream* suggests the plot of *Nymphidia*, where in place of the changling boy the complication is provided by a rival suitor for the Queen's favors.[11] The main plot—a court intrigue featuring the maneuvering and folly of Oberon, Queen Mab, and the rival suitor, the fairy-knight

Pigwiggen—furnishes the focal action. Almost as important as the plot however are the minutely detailed descriptive passages, a *sine qua non* of fashionable post-Shakespearean fairy poetry (see Jonson, Herrick, William Browne), which derive from the famous description of Mab and her chariot in *Romeo and Juliet*. The whole occurs in an English pastoral setting with the actions of the principals treated in mock-heroic fashion, paralleling the antics of the tiny creatures with the heroes of classic and romance. Further, the sophisticated reader is invited to delight in such mock-epic conventions poet and fairies blunder through as the invocation to a muse; Oberon's heroic frenzy, mad as Ajax or Orlando Furioso; the inventory of the hero's armor; the formal preparations for a trial by combat; and the intervention of a goddess in the climactic combat.

It seems likely that a large segment of Drayton's intended audience, including most youthful readers, would not be able to appreciate fully the literary humor of much of this mock-heroic. For the less sophisticated audience suggested by stanza two, however, Drayton offers pleasures of another kind. In addition to the broad-based appeal of the native fairy lore which Drayton generously loads into the interstices of the slender plot, the fairies' mock-heroic antics are genuinely humorous in their own right, without reference to literary models and allusions. The "minifying" technique,[12] popularized by Shakespeare's Queen Mab passage, results in descriptive passages of ingenuity and charm and the English pastoral setting keeps the poem in contact with the contemporary countryside and its folklore. It is primarily these features of the *Nymphidia* which, once the poem was in the house, were capable of imparting a special kind of pleasure to children. Of course there is much in *Nymphidia*, as there is in *Gulliver's Travels*, which children will not understand, but Drayton has pitched his poem at such a broad audience that there is much more in the poem to which a child will respond with alacrity and delight.

The fairy folklore which informs *Nymphidia* draws directly on the familiar materials of childhood, the tales of fairies and sprites learned at mother's or nurse's knee and passed about from child to child. Thus, although Drayton's fairies may derive from a larger European tradition and may mock sophisticated codes of courtesy and conduct in their love and war, they are still, simultaneously, the fairies of the English countryside. Puck and Tom Thumb are here; the beauteous Queen Mab is still she of the Night-mare (11. 53–56). The fairies engage in all the pursuits of traditional English fairy folklore—the pinching of mortals, the penny reward for cleanliness (11. 65–68), the stealing of changelings (11. 73–80). In combining the oral with the literary traditions of the fairy world, Drayton seeks to interest readers of every background, while incidentally providing for young readers a reassuringly familiar subject treated in a new way. Regardless of whether it was a part of Drayton's intent, in *Nymphidia* he created a bridge from the oral tradition of native folklore to the great world of European classical literature, a bridge most children of the time were constrained to cross in far more sober vehicles.

As the transition from one literary tradition to another might have challenged and excited the young reader of *Nymphidia,* so Drayton's descriptive technique, sharply detailed against the fantastic foreground, exerts a powerful imaginative appeal to the child in its equipoise of reality and fantasy. The stanzas describing the arming of the fairy knight Pigwiggen, who has challenged Oberon to combat, may serve as an example of this descriptive technique:

> And quickly Armes him for the Field,
> A little Cockle-shell his Shield,
> Which he could very bravely wield:
>   Yet could it not be pierced:
> His Speare a Bent both stiffe and strong,
> And well-neere of two Inches long;
> The Pyle was of a Horse-flyes tongue,
>   Whose sharpnesse naught reversed.
>
> And puts him on a coate of Male,
> Which was of a Fishes scale,
> That when his Foe should him assaile,
>   No poynt should be prevayling:
> His Rapier was a Hornets sting,
> It was a very dangerous thing:
> For if he chanc'd to hurt the King,
>   It would be long in healing.

11. 489–504

Here the ingenuity of Drayton's description of his diminutive warrior equipped with rustic weapons and armor stimulates the imagination in the combination of the familiar and the fantastic. By carrying through this minifying technique—far more regularly than Shakespeare does in *A Midsummer Night's Dream,* though with less mathematical precision than Swift would employ in Lilliput—against the native pastoral background, Drayton goes far toward the creation of a self-contained universe of fairyland with an atmosphere and logic all its own. As in most successful fiction, this atmospheric unity derives largely from the key elements of the narrative: plot and character.

Despite rich descriptive passages and folklorist interpolations, *Nymphidia* possesses a clear plot furnished with plenty of action. Flirtatious Queen Mab is the central figure with Oberon and Pigwiggen, abetted by their agents Tom Thumb and Puck, in competition for her favor. The presumption of Mab's infidelity causes Oberon to run mad, after the fashion of Orlando Furioso. But in Drayton's miniaturized world, Oberon's frenzied encounters become increasingly farcical: he mistakes a glowworm for a devil, at a hive of bees he is thoroughly bedaubed with wax and honey, he tumbles off an ant he has mounted into more dirt and slime, he collides with a molehill which he takes for a mountain, he scales the molehill and falls down the other side into a lake. Oberon's mock-heroic misfortunes are harmless, simple and physical, of the pie-in-the-face variety which would delight a child who had never heard of Homer, Ariosto, or Cervantes. This plot pattern of sound and fury eventuating in laughter dominates the narrative, establishes the poem's tone, and dictates the happy ending, where Proserpina (no less) intervenes in the trial by combat between Oberon and Pigwiggen, "For feare lest they too much should bleed, / Which wondrously her troubled" (11. 631–632), to set all right again through a judicious application of Lethe water. All exit "with mickle joy and merriment" (1. 702), in harmony with the atmosphere of good humor which pervades the poem.

Within Drayton's miniature pastoral cosmos, the elphine protagonists mimic human passion and folly, thereby highlighting both the pettiness and the humor of aspects of the human condition customarily treated seriously. Here too there is an appeal to children who might not fully comprehend the intricacies of the love plot. In *Nymphidia,* the fairies behave like many human adults, controlled generally by passion and impulse rather than reason, averting tragedy as they carom around their picturesque universe only through luck or the fortuitous intervention of a providence they can't remember. And unlike the motivation of the fairies in *A Midsummer Night's Dream*, which is relatively complex, with multiple perspectives on most issues including the royal quarrel, *Nymphidia* simplifies and de-emphasizes moral conflict by focusing on the ridiculous. Surely the spectacle presented by the fairies of adult posturing and folly in the name of love would delight all but the most unperceptive children.[13]

Nor is there a hidden moral lurking in the recesses of Drayton's fairy world to edify the unwary. The compulsive moralist might discern in the fairies' antics the old humanistic lesson of the folly and degradation of a life given over to blind passion. But if this is the message—and it seems criminal to abstract a moral so coldly from so lively and diaphanous a poem as this—it emerges only dimly and with difficulty.[14] Rather, the truth of the matter seems the obvious: *Nymphidia* is designed not to instruct but to delight by giving pleasure to different types of readers of widely diverse literary intelligence and comprehension.

In sum, *Nymphidia* possesses all the attributes of a successful fairy tale for children, even while it is demonstrably something other and more than that. It has fallen into neglect in our own time as the work of what one critic aptly calls "today the least fashionable of important Elizabethan poets."[15] If it is dismissed now as a narrative poem too long to fit comfortably into the standard anthologies of children's verse, it seems most unlikely *Nymphidia*'s rollicking good humor and capacity for imaginative stimulation would have escaped the notice of either Steele's friend Betty or the children of the preceding age. It is a work which deserves a prominent place not just in the annals of fairy poetry, but in the history of early English children's literature.

NOTES

1. F. J. H. Darton, *Children's Books in England: Five Centuries of Social Life*, 2nd ed. (Cambridge: University Press, 1958), p. 1. The usual critical procedure is to ignore altogether the preadult portion of the Renaissance reading public. Even such standard studies of the Renaissance English reading audience as Louis B. Wright's *Middle-Class Culture in Elizabethan England* (1935) and Edwin H. Miller's *The Professional Writer in Elizabethan England: A Study of Non-dramatic Literature* (1959) avoid any discussion of children and their reading habits.

2. *The British Essayists*, ed. A. Chalmers (Boston: Little, Brown and Co., 1856), II, 363.

3. Katherine M. Briggs, *The Fairies in English Tradition and Literature* (Chicago: University of Chicago Press, 1967), p. 175.

4. Darton, *Children's Books in England*, p. 33.

5. Oliver Elton, *Michael Drayton: A Critical Study* (New York: Russell and Russell, 1966), p. 137.

6. As late as 1909, for example, Drayton was still accorded a full chapter in the *Cambridge History of English Literature.*

7. *The Works of Michael Drayton,* ed. J. William Hebel, (Oxford: Shakespeare Head Press, 1961), V, 202. On the popularity of Drayton in his own day, see Bernard H. Newdigate, *Michael Drayton and His Circle* (Oxford: Shakespeare Head Press, 1961) and Joseph A. Berthelot, *Michael Drayton* (New York: Twayne Publishers, 1967). For the fullest survey of Drayton's reputation and the publication history of the poetry see Russell Noyes, *Michael Drayton's Literary Vogue since 1631* (Bloomington: University of Indiana Press, 1935).

8. Richard F. Hardin, *Michael Drayton and the Passing of Elizabethan England* (Lawrence: University Press of Kansas, 1973), p. 133.

9. *The Works of Michael Drayton,* III, 125. Subsequent citations from *Nymphidia* are to this edition with line numbers cited in the text.

10. Lillian H. Smith, *The Unreluctant Years: A Critical Approach to Children's Literature* (Chicago: American Library Association, 1953), p. 101.

11. See, for example, the discussion of Drayton's indebtedness in *Nymphidia* to Shakespeare in Minor White Latham, *The Elizabethan Fairies* (1930; reprt. New York: Octagon Books, 1972), pp. 203–206.

12. The term is Katherine M. Briggs' in *The Anatomy of Puck: An Examination of Fairy Beliefs among Shakespeare's Contemporaries and Successors* (London: Routledge and Kegan Paul, 1959), p. 58.

13. The objection that the plot of *Nymphidia* in its strong suggestion of adultery in the love triangle likely would not have interested or suited children seems specious. The theme does not seem to have kept Renaissance children from finding their way to Malory's *Morte d'Arthur*, for example, where the subject is treated far more seriously and graphically than in Drayton's poem, where it functions as merely the hinge for the mock-heroic burlesque. And Drayton's handling of the theme is light and deftly humorous without the salacious innuendo, for example, found in some of Herrick's fairy verse.

14. While diminished in most modern studies, attempts to extrapolate a "moral" from *Nymphidia* are not altogether past. Richard Hardin, for example, commenting on the poem's denouement where the timely application of Lethe water heals all wounds with the balm of forgetfulness, spies a useful lesson: "For men, whose bloodiest quarrels have origins that are usually just as insubstantial as the fairies', the implications are clear: almost all the kinds of problems met with in society . . . would vanish were it not for our memory of them. . . . With the detached, ironic view of man's pride and prejudice that is typical of his last years, Drayton has taken a momentary excursion into a world where the ancient curse of memory can be dispelled" (*Michael Drayton and the Passing of Elizabethan England,* p. 74).

15. *Ibid.,* p. v.

Samuel Johnson's The Fountains

The Fountains: A Fairy Tale

Samuel Johnson

> Felix qui potuit boni
> Fontem visere lucidum.
> —Boethius

As FLORETTA was wandering in a meadow at the foot of Plinlimmon,[1] she heard a little bird cry in such a note as she had never observed before, and looking round her, saw a lovely Goldfinch entangled by a lime-twig, and a Hawk hovering over him, as at the point of seizing him in his talons.

FLORETTA longed to rescue the little bird, but was afraid to encounter the Hawk, who looked fiercely upon her without any apparent dread of her approach, and as she advanced seemed to increase in bulk, and clapped his wings in token of defiance. FLORETTA stood deliberating a few moments, but seeing her mother at no great distance, took courage, and snatched the twig with the little bird upon it. When she had disengaged him she put him in her bosom, and the Hawk flew away.

FLORETTA shewing the bird to her mother, told her from what danger she had rescued him; her mother, after admiring his beauty, said, that he would be a very proper inhabitant of the little gilded cage, which had hung empty since the Starling died for want of water, and that he should be placed at the chamber window, for it would be wonderfully pleasant to hear him in the morning.

FLORETTA, with tears in her eyes, replied, that he had better have been devoured by the Hawk then die for want of water, and that she would not save him from a less evil to put him in danger of a greater: She therefore took him into her hand, cleaned his feathers from the bird-lime, looked upon him with great tenderness, and, having put his bill to her lips, dismissed him into the air.

He flew in circles round her as she went home, and perching on a tree before the door, delighted them awhile with such sweetness of song, that her mother reproved her for not putting him in the cage. FLORETTA endeavoured to look grave, but silently approved her own act, and wished her mother more generosity. Her mother guessed her thoughts, and told her, that when she was older she would be wiser.

FLORETTA however did not repent, but hoped to hear her little bird the next morning singing at liberty. She waked early and listened, but no Goldfinch could she hear. She rose, and walking again in the same meadow, went to view the bush where she had seen the lime-twig the day before.

When she entered the thicket, and was near the place for which she was looking, from behind a blossoming hawthorn advanced a female form of very low stature, but of elegant proportion and majestick air, arrayed in all the colours of the meadow, and sparkling as she moved like a dew-drop in the sun.

FLORETTA was too much disordered to speak or fly, and stood motionless between fear and pleasure, when the little lady took her by the hand.

I am, said she, one of the order of beings which some call Fairies, and some Piskies:[2] We have always been known to inhabit the crags and caverns of Plinlimmon. The maids and shepherds when they wander by moonlight have often heard our musick, and sometimes seen our dances.

I am the chief of the Fairies of this region, and am known among them by the name of LADY LILINET of the Blue Rock. As I lived always in my own mountain, I had very little knowledge of human manners, and thought better of mankind than other Fairies found them to deserve; I therefore often opposed the mischievous practices of my sisters without always enquiring whether they were just. I extinguished the light that was kindled to lead a traveller into a marsh, and found afterwards that he was hasting to corrupt a virgin: I dissipated a mist which assumed the form of a town, and was raised to decoy a monopolizer of corn from his way to the next market: I removed a thorn, artfully planted to prick the foot of a churl, that was going to hinder the Poor from following his reapers; and defeated so many schemes of obstruction and punishment, that I was cited before the Queen as one who favoured wickedness and opposed the execution of fairy justice.

Having never been accustomed to suffer control, and thinking myself disgraced by the necessity of defence, I so much irritated the Queen by my sullenness and petulance, that in her anger she transformed me into a Goldfinch. *In this form,* says she, *I doom thee to remain till some human being shall shew thee kindness without any prospect of interest.*

I flew out of her presence not much dejected; for I did not doubt but every reasonable being must love that which having never offended, could not be hated, and, having no power to hurt, could not be feared.

I therefore fluttered about the villages, and endeavoured to force myself into notice.

Having heard that nature was least corrupted among those who had no acquaintance with elegance and splendor, I employed myself for five years in hopping before the doors of cottages, and often sat singing on the thatched roof; my motions were seldom seen nor my notes heard; no kindness was ever excited, and all the reward of my officiousness was to be aimed at with a stone when I stood within a throw.

The stones never hurt me, for I had still the power of a Fairy.

I then betook myself to spacious and magnificent habitations, and sung in bowers by the walks or on the banks of fountains.

In these places where novelty was recommended by satiety, and curiosity excited by leisure, my form and my voice were soon distinguished, and I was known by the name of the pretty Goldfinch; the inhabitants would walk out to listen to my musick, and at last it was their practice to court my visits by scattering meat[3] in my common haunts.

This was repeated till I went about pecking in full security, and expected to regain my original form, when I observed two of my most liberal benefactors silently advancing with a net behind me. I flew off, and fluttering beside them pricked the leg of each, and left them halting and groaning with the cramp.

I then went to another house, where for two springs and summers I entertained a splendid family with such melody as they had never heard in the woods before. The winter that followed the second summer was remarkably cold, and many little birds perished in the field. I laid myself in the way of one of the ladies as benumbed with cold and faint with hunger; she picked me up with great joy, telling her companions that she had found the Goldfinch that sung so finely all summer in the myrtle hedge; that she would lay him where he should die, for she could not bear to kill him, and would then pick his fine feathers very carefully, and stick them in her muff.

Finding that her fondness and her gratitude could give way to so slight an interest, I chilled her fingers that she could not hold me, then flew at her face, and with my beak gave her nose four pecks that left four black spots indelible behind them, and broke a match by which she would have obtained the finest equpage in the country.

At length the Queen repented of her sentence, and being unable to revoke it, assisted me to try experiments upon man, to excite his tenderness, and attract his regard.

We made many attempts in which we were always disappointed. At last she placed me in your way held by a lime-twig, and herself in the shape of a Hawk made the shew of devouring me. You, my dear, have rescued me from the seeming danger without desiring to detain me in captivity, or seeking any other recompence than the pleasure of benefiting a feeling creature.

The Queen is so much pleased with your kindness, that I am come, by her permission, to reward you with a greater favour than every Fairy bestowed before.

The former gifts of Fairies, though bounties in design, have proved commonly mischiefs in the event. We have granted mortals to wish according to their own discretion, and their discretion being small, and their wishes irreversible, they have rashly petitioned for their own destruction. But you, my dearest FLORETTA, shall have, what none have ever before obtained from us, the power of indulging your wish, and the liberty of retracting it. Be bold and follow me.

FLORETTA was easily persuaded to accompany the Fairy, who led her through a labyrinth of craggs and shrubs, to a cavern covered by a thicket on the side of the mountain.

This cavern, said she, is the court of LILINET your friend; in this place you shall find a certain remedy for all real evils. LILINET then went before her through a long subterraneous passage, where she saw many beautiful Fairies, who came to gaze at the stranger, but who, from reverence to their mistress, gave her no disturbance. She heard from remote corners of the gloomy cavern the roar of winds and the fall of waters, and more than once entreated to return; but LILINET assuring her that she was safe, persuaded her to

proceed till they came to an arch, into which the light found its way
through a fissure of the rock.

There LILINET seated herself and her guest upon a bench of
agate, and pointing to two Fountains that bubbled before them,
said, Now attend, my dear FLORETTA, and enjoy the gratitude of a
Fairy. Observe the two Fountains that spring up in the middle of
the vault, one into a bason of alabaster, and the other into a bason
of dark flint. The one is called the Spring of Joy, the other of Sorrow; they rise from distant veins in the rock, and burst out in two
places, but after a short course unite their streams, and run ever
after in one mingled current.

By drinking of these fountains, which, though shut up from all
other human beings, shall be always accessible to you, it will be in
your power to regulate your future life.

When you are drinking the water of joy from the alabaster fountain, you may form your wish, and it shall be granted. As you raise
your wish higher, the water will be sweeter and sweeter to the
taste; but beware that you are not tempted by its increasing sweetness to repeat your draughts, for the ill effects of your wish can
only be removed by drinking the spring of sorrow from the bason
of flint, which will be bitter in the same proportion as the water of
joy was sweet. Now, my FLORETTA, make the experiment, and
give me the first proof of moderate desires. Take the golden cup
that stands on the margin of the spring of joy, form your wish and
drink.

FLORETTA wanted no time to deliberate on the subject of her
wish; her first desire was the increase of her beauty. She had some
disproportion of features. She took the cup and wished to be
agreeable; the water was sweet, and she drank copiously; and in the
fountain, which was clearer than crystal, she saw that her face was
completely regular.

She then filled the cup again, and wished for a rosy bloom upon
her cheeks: the water was sweeter than before, and the colour of
her cheeks was heightened.

She next wished for a sparkling eye: The water grew yet more
pleasant, and her glances were like the beams of the sun.

She could not yet stop; she drank again, desired to be made a
perfect beauty, and a perfect beauty she became.

She had now whatever her heart could wish; and making an
humble reverence to LILINET, requested to be restored to her own

habitation. They went back, and the Fairies in the way wondered at the change of FLORETTA's form. She came home delighted to her mother, who, on seeing the improvement, was yet more delighted than herself.

Her mother from that time pushed her forward into publick view: FLORETTA was at all the resorts of idleness and assemblies of pleasure; she was fatigued with balls, she was cloyed with treats, she was exhausted by the necessity of returning compliments. The life delighted her awhile, but custom soon destroyed its pleasure. She found that the men who courted her to day resigned her on the morrow to other flatterers, and that the women attacked her reputation by whispers and calumnies, till without knowing how she had offended, she was shunned as infamous.

She knew that her reputation was destroyed by the envy of her beauty, and resolved to degrade herself from the dangerous pre-eminence. She went to the bush where she rescued the bird, and called for LADY LILINET. Immediately LILINET appeared, and discovered by FLORETTA's dejected look that she had drank too much from the alabaster fountain.

Follow me, she cried, my FLORETTA, and be wiser for the future.

They went to the fountains, and FLORETTA began to taste the waters of sorrow, which were so bitter that she withdrew more than once the cup from her mouth: At last she resolutely drank away the perfection of beauty, the sparkling eye and rosy bloom, and left herself only agreeable.

She lived for some time with great content; but content is seldom lasting. She had a desire in a short time again to taste the waters of joy: she called for the conduct of LILINET, and was led to the alabaster fountain, where she drank, and wished for a faithful Lover.

After her return she was soon addressed by a young man, whom she thought worthy of her affection. He courted, and flattered, and promised; till at last she yielded up her heart. He then applied to her parents; and, finding her fortune less than he expected, contrived a quarrel and deserted her.

Exasperated by her disappointment, she went in quest of LILINET, and expostulated with her for the deceit which she had practised. LILINET asked her with a smile, for what she had been wishing; and being told, made her this reply. You are not, my dear, to wonder or complain: You may wish for yourself, but your wishes can have no effect upon another. You may become lovely by the efficacy of the fountain, but that you shall be loved is by no means a certain consequence; for you cannot confer upon another either discernment or fidelity: That happiness which you must derive from others, it is not in my power to regulate or bestow.

FLORETTA was for some time so dejected by this limitation of the fountain's power, that she thought it unworthy of another visit; but being on some occasion thwarted by her mother's authority, she went to LILINET, and drank at the alabaster fountain for a spirit to do her own way.

LILINET saw that she drank immoderately, and admonished her of her danger; but *spirit* and *her own way* gave such sweetness to the water, that she could not prevail upon herself to forbear, till LILINET in pure compassion snatched the cup out of her hand.

When she came home every thought was contempt, and every action was rebellion: She had drunk into herself a spirit to resist, but could not give her mother a disposition to yield; the old lady asserted her right to govern; and, though she was often foiled by the impetuosity of her daughter, she supplied by pertinacy what she wanted in violence; so that the house was in continual tumult by the pranks of the daughter and opposition of the mother.

In time, FLORETTA was convinced that spirit had only made her a capricious termagant, and that her own ways ended in errour, perplexity and disgrace; she perceived that the vehemence of mind, which to a man may sometimes procure awe and obedience, produce to a woman nothing but detestation; she therefore went back, and by a large draught from the flinty fountain, though the water was very bitter, replaced herself under her mother's care, and quitted her spirit, and her own way.

FLORETTA's fortune was moderate, and her desires were not larger, till her mother took her to spend a summer at one of the places which wealth and idleness frequent, under pretence of drinking the waters. She was now no longer a perfect beauty, and therefore conversation in her presence took its course as in other company; opinions were freely told, and observations made without reserve. Here FLORETTA first learned the importance of money. When she saw a woman of mean air and empty talk draw the attention of the place, she always discovered upon enquiry that she had so many thousands to her fortune.

She soon perceived that where these golden goddesses appeared, neither birth, nor elegance, nor civilty had any power of attraction;

that every art of entertainment was devoted to them, and that the great and the wise courted their regard.

The desire after wealth was raised yet higher by her mother, who was always telling her how much neglect she suffered from want of fortune, and what distinctions if she had but a fortune her good qualities would obtain. Her narrative of the day was always, that FLORETTA walked in the morning, but was not spoken to because she had a small fortune, and that FLORETTA danced at the ball better than any of them, but nobody minded her for want of a fortune.

This want, in which all other wants appeared to be included, FLORETTA was resolved to endure no longer and came home flattering her imagination in secret with the riches which she was now about to obtain.

On the day after her return she walked out alone to meet lady LILINET, and went with her to the fountain: Riches did not taste so sweet as either beauty or spirit, and therefore she was not immoderate in the draught.

When they returned from the cavern, LILINET gave her wand to the Fairy that attended her, with an order to conduct FLORETTA to the Black Rock.

The way was not long, and they soon came to the mouth of a mine in which there was a hidden treasure, guarded by an earthy Fairy deformed and shaggy, who opposed the entrance of FLORETTA till he recognized the want of the Lady of the Mountain. Here FLORETTA saw vast heaps of gold and silver and gems, gathered and reposited in former ages, and entrusted to the guard of the Fairies of the earth. The little Fairy delivered the orders of her mistress, and the surly sentinel promised to obey them.

FLORETTA, wearied with her walk, and pleased with her success, went home to rest, and when she waked in the morning, first opened her eyes upon a cabinet of jewels, and looking into her drawers and boxes, found them filled with gold.

FLORETTA was now as fine as the finest. She was the first to adopt any expensive fashion, to subscribe to any pompous entertainment, to encourage any foreign artist, or engage in any frolick of which the cost was to make the pleasure.

She was on a sudden the favourite of every place. Report made her wealth thrice greater than it really was, and wherever she came, all was attention, reverence and obedience. The ladies who had formerly slighted her, or by whom she had been formerly caressed, gratified her pride by open flattery and private murmurs.

She sometimes over-heard them railing at upstarts, and wondering whence some people came, or how their expenses were supplied. This incited her to heighten the splendour of her dress, to increase the number of her retinue, and to make such propositions of costly schemes, that her rivals were forced to desist from contest.

But she now began to find that the tricks which can be played with money will seldom bear to be repeated; that admiration is a short-lived passion, and that the pleasure of expence is gone when wonder and envy are no more excited. She found that respect was an empty form, and that all those who crouded round her were drawn to her by vanity or interest.

It was however pleasant to be able on any terms to elevate and mortify, to raise hopes and fears; and she would still have continued to be rich, had not the ambition of her mother contrived to marry her to a Lord, whom she despised as ignorant, and abhorred as profligate. Her mother persisted in her importunity; and FLORETTA having now lost the spirit of resistance, had no other refuge than to divest herself of her fairy fortune.

She implored the assistance of LILINET, who praised her resolution. She drank chearfully from the flinty fountain, and found the waters not extremely bitter. When she returned she went to bed, and in the morning perceived that all her riches had been conveyed away she knew not how, except a few ornamental jewels, which LILINET had ordered to be carried back as a reward for her dignity of mind.

She was now almost weary of visiting the fountain, and solaced herself with such amusements as every day happened to produce: At last there arose in her imagination a strong desire to become a Wit.

The pleasures with which this new character appeared to teem were so numerous and so great, that she was impatient to enjoy them; and rising before the sun, hastened to the place where she knew that her fairy patroness was always to be found. LILINET was willing to conduct her, but could now scarcely restrain her from leading the way but by telling her, that if she went first the Fairies of the cavern would refuse her passage.

They came in time to the fountain, and FLORETTA took the golden cup into her hand; she filled it and drank, and again she filled it, for wit was sweeter than riches, spirit, or beauty.

As she returned she felt new successions of imagery rise in her mind, and whatever her memory offered to her imagination, assumed a new form, and connected itself with things to which it seemed before to have no relation. All the appearances about her were changed, but the novelties exhibited were commonly defects. She now saw that almost every thing was wrong, without often feeling how it could be better; and frequently imputed to the imperfection of art those failures which were caused by the limitation of nature.

Wherever she went, she breathed nothing but censure and reformation. If she visited her friends, she quarrelled with the situation of their houses, the disposition of their gardens, the direction of their walks, and the termination of their views. It was vain to shew her fine furniture, for she was always ready to tell how it might be finer, or to conduct her through spacious apartments, for her thoughts were full of nobler fabricks of airy palaces and hesperian gardens. She admired nothing and praised but little.

Her conversation was generally thought uncivil. If she received flatteries, she seldom repaid them; for she set no value upon vulgar praise. She could not hear a long story without hurrying the speaker on to the conclusion; and obstructed the mirth of her companions, for she rarely took notice of a good jest, and never laughed except when she was delighted.

This behaviour made her unwelcome wherever she went; nor did her speculation upon human manners much contribute to forward her reception. She now saw the disproportions between language and sentiment, between passion and exclamation; she discovered the defects of every action, and the uncertainty of every conclusion; she knew the malignity of friendship, the avarice of liberality, the anxiety of content, and the cowardice of temerity.

To see all this was pleasant, but the greatest of all pleasures was to shew it. To laugh was something, but it was much more to make others laugh. As every deformity of character made a strong impression upon her, she could not always forbear to transmit it to others; as she hated false appearances she thought it her duty to detect them, till, between wantonness and virtue, scarce any that she knew escaped without some wounds by the shafts of ridicule; not that her merriment was always the consequence of total contempt, for she often honoured virtue where she laughed at affectation.

For these practices, and who can wonder, the cry was raised against her from every quarter, and to hunt her down was generally determined. Every eye was watching for a fault, and every tongue

was busy to supply its share of defamation. With the most un-
polluted purity of mind, she was censured as too free of favours,
because she was not afraid to talk with men: With generous
sensibility of every human excellence, she was thought cold or
envious, because she would not scatter praise with
undistinguishing profusion: With tenderness that agonized at real
misery, she was charged with delight in the pain of others, when
she would not condole with those whom she knew to counterfeit
affliction. She derided false appearances of kindness and of pity,
and was therefore avoided as an enemy to society. As she seldom
commended or censured but with some limitations and exceptions,
the world condemned her as indifferent to the good and bad; and
because she was often doubtful where others were confident, she
was charged with laxity of principles, while her days were
distracted and her rest broken by niceties of honour and scruples of
morality.

Report had now made her so formidable that all flattered and all
shunned her. If a Lover gave a ball to his mistress and her friends,
it was stipulated that FLORETTA should not be invited. If she
entered a publick room the ladies courtsied, and shrunk away, for
there was no such thing as speaking, but FLORETTA would find something to criticise. If a girl was more spritely than her Aunt, she was
threatened that in a little time she would be like FLORETTA. Visits
were very diligently paid when FLORETTA was known not to be at
home; and no mother trusted her daughter to herself without a
caution, if she should meet FLORETTA to leave the company as
soon as she could.

With all this FLORETTA made sport at first, but in time grew
weary of general hostility. She would have been content with a few
friends, but no friendship was durable; it was the fashion to desert
her, and with the fashion what fidelity will contend? She could
have easily amused herself in solitude, but that she thought it mean
to quit the field to treachery and folly.

Persecution at length tired her constancy, and she implored
LILINET to rid her of her wit: LILINET complied and walked up the
mountain, but was often forced to stop and wait for her follower.
When they came to the flinty fountain FLORETTA filled a small cup
and slowly brought it to her lips, but the water was insupportably
bitter. She just tasted it, and dashed it to the ground, diluted the
bitterness at the fountain of alabaster, and resolved to keep her
wit, with all its consequences.

Being now a wit for life, she surveyed the various conditions of mankind with such superiority of sentiment, that she found few distinctions to be envied or desired, and therefore did not very soon make another visit to the fountain. At length being alarmed by sickness, she resolved to drink length of life from the golden cup. She returned elated and secure, for though the longevity acquired was indeterminate, she considered death as far distant, and therefore suffered it not to intrude upon her pleasures.

But length of life included not perpetual health. She felt herself continually decaying, and saw the world fading about her. The delights of her early days would delight no longer, and however widely she extended her view, no new pleasure could be found; her friends, her enemies, her admirers, her rivals dropped one by one into the grave, and with those who succeeded them she had neither community of joys nor strife of competition.

By this time she began to doubt whether old age were not dangerous to virtue; whether pain would not produce peevishness, and peevishness impair benevolence. She thought that the spectacle of life might be too long continued, and the vices which were often seen might raise less abhorrence; that resolution might be sapped by time, and let that virtue sink which in its firmest state it had not without difficulty supported; and that it was vain to delay the hour which must come at last, and might come at a time of less preparation and greater imbecility.

These thoughts led her to LILINET, whom she accompanied to the flinty fountain; where, after a short combat with herself, she drank the bitter water. They walked back to the favourite bush pensive and silent; And now, said she, accept my thanks for the last benefit that FLORETTA can receive. LADY LILINET dropped a tear, impressed upon her lips the final kiss, and resigned her, as she resigned herself, to the course of Nature.

NOTES

1. A mountain in Wales.
2. Pixies.
3. Solid food in general, as opposed to drink.

The Fountains, *the Vanity of Human Wishes, and the Choice of Life*

Ruth K. MacDonald

The Fountains: A Fairy Tale is a delightful piece of Samuel Johnson's work which has had virtually no literary or critical acclaim. Originally published in *Miscellanies in Prose and Verse* by Anna Williams in 1766, it has not been included in any modern collections of Johnson's works. And with the exception of some earlier editions, it has been previously republished only once, in the *Baskerville Series* in 1927.[1] Both James Boswell and Lady Knight corroborate that Johnson was working on the tale for Mrs. Williams, but neither elaborates on the tale itself. Critics writing on the nature of Johnson's fiction have not considered the tale either. In fact, the only attention given it in this century are a *Times Literary Supplement* review of the Baskerville reprint on 5 May, 1927 (p. 314), which suggests that the tale is an allegory of Johnson's theme of the "vanity of human wishes," and a passing mention by Sydney Castle Roberts, who speaks of Johnson's inadequacy in imagining fairies as part of the natural setting much as Shakespeare imagined them.[2] In fact, *The Fountains* is an important part of the Johnson *oeuvre* both because of its similarity to *Rasselas* and *The Vanity of Human Wishes* in thematic considerations and also because of its unique accomplishments in the genre of the fairy tale.

As a fairy tale *The Fountains* is unique in a number of ways. First, the central figure of the story is a female. This in itself does not entitle the story to any particular praise, but Johnson has given this girl control over her future and responsible judgement with which to control it. Unlike most girls in fairy tales, this one is particularly active and assertive in controlling her fate. There is no Prince Charming to rescue her from her various predicaments. In most typical fairy tales such as "Snow White" and "The Sleeping Beauty," the heroines are actually ultimate figures of passivity, who are rescued from deathlike sleep by their male protectors. Johnson's little girl Floretta is not even guided by a smart and clever boy, as Gretel is by Hansel. In fact, there are only a handful of little girls—Gerda in Hans Christian Andersen's "The Snow Queen," who searches for and finally rescues her playfellow singlehandedly, and the girls of C. S. Lewis's *The Chronicles of*

Narnia, who actively combat the forces of evil in Narnia with sword, bow, and guile, are two of the very few—who actively pursue their fates. Johnson, through the agency of the fairy, gives to Floretta the ability to control her future according to her own wishes. Because Johnson lets Floretta take that option, he has in fact created a new kind of fairy-tale hero, or heroine to be exact, one who is unique in the genre.

Johnson's alteration of fairy-tale convention extends even further, in the device of the granted wish. In a fairy tale, it is the usual practice for some supernatural character—fairy godmother, witch, genie—to offer to a deserving mortal a specific number of wishes, usually three. Even if the number of wishes is unspecified, as with a magic lamp, it is never within the power of the mortal to undo the wishes. Even if one tries to undo the harm with another wish, the situation that results is even more complicated than the earlier one. Johnson, however, has recognized that fairy wishes have been the ruination of many a favored fictional mortal. He therefore restructures the whole wishing device with a new set of guidelines. Floretta may make a wish and then retract it,—first by drinking of the fountain of joy and then by drinking the mitigating waters of the fountain of sorrow. The result is a workable device of plot which saves Floretta from destruction by one false step. It is a device particularly suited to Johnson's didactic and moral intentions as well as to his intention to please and delight his reader. Using her power to both wish and unwish, Floretta can learn by experience and yet not be permanently damaged by it. Johnson thus escapes an excessively sentimental situation at the end of the story because his sympathetic heroine need not be utterly ruined by her adventures. He can avoid excesses of pity for Floretta, and he can also avoid the negative reader reaction which might have occurred if he had disfigured her.

Floretta is a particularly suitable little girl for this role, again emphasizing her uniqueness in the fairy-tale genre, because she is so tractable and able to learn from her mistakes. She is, in fact, a miniature grownup who simply lacks worldly experience. In the beginning of the story she evinces charity unalloyed, and for this charity she is rewarded. She rescues the fairy because the fairy deserves pity and help and not because she has any ulterior motives in the capture. She is not an impulsive, possessive young girl. In fact, her generosity in letting the enchanted fairy, who is con-

demned to take the shape of a bird, go free after she has rescued
her is juxtaposed to the shortsightedness of her own mother, who
would have caged the fairy and therefore destroyed the possibility
of fairy reward for services selflessly rendered. Neither is Floretta
so willful that she would refuse the bitter waters from the fountain
of sorrow. But rather she takes her punishment like an adult who
knows what is good for her. She is also smart enough to ask for
sensible things, like money or handsome looks, rather than for
power to rule the world or something equally preposterous. This is
no screaming, tantrum-throwing, spoiled little girl but, rather, one
who is the best kind of pupil for what she will learn.

Johnson also alters fairy-tale convention further by inventing a
whole new set of motivations for his fairies. Heretofore, fairies had
been, like Shakespeare's Puck, mischievous spirits who caused
minor domestic calamities simply for the fun of manipulating the
situation and then watching mortals try to right matters again. But
Johnson's fairies are different; they are instruments of ultimate justice. They precipitate calamities because the humans to which
these disasters occur deserve their punishment. In her youth, the
fairy Lilinet behaved more benevolently toward humans because in
her innocence she knew no better. Her overestimation of the goodness of mankind resulted in rewarding the evildoers and promoting
the victimization of the innocent. She assisted rather than hindered
a man on his way to seduce a virgin; she guided a crooked corn
merchant to his next victims; and she helped a farmer to deprive
the poor of their customary charity of the leavings from his harvest. Johnson has in fact humanized the realm of faery, giving the
fairies feelings of justice and compassion. And in so doing he has
made faery action comprehensible to humans. Lilinet thought that
in her benevolence toward humans she was helping them; but she
acted without understanding the whole situation and therefore
helped those humans to take advantage of other humans, in spite of
her good intentions.

Finally, the tale is unusual because it has neither the catastrophic
nor the happy ending one would expect in a typical fairy tale. The
ending is a sad but tranquil resolution of Floretta's difficulties in
dealing with her desires to control her life. She simply resigns herself to whatever may happen, without designing or hoping for anything else. The ending is an anticlimax to all the experiences that
Floretta has had. She has not been permanently damaged. Her

beauty has not been scarred; nor has she been turned into a disagreeable old crone or a frog for wishing immoderately. Nor does
she marry wisely and well, as one would expect for a girl who has
behaved well in a fairy story. The girl simply resolves herself to
going on with life, no matter what it might bring in hopes that some
small happinesses may be found and major griefs may be avoided.

That the ending is not hopeless is foreshadowed in the epigraph,
"*Felix qui potuit boni / Fontem visere lucidum*"—"Happy the man
who has been able to look into the bright fountain of goodness."
This is what happens to Floretta; she sees through the delusions of
wealth, grandeur, and happiness offered by the fountain of joy. And
by seeing through these delusions, she is freed from them. This
freedom bestows a modicum of happiness in itself. Floretta has six
wish experiences through which she continually grows. Her first
wish is for beauty. On the surface it would seem that the lesson to
be learned here is simply to be moderate in one's wishes. Her wish
to be agreeable and regular in feature is commendable, but it is the
wish to be beautiful that undoes her. She consequently drinks from
the spring of sorrow until she is only tolerably attractive. Her second wish, for a faithful lover, seems to be a more solid, commendable kind of wish, less material and vain, more intellectually and
emotionally satisfying. But even here she finds that the lover is
finally unsatisfactory and she cannot depend on the love of others
to make her happy. The lesson learned is that one must look for
more dependable happinesses within oneself; no amount of wishing
can influence others. Her third wish, for the spirit to do her own
will, disrupts her filial relationship with her mother. Aggressive
willfulness will not do because the opposition one may meet can
destroy what is otherwise precious and because it makes one disagreeable both to oneself and to others.

By the time she has her fourth wish, for money, Floretta has
apparently learned to moderate her desires. She finds the taste of
the wish for riches less sweet than her former wishes, so it is easy
to be temperate this time. The temptation to overindulge is not so
great. And after a time she decides to drink of the spring of sor-
rows on her own even though she is still enjoying her wealth. For
her self-control she is rewarded by the fairy, who leaves a few of
the jewels behind. Her fifth wish, for wit, is the most tempting, for
the draught is sweeter than any of the other wishes. It is through
this wish that Floretta learns most about society and life in general,

for she sees through the social conventions to the baseness of the humanity beneath. Johnson in no way counteracts or softens this estimation of life. The result of so much insight is devastating, and Floretta becomes a very disagreeable person, rejected by all because of her scathing tongue. Yet the remedy for wit is so bitter that she resolves to keep her wit in spite of the pain it causes her. Her last wish, for long life (which unfortunately does not include attendant youthfulness), does not improve her prospects. For in using long life to further survey mankind, she finds that no matter where she looks there are no new entertainments to occupy her. In fact, she suspects that long life is really a threat to virtue, since by living long one might become tolerant of vices because they are so common. At this point she finally realizes the futility of all that she could wish for with the fountains. She resolves to visit them no more and let life go on as it will since it cannot be improved by wishes. Although there is no direct promise that Floretta will now be happy, at least we know that she sees life for what it is and has resolved to go on living—this time with no great hopes for happinesses or ultimate solutions.

The ending is of course very Johnsonian: it illustrates the "vanity of human wishes" in bringing lasting happiness and the ultimate inconclusiveness in trying to make the final and irrevocable "choice of life." Given the fact that she is human and has not demonstrated any particularly convincing instances of stoicism, one suspects that Floretta will not stop desiring and hoping. One is sure though that she will not now be driven through her life by her passions.

The story is in fact very much like *Rasselas* in "The conclusion, in which nothing is concluded" (chap. 49).[3] Like Rasselas, Floretta is introduced into society and from her experience learns that there are no conclusions ultimately and finally to conclude upon. She has her fairy as her Imlac-figure to guide her. The fairy tells the story of her own maturation, which is very much like Imlac's story of his childhood. Both Imlac and the fairy learn of the corruption of human nature and of the need to moderate desires; yet neither's pupil learns from the experience of the older, more worldly-wise teacher and very seldom heeds the teacher's advice. Both pupils must learn for themselves about the futility of wishing and about the difficulties inherent in living.

There are also a number of significant differences between the two stories. The most striking dissimilarity is the absence of Christian consolation at the end of *The Fountains*. In *Rasselas* (chap. 48), the discussion turns to the question of the supreme being, and all the characters show reverence for Nekeyah's resolution that "the choice of life is become less important; I hope hereafter to think only on the choice of eternity." *The Vanity of Human Wishes* is an even more definite statement of the need for prayer and faith in God in order to sustain one in an existence that is inherently disappointing and disastrous. For Johnson, life was not to be enjoyed, but only endured; and it is made more endurable only by faith and prayer. However, Floretta makes no such determination as Nekeyah makes at the end of *Rasselas*. Floretta is, like Imlac and the astronomer, determined "to be driven along the stream of life without directing their course to any particular port" (chap. 49). Essentially Floretta is condemned to live without consolation. The single implication, only vaguely hinted at in *The Fountains*, that there is any ultimate eternal life to aim for is in the epigraph from Boethius, whose *Consolation* also aimed at a life removed from the earthly one. And that hint is further obscured by its Latin delivery.

The elimination of Christian didacticism at the end of *The Fountains* is a variation from the typical Johnsonian ending and suits the fairy tale well. The ending of *The Fountains* is much more palatable than the ending of *The Vanity of Human Wishes,* which is oppressively heavy with only the glimmer of Christian consolation to mitigate the gloom. Although *The Fountains* ends sadly, the tale does not verge on tragedy because the reader feels that somehow Floretta will find life bearable, even though just how is not explained. It is a much more hopeful ending, certainly suitable for children who do not yet know the oppressiveness of living. And the moral intention for the child is not complicated by philosophical and religious problems.

Other alterations that Johnson makes from *Rasselas* to *The Fountains* also benefit a juvenile audience. There are no essaylike digressions. Nor is Floretta a passive observer like Rasselas, who is acted upon and then comments on the action. Floretta is a full participant in an active story line; she becomes her choice of life and then rejects that choice on the basis of experience. Nekeyah, on the other hand, does not marry in order to find out what marriage is really like. Instead she relies on her assembled data. Floretta is also considerably smarter than Rasselas, less given over to idle speculation, and much quicker to learn from her mistakes and rectify them. The effect of all these alterations is to improve upon the static quality of *Rasselas,* to make the story more vivid and more demonstrative. Pointed compactness, combined with Johnson's uniquely eloquent diction, is the key to the moving quality of the tale and to its fitness both for an adult and a juvenile audience. The miscellany tradition in the eighteenth century does not suggest however that *The Fountains* was necessarily designed for a juvenile audience. But the simplicity of the style and the obvious alterations of plot and character, from complex to simple, in *The Fountains* certainly suggest that Johnson was deliberately simplifying his method so that the tale would appeal to a wider audience—an audience which would certainly have included children. All three works, *Rasselas, The Fountains,* and *The Vanity of Human Wishes,* deal with Johnson's idea of the essentially problematical nature of living. All use the same clever logic, each with a different tone and different degree of seriousness. In *The Fountains* we see Johnson's unique tailoring of his ideas to suit the genre of the fairy tale for a less sophisticated audience—perhaps even a juvenile audience.

NOTES

1. *Baskerville Series* (London: Elkin Mathews and Marrot, 1927).

2. *"Dr. Johnson and the Fairies,"* in *Tribute to Walter De la Mare on His Seventy-fifth Birthday* (London: Faber and Faber, 1948), p. 191.

3. Quotations from *Rasselas* are cited in the text by chapter number from *Eighteenth-Century English Literature,* Geoffrey Tillotson *et al.,* eds. (New York: Harcourt, Brace and World, 1969), pp. 1020-1065.

Between 1776 and 1976

The World of Children in an American Commune of the 1890s*

Francelia Butler

In November 1897, "Uncle Herbert," editor of the Children's Column in the newspaper of a commune in Tennessee, observed: "These colonists have forsaken an artificial civilization and have gone back, or rather forwards, to a simpler and more natural life. It is a curious mingling of 1776 and 1976, of backwoods and millenium." Now, as we look back from "millenium," most of the children of these colonists, who once loved the experiment in natural living, have seen it fail, lost faith in it, and are dead.

Many of the political and social problems, fads and innovations that made headlines in the 1970s were familiar to at least one group of children of the 1890s. In the commune of some 500 people of the Ruskin, Tennessee Cooperative Association, thirty miles south of Nashville, children joyously experienced open education, covertly listened to the discussions of their parents about sex outside marriage or read about free love in the communal library, demonstrated against war, espoused health foods and mysticism, wrote letters to the editor about the pollution of air and water by factories, and shared a life of equality with other human beings without regard to sex or race. Children lived through these experiences, saw the commune fail, and seemingly grew up and forgot. But now, three generations later, like slow-germinating seeds, these interests are sprouting up everywhere.

Idealists in the commune, which was composed mainly of factory laborers from New England and miners and farmers from the West who were thrown out of work by the Depression of 1893, tried hard from 1893 to 1901 to arrange an unusual system of education for children. But quarrels within the commune, mainly over free love, separated the members. About half—the anti-free-love contingent—left in September 1899 to establish another Ruskin near Waycross, Georgia, at the edge of the Okefenokee Swamp. Typhoid fever and starvation—colonists were reduced to eating stray alligators and cornmeal shaped and fried to look like pork

*This article will appear as a chapter in *Comrade Wayland and the Cavedwellers*, to be published by Stonehill Publications, New York. The work was co-authored by Francelia Butler and Jan Bakker.

chops—concluded the experiment toward the end of 1901. Those tolerant of free love scattered to other places, including the art colony at Fairhope, Alabama.

Information about life in the commune has to be ferreted out of the columns of *The Coming Nation,* the weekly newspaper of the commune, the files of which extend from 1893 through 1901 and are preserved in the Draper Collection of the State Historical Library in Madison, Wisconsin. The writings of Ruskin, Marx, and other socialists were quoted in the paper and sold by the commune, which was certainly one of the first to be influenced by Marx. Considerable material can be found in Special Collections in the University of Tennessee Library. Some is in my possession, since my father-in-law was one of the printers of *The Coming Nation* and my late husband, Jerome Butler, was born in the commune.

Perhaps the most radical innovation in the commune was a form of open education. Accounts in *The Coming Nation* and interviews with aged persons who were children in the colony make it clear that children were given wide freedom to pursue individual interests. No special emphasis was put on having to learn specific academic skills such as reading. Rather, the hope of the Ruskinites was that their children would learn some practical work-skill and also some art, such as painting or music—the latter because they espoused Ruskin's theory that creativity would flourish better in a free, secure environment. If a child was so inclined, Ruskinites wanted him to have every opportunity for a higher education. After a free education, many Ruskinites believed that a normal child of ten should be able to lead a happy, balanced life with the skills he had attained up to that point.

Various work and study areas were arranged on colony grounds: woodworking area, communal garden, studio for sculpturing and painting, printing and newspaper work area, tailor shop, kitchen, library, music room, as well as an area for study of the traditional reading, writing, and 'rithmatic. And there were facilities for simple scientific experiments. In general, supervision of these areas was excellent. For horticulture, the famous Walter Van Fleet taught such skills as grafting and hybridization. The noted artist and sculptor, Isaac Broome, directed the efforts of children to shape interesting figures out of the moist Fuller's earth from the floor of the great cave owned by the commune. Girls as well as boys—the commune had equal opportunity regulations before the state or the United States—studied woodworking or did scientific experiments under the tutelage of the communal physician, Dr. H. C. McDill.

There was public criticism of some other facets of colony life—the free-love contingent among adults, the atheism of most colony members, the mysticism of others, the way they dressed (women sometimes wore slacks and men worked stripped to the waist), and their attack on the establishment (especially when it took the form of setting off homemade bombs). But nobody to this day has ever criticized the schools. The system worked, and old timers who recall it still pronounce it excellent.

Walter Wayland, son of the founder of the colony, Julius Wayland, lived in the commune from 1894 until he was ten. He later wrote music as well as articles for a paper published by his father. When I interviewed him in Girard, Kansas, Wayland, who is now over ninety, told me he recalled the excellence of the commune's school system. Annie Ennis Lewis, also nearly ninety, praises the school highly. "Not only did one learn a lot but it was fun." She recalls that a room in the Center was divided off into sections, some for painting, some for woodwork, and so on:

Boys—girls, too—learned to turn, square, and fit, to construct little water wheels and other contrivances—whatever their fancy suggested. I think the whole system was partly theory, partly necessity. Every enterprise in the commune could use an extra hand and, of course, it was better to have a willing hand. On the theoretical side, there was an exhilarating feeling of freedom in the air—as if we were all going through life in a free-form dance. Whenever we were tired or bored, any of us—boys or girls— could go for a dip in Yellow Creek, which was a beautiful spot, like the Golden River in the fantasy by John Ruskin. We all read that in the communal library and made statues of Ruskin out of Fuller's earth.

The adults lived in crude shanties, like large corncribs—they and the older children. The babies were taken care of in the nursery on the third floor of the Center. When we wanted to do paintings, we were always allowed to put them up on the walls of the shanties, and the walls were papered with our pictures.

As a perusal of the catalog indicates, the Ruskin Library was well-stocked with such staples of children's (or adult) literature as *Swiss Family Robinson*, *Robinson Crusoe*, *Tom Sawyer*, *Black Beauty*, Grimm's *Fairy Tales*, *Little Women*, Marryat's *Masterman*

Ready, Gulliver's Travels, House of Seven Gables, Jane Eyre, Les Miserables, Last of the Mohicans, and Dickens' *Child's History of England, David Copperfield, Great Expectations, Little Dorrit, Martin Chuzzlewit,* and *Our Mutual Friend.* There were also anthologies of poetry and biographies. Once children could read, they were free to read anything in the library that appealed to them, including the political and free-love books, or treatises on atheism, mysticism, vegetarianism, nature, and gardening.

The only things children in the commune didn't understand, some colonists boasted, were the meanings of such words as "tramp" or "poverty." In fact, the experiment in education proved so successful that no one contemplated changing it, even in 1898, when the commune had become a flourishing town with assets of nearly $100,000, or after the Tennessee experiment had failed and the commune had moved on to its new site in Georgia.

Besides the books in the library, the children read the Children's Column of *The Coming Nation.* The column was established in 1898 by the editor of the paper, Herbert Casson, who shortly after was married to Lydia Commander, editor of an astonishingly avant garde Women's Column in the same paper. Their beautiful, but unorthodox, marriage service—very much like that of "hippies"— took place in the meeting hall of the center. Miss Commander retained her maiden name.

Under the pseudonym Uncle Herbert, Casson took up in the Children's Column certain political problems such as war, particularly the impending "Cuban" (Spanish-American) War; economic inequality and the "nefarious" effects of traditional religion; social problems, including racial discrimination; and ecological problems, particularly pollution. Uncle Herbert did not talk down to children, and as a result, they talked back. In "Letters to the Editor," they added their own observations. In the column as in the commune, education was a process of osmosis in which children mingled their fresh impressions with the more experienced observations of adults.

One of the major subjects discussed in the Children's Column was war. On 18 March 1898, about a month after the blowing up of the U.S.S. *Maine* in Havana harbor and a month before the declaration of war against Spain, Uncle Herbert printed a letter from Dora May Engle of Sharon Center, New York:

> We are glad you have started this children's column, for now we can get acquainted with lots of good Socialist boys and girls

from all over the United States and maybe from other countries, too. How we pity those poor destitute children in Cuba! I wish some of them could write you a letter so we could read it. What an awful thing it was to have our warship Maine blown up in the night when all were asleep! Papa believes that it was no accident.

Many people believed and still believe that the destruction of the *Maine* was rigged by the United States to trigger a war which reputable historians still regard as totally unnecessary. Requesting that readers send *The Coming Nation* to Cuban and other children, Uncle Herbert observed: "We don't believe in hitting anybody or in going to war with Spain or any other country. Socialists believe in teaching people to do right, and in preventing all greedy millionaires from grabbing what does not belong to them."

Attacks in the Children's Column on the war paralleled those on the front page of *The Coming Nation* and continued spasmodically until the end of the year, by which time Spain had been forced, in formal agreements, to relinquish not only Cuba, but Puerto Rico and the Philippines as well. On 19 March 1898 (war would be declared in less than a month), Uncle Herbert wrote the children:

My Dear Nieces and Nephews:
I wonder if all the newspapers in the towns where you live have been talking about war. You know whenever the working people get very poor, the papers begin to talk about war to prevent the people from thinking about poverty. The papers try to protect the millionaires, so they stir us up to pitch into Spain or Italy or England or some other country a long ways off. I hope none of my nephews will ever be so foolish as to join an army and fight against any other nation. There are lots of jolly boys and nice girls in Spain, and we don't want to kill their fathers and make them orphans. We want to stop the war in Cuba and to teach people to be kind to one another. We love America too well to want it to be a fighting nation. Our stars and stripes ought to be a peace flag. . . . Did you ever see a man run over by a train and cut into little pieces? . . . That is what war is like.

Uncle Herbert, then in his twenties, was not in the Civil War, which ended in 1865. Nevertheless, like youth in the 1960s, he was violently against any form of participation in war and conveyed his feeling to his young readers.

On 23 April 1898, the week that war was declared, a child wrote from Lynn, Massachusetts: "Don't you think it is a shame to have those Cuban people starving? I do. I can't see why we Socialists can't do something towards giving the Cubans something." And the week after that a child wrote: "I believe there are as many starving in Pennsylvania as there are in Cuba. It is all right for the rich man to cry war but the poor man has to lose his life. And the rich men get the glory of it."

Perhaps it was this attitude on the part of the children that inspired a sermon Uncle Herbert gave about this time at the Lynn, Massachusetts, Labor Church, where socialism was a religion. The subject of his sermon was "The Foolish Games of Our National Childhood." The games he referred to, of course, were War and Business, and he quoted John Ruskin as saying: "There is no physical crime so far beyond pardon . . . as the making of war machinery. . . . Men are enlisted for the labor that kills—the labor of war. . . . Let the officers of troops of LIFE be held as honorable as the officers of troops of DEATH."

Again on June 4, Uncle Herbert took up the war in his Children's Column and quoted from an antiwar letter received from a child in Camden, New Jersey. On June 18, he urged children to send copies of *The Coming Nation* to soldiers:

> If you know the address of any soldiers at Tampa, or anywhere else, I wish you would send them a *Coming Nation,* because they have plenty of time to read, and one paper may be handed round through a whole regiment. Besides, we want to teach these soldiers that there is something else to fight besides Spain. When they come back from Cuba, they ought to march after Mark Hanna and put him out of the Senate. We want to let them know that there are millions of poor people in our country who need justice just as much as the Cubans do.

Uncle Herbert spoke out against letting children play war games. He had seen some children in Toronto playing out the Spanish-American War. The following week he printed another attack on the war with Spain, questioning whether any tyranny was worse than the tyranny of American imperialistic monopoly. Eerily prophetic was his comment on July 23: "There will be a time come as true as the sun shines, when they (the Cubans) will raise up in their might and free themselves from the tyranny of monopoly."

Lack of respect for the government reflects itself in lack of respect for what the American flag stands for. No flag burning was reported in the column, but from time to time a child complained that he no longer looked up to the flag with pride. Uncle Herbert printed a poem entitled, "Our Flag." According to the poem, the red stripes stood for the blood of the poor, the white for their anemic faces, the stars for their tears on a blue background—the color tone of chains.

Though often related to the war, economic problems were also taken up in more general terms. Uncle Herbert, for instance, warned children about the dangers of pawnshops. He called them places "where you have to pay eight cents for a nickel." You pawn a watch. They loan only on a small portion of the value of the watch, and if you can come to reclaim it, they charge an exorbitant rate of interest. The three balls outside a pawnshop stand for "Rent, Profit, and Interest—the three ways that working people lose their money."

Flagler and Standard Oil were the butt of many barbs. On 5 March 1898 the column printed a joke about a little girl in Palm Beach, Florida, a place "owned by Mr. Flagler of Standard Oil Company." Told she could not go bathing because the waves were too high, she wanted to know, "When will Mr. Flagler let the waves go down?" Then there was the story later on in the month about how Miss Flagler, "the millionaire's daughter in New York," shot a little Negro boy in the back for picking a few flowers from her garden.

On 26 March 1898, Uncle Herbert told a version of the story by the Brothers Grimm about the magic pot that kept producing soup. He shared with the children the wish that every family could have a magic pot. The following week, he began a contest for children for the best definition of socialism. Hundreds of children were reputed to have replied, and dozens of replies were published in the Children's Column. Uncle Herbert expressed the opinion that some of their definitions were considerably better than those of some college professors. At least, he said, children tell it like it is and don't talk about "the unity of the multiplicities of self-expression," as one college professor did.

A moving dialogue appeared in the May 28 column, in which a little boy asked his father about the life of the men who worked in his father's brickyard. At first encouraging his son's candid questions, the father was finally unable to tolerate their penetrating nature. They revealed altogether too clearly the low living conditions of the men and the father's responsibility for their misery and

for the tragedies that sometimes occurred. Abruptly, the father
ended the dialogue with, "Don't ask foolish questions, boy!"

Children at Ruskin were quite capable of understanding the sa-
tiric nature of such a dialogue. Through their freedom to choose
their education, they were "naturally disciplined," they knew what
were fair conditions for work. Children worked hard in the commune, Uncle Herbert revealed, but they enjoyed it. Children outside the colony often wrote expressing admiration for the way of
life of children in the commune, as described in the column. They
too would have liked to go to school in Ruskin. Uncle Herbert
invited them to visit Ruskin. In return for a certain number of paid
subscriptions, he sent leather suspenders made in the commune to
the boys and belts to girls. He also sent them pamphlets about
Socialism. For a short time, he did in fact develop a strong Junior
Socialist movement throughout the country. It was hoped that
through the effort of youth and adults to establish small socialist
communes, America could peacefully be converted into a Workers'
State with Ruskin as the center.

On 25 February 1899 the front page of *The Coming Nation*
printed a story about a poor little girl who froze to death in Dayton,
Ohio. It was typical of the paper that the tragedy was mentioned in
the Children's Column as well. Economics and politics were not
merely the province of adults. Uncle Herbert suggested to the children that even the Presidency might not be immune from corruption. He printed the story about how George Washington never
told a lie and became President—and added, "but times have
changed." This attitude reflected that in the regular columns of the
paper, wherein the President of the United States (McKinley) was
accused of surrounding himself with corrupt officials and using the
church in the person of a revivalist (Moody) to reinforce the power
of the imperialistic monopolists.

Indeed, religion in relation to economics, racism, and war was
the subject of some bitter comment. A little girl prayed for her
daily bread—and asked her mother if it was all right to pray for a
little butter too. Uncle Herbert had a talk with his cat in which the
cat admited terror of the big dog in the sky but said she was going
to concentrate on uniting all the cats of the world (The slogan
under the masthead of *The Coming Nation* was sometimes:
"Workers of the world, unite! You have nothing to lose but your
chains." On 5 March 1898, Uncle Herbert published a letter from a

high-school boy in Toronto. The letter attacked religious hypocrisy:

> Dear Herbert—We have a teacher in our high school who is a sleek, oily, religious crank. . . . Well, this beautiful Christian pharisee goes around at recess picking notes off the floor and reading them. I think the man who is above such petty things and says "damn" occasionally has a better chance to flap his wings and play his golden harp than a hypocritical pretender has, don't you?

The Editor's comment to this disillusioned student was: "Good for George. He is bound to grow up to be an agitator and a useful reformer."

Sometimes religion was savagely treated as in this "hymn":

> Are you coming home tonight? Bang, bang
> Are you coming home to Jesus
> Out of darkness into light? Bang, bang

At other times, religion was parodied with impudence or gentle humor, as in the Ten Commandments for Sparrows:

1. Find your own food and lodging
2. Keep away from people, especially boys.
3. Don't associate with crows.
4. Stay in your own town.
5. Beware of cats.
6. Go to bed early and get up when the sun does.
7. Bathe every day.
8. Keep your nest hid.
9. Feed your children 'till they can fly.
10. Be sociable, and always sing with the crowd.

Social problems, including racial discrimination, often were taken up in the paper. The plight of the dark-skinned Spanish workers, suffering through the exigencies of the Spanish-American War, led the colonists to consider the plight of black workers and their children. On 2 April 1898 the paper reported the murder of a Negro and his child in Georgia. The report was bitter and sarcastic:

> An unknown party fired through the window, killing Henry Raines and his two-year-old child, while the father was in the act of kissing the baby. This little incident happened near Quitman, Ga. Raines had committed the unpardonable crime of being born

with a black skin. This being the case, he had no right on earth. Hence someone removed him, together with his offspring, in the manner before described. God made the niggers for white men to kill. Why not line them up and slaughter as many as possible at one shot, so as to save ammunition? Why let anyone live but We, Us, & Co.? See the selfishness, degradation, and intolerance the competitive system breeds? There is room a plenty for this Negro and his child—Mother Nature would pour forth unstintedly for their necessities in return for their labor—and this dispatch does not state that he had refused to work. "Hate" is the coat-of-arms for today.

The following month, on May 7, an address appeared in the regular columns in which the speaker, Bolton Hall, was quoted as saying that the condition of the Cubans was no worse than the condition of the Blacks in this country: "The cruelty exhibited in Cuba is not peculiarly of the Spanish race. Within the past few weeks instances of cruelty to Negroes have occurred in this country which equal if they do not surpass anything which has occurred in Cuba."

Women, blacks, and children could not vote. This injustice in respect to women and blacks was pointed out more than once, and the children were not forgotten either. "Children have no votes anywhere," observed the editor of the Women's Column on December 10. For this reason, *The Coming Nation* had developed "the best children's column in America." This was not an idle boast—other columns tended to be sloppily sentimental, falsely protective, laden with severe, moralistic poetry. The basic economic issues confronting adults are not so complex but what children can understand them, as evidenced by a child's comment in the 18 February 1899 Children's Column: "We children must seem to the birds and dogs and cats just like the big monopolists seem to our fathers."

On 11 March 1899, the Reverend Dwight L. Moody, the "Billy Graham" of the day and close to the President, was reported to have berated and denounced Jews in a revival meeting in Boston. A young Jew in his audience effectively defended his race, so effectively in fact that Moody was made a laughing stock and suddenly left town. Surely such an incident would have been discussed by colonists of all ages, especially since some of the colonists were Jews (though there were no blacks, so far as I can determine). In the same paper appeared a parody of Kipling's "White Man's Burden":

> Pile on the brown man's burden
> Compel him to be free
> Let all your manifestoes
> Reek with philanthropy.
> And if, with heathen folly,
> He dares your will dispute,
> Then in the name of freedom,
> Don't hesitate to shoot.

An "eye witness" in a letter almost too naive not to be true reported the "slaughter of every man, woman, and child in whole villages in the Philippines." And, the witness added, "I am in my glory when I can sight my gun on some dark skin and pull the trigger."

On 1 July 1899 the colonists reminded each other: "Each man is his brother's keeper and must give him all the rights we claim for ourselves . . . regardless of the color of skin."

Not all children's crusades were political and racial. The commune understood ecological problems, and a plea for environmental purity appeared in the Children's Column on 6 August 1898:

> You know air is to us what water is to the fishes. It is what we live in and unless we can get it pure, we become sick and weak.
> Whenever a sawmill is built besides a river, and the river is filled with sawdust, the fishes all move away to where the water is clear and pure. They know that if they live in dirty, unhealthy water, they will die. So you see, they are wiser than we are in some things.

Children were constantly taken on excursions to study wildlife, flowers and trees, and the terrain itself, particularly the two caves: one a mammoth limestone cavern in which the colonists first took shelter before buildings were completed and the other a brilliantly colored stalactite cave (now called Jewel Cave).

Once, according to the Children's Column, the children made an excursion through the Stalactite Cave, at that time scarcely explored. One by one, they descended into a large hole, climbing down a long ladder. Inside, they saw "domes that looked like the inside of huge bells, tiny lakes of clear water, a long stone shelf or table covered with stalagmites and so near the low roof that the stalactites on the roof reflected their shadows on the table when we put up our candles to view the beautiful sight."

Picnics, which often included berry picking, were instructive and useful as well as delightful. Week after week, the column ran descriptions of the natural beauties children could search out and enjoy on such expeditions. Visitors frequently reported how bright-eyed, happy, and healthy the children at Ruskin looked.

On 3 September 1898, for instance, Uncle Herbert reported that some of the children were having a taffy pull in the big cave, some were playing in the hall at the center, others were picking berries in the woods or wading in the creek or climbing cliffs or shooting marbles under the shade of a tree or helping with the canning or practicing plays, songs, and the telling of original stories for the evening entertainment of the Progress League. And this was during vacation!

Three weeks later, Uncle Herbert reported that within the past five days there had been three concerts, two parties, and a baseball game. And the children always got the best seats for concerts because they got there first. He also reported that the children had made a long exploration of the big cave but had not found the end of it. They had discovered, however, a new room over 200 feet square.

In the late autumn, the children were busy gathering nuts—hickory nuts and black walnuts—and fruits—persimmons and pawpaws. And always running with them was their black dog, Sport.

Meanwhile, corny jokes and riddles—but not without their purpose—filled the Children's Column. One was about a boy who claimed that a kitten he was trying to sell was a Democrat. Later, he told his prospective buyer the kitten was a Republican. Finally, the man took the cat and the boy changed his mind again: "It's really a Socialist." But the man protested, "I thought you said it was a Democrat or a Republican." "It thought it was before," the boy said, "but now its eyes are open." Another joke was about a boy who got his arithmetic problems done by taking them to the store, getting the total of the items, and then running before he had to pay. At least, he showed ingenuity! On 11 March 1899 the column ran a long, nonsense story which ended with someone making an apple pie out of a salmon.

Two weeks later, the children were back in the woods and returning from their jaunts with their arms full of spring beauties, bloodroot, and violets. It was fun for them, too, just to contemplate, to lie on the grass and hear the birds sing "with glee." According to the column, the rule of children at Ruskin was to treat birds, animals, and people alike.

Comrades in Stalactite (now Jewell) Cave on communal property, 1895.

Besides the excursions into the natural surroundings, there were elaborate celebrations, especially on Christmas and the Fourth of July. In Tennessee in the big communal hall on the third floor of the communal center, the busts of Marx and Ruskin which decorated each side of the stage would be carefully stored at Christmas and a great tree put up to be decorated with popcorn, tinsel, and gingerbread. Santa Claus (on concealed stilts) was ten feet high! Each child received a homemade gift. Simple things satisfied them—a homemade Christmas card was greatly treasured. There was round dancing, something imported from the North and frowned on by the square-dancing natives. Children also participated in special plays, recitations, and lantern-slide presentations.

Even bigger than Christmas was the celebration of the Fourth of July—perhaps somewhat of a defense mechanism on the part of the colonists to assure outsiders of their patriotism, though Marxism was not really regarded as a menace until after the Russian Revolution in 1917. The center for the festivities was the Great Cave near the center. The cave looked like a medieval hall. One entered it through a gaping hole in a 350-foot limestone cliff, and one could stroll past the "bottomless" lake where the colonists did their canning and washing, past the little chambers used for the storage of ice and food or the growing of celery, past another sinister-looking lake, and into other halls, possibly extending two miles.

In the cool main hall of the cave on the Fourth, plays were put on. One was *Hercules,* in which the hero, the Working Man, subdued the iron horses of the Railroad Trust and assorted capitalist dragons. That particular play attracted a crowd so large that it had to be run again and again. Crowds of 3,000 were not uncommon. The girls of the colony performed a "Joan-of-Arc" quadrille—their own invention. Gallons of strawberry ice cream, cranked out in advance, were produced and dispensed from the cool recesses of the cave, along with balls of shaved ice flavored with wild blackberry juice.

From all these accounts, one might think that education was not taken seriously by the colonists. On the contrary, it was the cornerstone of their existence, symbolically represented by the actual laying of the cornerstone of the proposed Ruskin College of the New Economy. While the children were growing up, work was progressing towards their higher education. A quarry near the college site had been opened early in the spring of 1897 and constantly worked. Excavations had been made and foundations for one wing of the building were well-advanced. Drawings of plans depict a massive structure, something on the order of a state capitol.

On Saturday, 19 June 1897, a beautiful day, at noon, several hundred colonists and officials had a big dinner in the center and then puffed their way up a hill nearby to the site of the new college. Here, a fine piece of Ruskin marble had been selected for the cornerstone, polished, and lettered, "R.C.N.E., 1897." A cavity had been cut in the bed of the stone, and in it had been deposited the charter and bylaws and an historical sketch of the commune, an anniversary number of *The Coming Nation,* and Ruskin scrip. (Pay was based on labor. Ruskin printed its own money, so that members received ten hours a day—children also were paid in accordance with their work hours—and bills of one-, five-, and ten-hour denominations could be exchanged for goods in the communal store.) The cornerstone also contained the program for the day and Henry Demarest Lloyd's calling card. Lloyd, a famous economist and writer, author of *Wealth vs. Commonwealth,* then delivered a grandiloquent, two-hour address. The photographer took official pictures, and the chorus sang "100 Years from Now."

Everyone was "dewy-eyed." They had a feeling they were a small group participating in an extremely important event—the establishment on American soil of the first university dedicated to the study of industrial freedom. Work had begun on that first building Monday morning, April 5, and every act was chronicled, for the event was believed to be a landmark in the development of culture.

Though most of Lloyd's address was a string of literary quotations, drawn perhaps from an anthology, he did relieve the recital with the story of a bricklayer George Smith in Coalville, Stafford, England, self-educated from the age of five to eighteen by the light of the kiln fires he tended. Smith wrote a letter to influential men about the treatment of children, and as a result, laws were passed protecting "brickyard" children. Gradually, Smith rose out of his condition to become wealthy, then lost his money in his crusade to rescue canal-boat children, who were being exploited. He made a decent life possible for tens of thousands of children on canal boats. He himself died poor but beloved. By then he was known as "The Children's Friend."

Lloyd said that the living standards of the people living in the Ruskin commune were appreciably higher than those outside the commune and indicated that this was the case in other communistic societies in America.

Neither he nor his audience could foresee that, ironically, as a result perhaps of being taught cooperation, the children of members of the Ruskin commune might become traditionalists when they became members of the larger society outside the commune. None, so far as I can determine, became agitators or reformers. For instance, Walter Wayland, son of the founder of the commune, is now a retired store owner in Girard, Kansas. He was an ardent Goldwater supporter and a pillar of the Presbyterian Church. Annie Ennis Lewis, daughter of commune member John Albin Butler, is deeply religious and conservative in her political views. She worked for several years as a secretary-typist. One of her brothers, Charles Butler, became an insurance agent and country-club member, and another brother, John Butler, became the printer of a racing sheet. The interest of the third son, my husband, Jerome Butler, in social problems was somewhat ambivalent. In 1938, he tried hard to start a union among the workers on the *Paris Herald,* and corresponded with Heywood Broun on the subject. On the other hand, he worked for a time as an editor of a McGraw-Hill magazine *Aviation News.* For awhile, he was a featured reporter for the Hearst papers. He became Washington bureau chief for the *Chicago Journal of Commerce* (now defunct) and even did a feature for the National Association of Manufacturers.

Though some of the colonists did feel that their experiment was a temporary one, even they thought it would have permanent impact on social history. Yet so far as I can determine, the only youth influenced by the commune was Eugene Debs, who as a young man sold subscriptions to *The Coming Nation.* Later Debs wrote articles for *The Appeal to Reason,* a socialist paper established in Girard, Kansas by Julius Wayland, founder of Ruskin. Debs, of course, became one of the most powerful American labor leaders. But he did not spend his childhood in Ruskin.

So forgotten are the aspirations of the Ruskin commune that in the summer of 1972, Robert G. Miner, Jr., J. Bruce McWilliams, and I spent an entire day in a close inspection of the ground where the dedication service of the Ruskin College of the New Economy took place and could not find the cornerstone or even any sign of the foundation. In fact, we had considerable difficulty locating the site. The situation lends stinging irony to the fact that the colonists had indeed done what Uncle Herbert said: "gone back, or rather forwards, to a simpler and more natural life . . . a curious mingling of 1776 and 1976, of backwoods and millenium."

Individuation in "La Chatte Blanche"

Jane Merrill Filstrup

An important custom for women in seventeenth-century France was to gather at the bedside of a woman with child. The visiting ladies would redact news and gossip to the woman confined, and their presence reassured her. Often relatives and neighbors sat in on the event of delivery, and a parade of visitors came to peer at the infant and offer congratulatory and cautionary remarks to the bedridden mother. Not only were girls child-brides at twelve, but they were often promised from the cradle; so women were keenly interested in girl babies of means. Women gave birth year in and year out, so that nannies (*mies*) and as well the custom of storytelling (*mitonner,* which took its name from the artistry of these storytellers) were familiar even to salon visitors.

The first prose fairy tale published as a discrete literary unit, Perrault's "Belle au bois dormant," made famous the formal occasion of parturition with its attendant fairies. Mme. la Comtesse d'Aulnoy (1650–1705), who played a central role in creating the fairy tale as a French literary genre, in many of her stories makes the tacit connection between fairy power and the particularly felicitous occasion presented by the rite of birth. Ten of her fifteen *Contes des Fées* and five of her nine *Contes Nouveaux* take the conventional birth or name-giving ceremony as the initial peripeteia. In each instance in which birth provides the initial action, the event somehow goes asunder—typically as an awryness either in the pregnancy desire of a previously childless woman or in the conferring of blessings by the fairies.

Just as central characters in her stories come into reality in extraordinary circumstances, so Mme. d'Aulnoy's own experiences of *accouchement* were tumultuous and irregular. The countess gave birth to six children. The first two, born in the first and second years of her marriage to the Baron d'Aulnoy, a profiteer in war who purchased his barony and whom she and her mother considered a moneyed boor, died in infancy. The baron wrote *le père absent* on the birth certificates of the next three children: their true father is unknown. Mme. d'Aulnoy tried to dispose of her husband by falsely accusing him of *lèse-majesté,* and they were definitively separated. At the date of the arrest of her husband in 1669, Mme. d'Aulnoy was seven months pregnant. The trials showed her guilty of perjury against the baron. And since she was unable to make a midwinter escape with her mother to Spain, the authorities imprisoned the notorious and very pregnant young woman in a gentlewoman's cell in the Bastille. Her fairy tales, written after she had retired to the quiet of a convent, were intended as an amusing commentary on love for girls of the salon. They also fortified the girls for the experience most hazardous and most honorable in a woman's life, giving birth. By rehearsing with them the event and aftermath of giving birth, she taught them how to face the sexual and societal assaults on their selfhood presented by marriage and childbearing—which occurred in most of their young lives by the mid-teens.

Unlike the Grimm brothers a century later, Mme. d'Aulnoy did not merely collect and redact oral tales (*Märchen*) but modified them to suit the literary tastes of salon audiences. From the building blocks of oral folk tales, Mme. d'Aulnoy constructed literary works which treat love and individuation in a fashion markedly different from the oral material. Whereas the oral folk tale exhibits a mythical sense of naïveté, the fairy tales taken by Mme. d'Aulnoy from Norman sources reflect a sense of self-consciousness and irony appropriate to an author who stands somewhat outside the oral tradition. Her fairy tales lie between a traditional literary form and the fiction of romance and novels. They recognized and suggested solutions for problems preoccupying the female listeners.

Of Mme. d'Aulnoy's fairy tales, "La Chatte blanche" is the most successful admixture of folk material and literary art.[1] "Chatte blanche" is the story of a princess who gains an inner freedom to mature during a bittersweet metamorphosis outside conventional time and space. Brought up in a tower which none but the watchful fairy may enter, the princess is seen and wooed by a prince who rides by on a hunt. Her confidantes, a dog and a parrot, help bring about a private wedding, but the fairy, who had favoured her own hideous candidate, casts a spell on the rebellious princess, transforming her into a cat. The fairy's dragon devours the groom. And so, it is as a mysterious widow that the cat reigns in an enchanted realm until another stranger-prince pays her court and gradually grows to love her. She both fetes him and tests his patience. His final and hardest task, to cut off her head and tail, releases the cat princess from the fairy's spell. She then divulges her uncommon infancy and the history of her tower life.

In this story Mme. d'Aulnoy combines the plots of "Rapunzel" and the *Arabian Nights'* story of Prince Ahmed and the fairy Pari-Banou (the Grimms'-type "Three feathers") to form a biography of a princess-heroine. She adapts each plot to develop themes of a courtship and feminine individuality. Rapunzel serves as the model for the life of the princess from birth to the onset of puberty and takes in the episodes of pregnancy-wish and delivery; Prince Ahmed is the pattern for her life from puberty to the achievement of adulthood. This eclectic juxtaposition of stories is heightened by Mme. d'Aulnoy's use of a story within a story to reconstruct, from the vantage of full adulthood, the princess' early Rapunzel-type life.

The fairy tale works its meaning in the unconscious, where beginnings and ends are interchangeable like the length of a Möbius strip. Although "Chatte blanche" begins with the princess already transformed into a cat, the internal chronology—following the model of "Rapunzel"—begins with the conception, birth, and loss of the child. Only after she has regained her human shape, do we learn of the princess' childhood, which she narrates as a frame-story. Mme. d'Aulnoy distances her audience from the fairy tale by channeling the story through a character's recollection. Unlike the Grimms' *Märchen,* which directly confront the audience with a time-space reality other than the one we conventionally negotiate, Mme. d'Aulnoy's fairy tale moves back and forth between the real and the faerie, delighting in the marvelous but always conscious of the unreality of the fairy tale's symbols. The self-conscious stance of the former tends to reduce the mythic elements of *Märchen* to metaphors in which archetypal patterns are manipulated to explore, more or less consciously, psychological realities.

The plot of "Rapunzel" hinges on desire, which motivates violation of defined space.[2] In the world of the Grimms' *Märchen,* the realm of the witch is absolute: the garden of the witch cannot be violated without a response. Since the nature of things is magically fixed, the pregnant woman's desire for lamb's lettuce ("Rapunzel") generates an anxiety based on the unshakeable logic that infringement of the witch's domain triggers a chain of events which will deprive the frail poachers of what they want most. Because the wife's pregnancy-desire is so deeply human, her fate is all the worse. In the exhilaration of her fecund state, she forgets that she is safe only in the context of human space and emotions. One might eat too much rampion, or one might steal from a neighboring farm and still bear good fruit. The human world gives and forgives. But the realm of the witch is static, a *Tötenreich* rigid to the degree of invulnerability. The slightest poaching requires the dearest recompense.

At the beginning of the *Märchen* we feel the tug of the ending. The denouement of the husband's capture and ransom acts out a fate that cannot be prevented, however terrible. When the husband crosses into the lettuce field, the moment shivers with anxiety. Caught in the act, the wife and husband hand over the child without a murmur of protest. So absolute is the witch's power over the relative world, when it intrudes, that the once hopeful couple vanishes from the story. They disintegrate under the impact of the witch's claims. The husband does not heroically give his life for the safety of the child because the world in which he is caught recognizes no heroes. The witch's power, by the same token, does not reside in some quality of personality such as learning or bravery or even trickery. In the traditional *Märchen,* a witch is a witch because she is. Her sheer existence defines her. She could no more respond to an act of heroism than could a wall. Because they are ineffectual in the world of *Märchen,* emotions do not come into play. The hubris of the pregnant woman leads to a cold, impersonal nemesis.

In Mme. d'Aulnoy's "Chatte blanche," the preparturition biography of the princess varies in several ways from the more linear traditional story. The beginning of the story establishes the expectant queen as a more complex personality than the mother of Rapunzel, for whom the intense pregnancy-desire blots out all other facets of personality. The queen, though pregnant, journeys to a far mountain in search of surprises—an urge for freedom distinctly more civilized than Rapunzel's mother's appetence. There she falls victim to an overwhelming pregnancy-desire. Whereas Rapunzel's mother catches sight of the forbidden fruit across her backyard fence, the queen orders her servants over insurmountable walls. Since the fruit is physically isolated from the world, the queen's orders to raise ladders ever higher are capricious and arbitrary. All attempts to breach the walls fall short, and the queen falls ill with anorexia and insomnia.

Mme. d'Aulnoy elaborates upon the traditional motif in order to modernize the story fabric. There is a striking difference between the folk treatment of the pregnant Rapunzel and Mme. d'Aulnoy's treatment of the queen. In "Rapunzel" the wife personifies desire to the exclusion of all else. But Mme. d'Aulnoy's queen is a salon lady with many interests and a penchant for novelty. Her pregnancy desire is less rabid than the simple wife's. Her desire for fruit of exotic species stems from royal status and educated curiosity, as well as from her pregnancy. Since the collective authors of "Rapunzel" are not interested in the perplexities of the wife's relationship to the world, she receives her request. But in "Chatte blanche," the queen fails initially and to the complete disregard of her unborn child eschews eating and sleeping for six weeks. Typically restructuring fairy events, Mme. d'Aulnoy introduces the relationship of the mother to her child in order to define the queen as a worldly personality. Her inanition raises doubts about her feelings toward motherhood and, as we see later, toward marriage. Such a multifaceted treatment, however terse, departs radically from the simplicity of the *Märchen*. In "Rapunzel," personality resides in the story as a whole, each person exhibiting a facet. In "Chatte blanche," the queen, though not fully developed, has a life of her own independent of the logic of the story plot.

Like Rapunzel's mother, the queen must pay for her obsession. One night a fairy appears and offers the queen access to the fruit in exchange for the fetal child. Rationalizing that if she does not eat and therefore dies the unborn child will not persist anyway, the queen agrees. In "Rapunzel" the agreement of the husband to yield the child climaxes the episode. The womb-fruit is handed over without a word, for the couple's loss of their child merits no elaboration. But in Mme. d'Aulnoy's story the promise of the queen is brought to bear on her marital relationship. The court celebrates the queen's return with feasts and balls, but the gaiety cracks under the growing weight of the queen's anxiety. Gestation is fraught with the inviolability of her promise to the fairies. The queen's disclosure of her disgraceful promise shifts authority to the king, who summarily locks her in a tower for agreeing to give up an heir for *deux ou trois pommes*. This late revelation of the couple's childlessness still more pointedly marks the queen as a woman out-of-touch. To her, childlessness presents no hazard, but the king must think of an heir.

"Rapunzel" moves abruptly from desire to breach, to capture, to loss of the child. In a sense it can be comprehended at a single glance. Because each element in the *Märchen* is so dependent on the others, the plot does not tarry. Events succeed one upon the other in a trice. The *Märchen* has the mythic capacity to draw the hearer or reader out of the real world and into a network of symbols animate with some universal experience. Since it is an event of the subconscious, one must participate in order to understand. Mme. d'Aulnoy's fairy tales, on the other hand, distance the reader by undertaking a more extensive examination of human motivations. She slows down the narrative pace in the first, preparturition section of the story in order to augment personalities and personal relations. Her tales are modern in the sense that she and her audience keep one foot in the conventional world. The king takes on proportions unsuited to the *Märchen,* which is a world unto itself. He acts against his wife because he is a man of the world. Yet against the fairies he is no more effective than the misguided queen. By substituting queen-in-the-tower for daughter-in-the-tower, the king does not placate the fairies, who want their prize. The fairies send a delegation of dwarfs to the king; he treats them uncouthly, and the fairies set loose a malevolent dragon to lay waste to the land.

As the queen once gathered fruit from the bewitched garden, the dragon now claims human lives. The king—ex officio no daring knight—never imperils his own safety in the struggle against the dragon. The fairies remain aloof from the central combat. A fairy confidante persuades the king that all strategies against fairies are futile. This "ambassadress of good sense about fairies" symbolizes an intermixture of fairy and human realms not found in "Rapunzel," where the spaces of the witch and the expectant couple lie side by side but are disharmonious. When the husband enters the lettuce garden, he collides with the witch's sovereignty of that territory. Face to face with the numinosity of a demonic being, the expectant father is grateful to retreat from otherness—still integral in his own space and suffering only the loss of his dearest possession. Mme. d'Aulnoy, in expanding her characters' personalities beyond folkloric type-molds, strengthens them to resist the power of the fairies. The fairies must work at bending the will of the king. Unlike the witch in "Rapunzel," the sheer existence of the fairies is not sufficient to subject mankind to their will. In the end their hold on violators is decisive, but only through the agencies of the dragon and the fairy-in-residence. As if concluding a bargain, the fairies promise to treat the child humanely and so check further entanglements with the king. Although the countess is correct that every king needs an unhuman advisor, such an alliance belongs to the manifest world of politics, not to the inner world of the traditional fairy tale. Traditional *Märchen* view fairies and humans as oil and water; Mme. d'Aulnoy sees them as oil and vinegar, which, when blended, become a sapid garnish for the human palate.

A third modernization of the preparturition section of "Rapunzel" is a marital quarrel which, as an opportunity to comment on the psychology of family life, Mme. d'Aulnoy interjects before the family relinquishes the spotlight to the development of the daughter. The child, even in the womb, alienates husband from wife because the wife is unaccepting of her redefinition into a passive role. Rapunzel's mother is an archetypal tomato; the queen is a free spirit to whom childbearing is only one of many life activities. After the king releases the queen from her tower internment—a political punishment which, like all of his realpolitik strategies to destroy the witches, fails—mental tension lies closer to the surface. King and queen again quarrel over whether the king will surrender or the queen will retain the baby, which leads their daughter to remark years later, "Il semblait que quelque fatalité s'en mêlait, et que je devais toujours être un sujet de discorde entre mon père et ma mère."[3] This psychological lacing of the episode is alien to the Grimm-type fairy tale's "Kunst der Fläche," where self-reflectiveness is equated with a block to action, like fear or cowardliness.[4] Yet, Mme. d'Aulnoy's psychological lacings give the fullness of romance to the story. In novelistic fashion, the daughter is admired for her perspicuity. And by correctly assessing her never-seen parents, she belatedly gives a finishing touch to their strange life histories.

Mme. d'Aulnoy's modern adaptation of the traditional motifs is further apparent when the king and queen officially surrender the infant. The creche, adorned with jewels, is paraded to the meeting place with all the pomp of a Versailles baptism. The fairies collect the cradle and place it on the dragon, now leashed in diamond chains. As the dragon spreads its wings and takes to flight, the queen cries out for safety of the child. This would be nonsensical in

Märchen, in which the human and fairy realms are so distinct that neither the figure of the queen nor her sensibilities vis-à-vis the child's destiny in the other mirror-work realm would be recorded. In "Rapunzel" the action of passing the infant from one realm of control to another is utterly decisive. Once accomplished, feelings of sympathy or regret miscarry a story listener to inattention, leading to a state of being detached from rather than lost in story—an antiepisodic reaction which the *nouvelliste,* not the reciter, encourages. Rapunzel's mother does not presume to fret over the fate of her progeny. Her loss teaches her to mind her place. The queen, too rich in ambition to acquiesce silently, yet too skeletal to be tragic, asserts herself to the last in "Chatte blanche."

Once the child moves from her parents to the fay, both king and queen, like Rapunzel's parents, vanish from sight leaving the daughter a queen unawares and *in absentia.* Mme. d'Aulnoy alters the life-in-the-tower setting to further isolate the princess. Instead of having a personal name like Rapunzel or Persinette (parsley) which links the child to the pregnancy-desire, the queen's daughter is born and grows up *"la princesse."*[5] This shifts her status from surrendered child to captive heiress. The lack of a proper name reminds us that we are following the career of a royal figure, not of just another nubile maiden.

The metamorphosis of the princess now commands our undivided attention. Her playful, new feline body reestablishes continuity with the prepubertal body which she has always known, just as her new societal "envelope" offers redress of injury to her developing self. While Rapunzel waits listlessly for the happenstance impingement of her noble spouse, the princess in "Chatte blanche" undergoes a complex initiation into the human world. Metamorphosis and retransformation are part of the trial through which she becomes queen and ruler of her destiny.

The third part of "Rapunzel"—consisting of the wandering of the prince, his reunion with Rapunzel, and the restoration of his sight—is almost an afterthought. Since the central theme of the story treats the miscarriage of young love, the ending seems a cheerful non sequitur. In place of this episode, Mme. d'Aulnoy adapts another folk-story type, derived from the Prince Ahmed–Pari-Banou story of the *Arabian Nights* (called "The Three feathers" in Grimm) and radically slows the process of reunion in order to explain the development of the princess in her second exile from the mundane world. Since Antoine Galland told many of the stories of *Mille et une nuits* in salons well before he published them in 1704–11, it is likely that Mme. d'Aulnoy heard the story in his or in another salon and adapted and amalgamated it with the story of Rapunzel. Mme. d'Aulnoy's version, the opening part of "Chatte blanche," is narratively similar to "Three feathers" which may in fact be a derivation from her version of the *Nights* story.[6]

"Chatte blanche" opens with an elderly king and his three sons. The female side of the family is absent. But Mme. d'Aulnoy twists the aging-king theme, for the father has no intention of relinquishing his rule. On the contrary, by sending his sons on a merry dog chase, he hopes to distract their attention from his increasing agedness. The contest is chimerical, for the king cares not a fig about little dogs. He hopes the rivalry will exhaust his sons and end in a no-show. When the youngest son returns with the loveliest of all dogs, it is the king, not the brothers as in "Three feathers," who extends the competition to another contest. After this second contest results in another victory, the king again equivocates. And even after the last search, for the fairest maiden, produces a worthy queen, the king keeps his throne. A sense of rococo play inheres in this overall structure, for though the sons move about the realm exposing this treasure and that to the surface, the familial and political girdings remain unaltered.

Mme. d'Aulnoy uses an arabesque pattern of story plot in order to lend the transformed princess sufficient story space to court the prince, resolve her ambivalent feelings toward sexual conjoinment, and gain his commitment to her welfare. The end of each episode returns to the starting point whence another narrative tendril swirls forth. In the *Arabian Nights,* Prince Ahmed and Pari-Banou marry upon first sight. In "Three feathers" the youngest son does not court his toad-lady. In "Chatte blanche" the pace of the frame competition slows down to a contest per year, the great part of which the Chatte and the prince spend in leisurely togetherness, resurrecting the princess's earlier sexual feelings in a qualitatively new relationship.

The prince comes upon a great palace decorated with tiles depicting all the fairies since Creation—stories of fairies including "Peau d'âne" and "La Belle au bois dormant" by Perrault and four of Mme. d'Aulnoy's own *contes.* In the reception hall he stops before a gallery of cats—paintings of Rabelais' *Rodilardus,* Perrault's *Chat botte*, sorcerer-cats, and La Fontaine's cat-turned woman—which adumbrate the subjective experience of feline fairies for the prince. The cat, veiled in black and melancholy, enters the reception hall and invites the prince to dine with her. The presence of cooked mice alongside his roasted pigeon repulses the prince. The cat assures him that his cuisine is prepared *à part*. Together with the processional caterwauling of a chamber ensemble of cats, the commensual event serves to test the youth's adaptability to the strangeness of the feline court. It is a game of etiquette, but a serious game, for the cat must establish her identity as something other than man or cat. Otherwise the prince will not engage her felinity seriously enough to undo it. In order for the white cat to regain her human form, she must engineer a courtship in which she prepares herself and the prince for royal responsibility.

The prince sets out in search of a treasure three times. After each assignment he enters the palace of the cat where he spends a year. In each of these years the cat introduces the youth to an event which authenticates her otherness as an animal and independence as a personality. The morning after their first meeting, the cat doffs her veil, mounts an ape, and together with hundreds of other felines ravages the rabbit and bird population of the neighboring purlieus. The cats frolic in total abandon; the cat is a sorceress and the gathering is likened to a sabbat. The intended effect of impressing the prince with the bestial willfulness of the cat is heightened by placing him on a wooden horse, despite his protests that he is no Don Quixote. The move to the hunt displays the new energy of a creature whose earlier experience has been stamped with ordered constraint, but who as an adult periodically relaxes.

The white cat is a formidable mate for the innocent prince. During the first year's sabbat, the prince carefully sits to the side. But in the second year he intervenes to free the cats who have been condemned to capital punishment for nibbling from the Chatte's *quisquilliae*. He prevents monarchial overkill and the collapse of justice. This first act of state of the prince makes humane the judgment of the animal world. By taking a stance against the Chatte, the prince allows her to resist the animal in which she is captive. When he dissuades her from executing innocent subjects, the couple takes the first steps of a minuet in which the female leads the male toward maturity in order that he can free her. The maturation of the prince and the anticipation of the Chatte encourage and restrict the movements of each other as they dance toward the moment of truth.

In the third year the cat treats the prince to a staged battle between cats and rats. This military spectacle favors cats, but the watery arena in which it takes place is an equalizer. Rats in eggshells evenly battle cats on cork platforms until Minagrobis (named after Rabelais' scary puss), admiral of the cats, eats the rat admiral, an old salt who has thrice stowed his way around the world. Cats against rats is a mere entertainment for the white cat who, because she has *la politique,* spares the murine survivors, lest her subjects fall into "une oisiveté qui pourrait lui deviner préjudiciable" from lack of sport.[7]

In each of three sojourns at the palace of the white cat, the prince passes his time being caressed by the luxuries and pleasures of the court. A reborn version of the first suitor, the prince is an adolescent with a capacity for affective response, which complements the growing ability of the cat to conceptualize her freedom. The prince forgets his father, brothers, and the rivalry. For him, life in the palace is blissfully insensible. Like his predecessor (successor in the narrative account), he desires to enter the tower room, to live and love without the exigencies of adulthood. When the hour of departure approaches, the prince asks to stay, even, to become a cat. The princess is wiser and puts him off with "responses obscures."[8] To the prince life with the charming cat is carefree, but to the white cat it is a captive mourning and bondage to a personal past that is both unknown and basically incomprehensible to the prince. To the white cat, the moment is of little import. Only internal, psychic time matters for the reaffirmation of her femininity and royalty. She must shed her nastiness; the prince must attend to her words and gain experience. Each needs the other's support.

In the palace, the white cat is a kept animal. Her place is in the home, but she lacks a master—leaving her in a netherworld between the jungle of the *chat sauvage* and full domesticity. When the prince returns the second year he caresses her, but she never becomes his pet. The fairy power controls the human, not vice versa. Yet most of each of the three years passes quietly, as unremarkably as a cat sleeps on its favorite chair. As long as it takes for the cat to work her escape, she leads a limited domestic life. But her realm is destined to grow, making her the master and men her pets.

During the first year at the fairy court the white cat delights the prince with masques and balls. During the second year her learned discourses on books, paintings, and antique medals (Perrault's hobby) dazzle him. In the third year he is convinced that she is no *chose naturelle* but a prodigy even among marvels. When the time to depart approaches, the cat awakens the insouciant youth to his worldly task, prodding him to compete for the throne. The prince declares his love for her and asks to stay. While the "Rapunzel" substory is the stage for the female's development, the cat story is the stage for the male's coming to consciousness, albeit with the cat as mistress of ceremonies. Her philosophical disclaimer to the petitioning prince, "Je te tiens compte de l'attachement que tu témoins pour une petite Chatte Blanche, qui dans le fond n'est propre à rien qu'a prendre des souris," is not a departure from the festive diversions which she has afforded the inamorato, but a minute strategem.[9] To win this mouser the prince must snatch the crown.

The prince moves between a trickster father and a sphinxlike lady, neither of whom is willing to shelter him. He is in effect a shuttlecock in a game of reconnoitering between the father and the daughter-in-law. Like Prince Ahmed and the simpleton son in "Three feathers," this prince succeeds only because he relies on the fairy animal. The cat supplies him with the winning objects, but the contest is illusory. At home court he asserts himself over his brothers but never enough to become king. Indeed the king's realm appears prosaic by juxtaposition with the fairy cat's palace. The prince's role at every move of the tale is to release the princess from enchantment and to become husband to the queen, not to be the ruler himself.

When the prince returns for the third time, the cat receives him outside the palace in a pavilion *à la mode persane*. This is her first step outside fairy walls. The princess's court meow their ecstasy from the palace gutters, a stereotypic place for feline lovemaking, humorously slanting the Chatte's court as a court of love. Her abortive, unhappy first-love experience has until now rendered the white cat prudent, in agreement with the contemporary proverb: "cat échaudé craint l'eau froide."[10] But the third arrival of the prince initiates preparations for retransformation and overt sexual encounter. The white cat, once demure in mourning, exhibits her charms, and servants, once hushed, make ready to mate. After a year of hunts and chess, the prince presses the cat to bare her secret. The prince seeks neither toy doglets nor beautiful cloths but a wife. This prize joins the careers of the prince and princess. The innocence of the fairy world shatters as the prince, probing the surface of this extraordinary creature, asks her whether she is a fairy or a human in a feline metamorphosis. Such a stark attack of the self-conscious manipulator of symbols on a mythical symbol set reveals the means by which Mme. d'Aulnoy distances herself from the assumptions of folk-tale formality. Out of exasperation, the prince speaks the mind of an urban elite familiar with the Cartesian image of a mathematically defined universe and a rationally structured homo sapiens.

The prince aims his query from outside the story with a detachment of belief unknown to traditional *Märchen*. He resembles a person who awakens from a dream and asks what the dream meant. The prince entreats the white cat to cease with dreaming. At first she again delays. Her world makes but distracted sense from a rational perspective, but she must engineer the exit. The symbols are psychologically important. The outside observer may question the sense of the whole set of symbols, but he cannot move another's personality from one mode to another through bypassing the symbols altogether.

On the eve of the prince's return to his father's court, the white cat makes her move: the prince must exscind her head and tail and cast them into the fire.[11] The prince is repelled by such a barbarous request. The white cat next resorts to the solid interdependence between the prince and herself, pleading with him to obey her as a "chatte de bien et de honneur."[12] She lowers the legitimization of murder to herself, to her word of honor. At issue is the prince's assessment of her trustworthiness. Still he vacillates. As a last recourse, she throws him back on himself: if he wishes to defeat his brothers in rivalry for the throne, he must accomplish her decapitation. At issue is the princess's assessment of the prince. Is he ready to kill in order to live?

The prince dismembers the cat and throws the head and tail into the fire, releasing the princess into a beautiful lady. After she relates her childhood, the "Rapunzel" section of the tale, the couple travels to the prince's court for the final contest. As the king graciously bends down to open the cat's cage, the queen bursts forth "comme le soleil qui a été quelque temps enveloppé dans une nue."[13] She is no longer *la princesse* but *la reine.* The king, awed by such beauty, cries out that this fairy deserves the crown. But the radiant queen desires not the king's land. Rather, displaying *noblesse oblige,* she parcels out bits of her kingdoms to the father and the brothers. The queen simply removes the youngest son from the father's realm to hers, where she rules and he reigns. Unable to overcome the father, the son remains a subject to the queen. She on the other hand embraces her right to rule. She has survived life in the tower and life in the *chatterie.* She has earned her freedom. Whereas her mother was capricious, she is prudent; where the king failed, she succeeds. She is the salon's answer to the philosopher-king—the enchantress-queen.

The white cat metamorphosis connects the birth of awareness in the princess and the fulfillment of ambition in the queen. Her life as a cat is an interlude of patient wait for the male to return to the scene and free her, what Bruno Bettelheim describes as an "era of recovery."[14] Until this happens she fluctuates between domesticity, symbolized by the elegance of her court, and feline exertiveness. In the court the cat is veiled, demure, unable to break out of her past. When she does strike out, her actions are debased to the level of the sabbat or the petty enjoyment of watching cats eat rats, until the disparate aspects of her personality are integrated. While she maturely runs a mini-realm during her confinement, her inner development takes place. She controls her new romance. Her state of mourning symbolizes her bondage to the past and limited access to the world and her conviction that someday her "Rapunzel"-husband will return and rescue her. This mood of mourning is broken only once, at the sabbat, when her veil of *pudeur* is thrown back revealing to herself and the prince an exciting inner freedom. The white cat is an interface between the basic cut of the Rapunzel-like childhood and the final fitting of responsible adulthood. The cat figure acts as the piece of cloth which allows a garment to be contoured and which then lies hidden beneath the surface. When the inner and the outer cloths are joined, the cat disappears.

When she is released from the spell, she becomes manly—fully exercising her animus. At the king's court, she bursts from her cage like a sun, a heavenly deity. She sheds the light of rationality on the scene of illusion. Where the career of the prince lacked meaning because the contests were false, the new queen makes sense of the whole. She brings the silliness to an end by adding her lands to the prize. Once petlike, she now throws tidbits of land to the king and his sons. Since the prince is unable to come into his own in the arena of his adolescence, the queen whisks him away. She provides the rational therapy which checks his frustration. In all these ways, the queen operates like a man. The crucial syzygy in Jungian terms of anima and animus takes place, but in a highly feminist way. Within the fantasy, she becomes her own institution, monarch. She becomes part of the world and uses it. Yet she retains a feline independence of all men, an aura of virginity in the Classical sense. Once she is disenchanted, she enchants. Men love her. But because the animus of each prince is so weak, she cultivates only herself. The union of her anima and animus obviates the role of the prince. The queen is a Diana of fairies, above the peripeteia of human romance.

NOTES

1. d'Aulnoy, "La Chatte blanche," *Contes des Feés* (Paris: Mercure de France, 1956). II. pp. 111-145. For prior critical treatment of the story see Renée Hubert's "Poetic humor in Mme. d'Aulnoy's fairy tales," *Esprit créateur,* III, No. 3 (Fall, 1963), 123–29. Hubert suggests that the *conteuse* entered love's labyrinth with a different thread in each story. Emphasizing that Mme. d'Aulnoy values love as the ultimate human refinement, Hubert situates the burlesque moments and the metamorphosis which are love's troubles in the Petrarchan tradition.

2. The strong parallels between the plots of the two fairy tales examined in this study are pointed up in the following broad outline. Italics indicate the story within a story.

"Rapunzel" (*KHM #*12)

I. Pregnancy-desire and loss of child
    A. Pregnancy-desire and breach of garden
    B. Husband captured and freed with lettuce in return for womb-fruit
    C. Witch takes child
II. Life in the tower
III. Wandering and reunion

"La Chatte blanche"

I. *Pregnancy-desire and loss of child*

    A. *Pregnancy-desire and abortive*
       attempt to breach bewitched
       garden
    B. *Queen falls ill*
    C. *Queen is cured, takes fruit in*
       return for her womb-fruit
    D. *King discovers wife's barter,*
       take possession of womb-fruit
    E. *King resists witches and fails*
    F. *Fairies take child*
II. *Life in the tower*
III. Life as a cat

    3. "Chatte blanche," pp. 133–144.
    4. Max Lüthi, *Volksmärchen und Volkssage*, 2nd ed. (Munich: Francke [1966]), p. 14.
    5. The "Rapunzel" story was likely known to Mme. d'Aulnoy in the version whihch Mlle. de la Force borrowed from Basile's "Petrosellina" (Day 2, Tale 1). This was published the year before "Chatte blanche" and entitled "Persinette" (*Cabinet des Fées*, Paris, 1789, VI, 43–54).
    6. The plot similarities of the Arabic story and "Drei Federn" ("Three Feathers") are significant enough to argue for some causality, perhaps through Mme. d'Aulnoy's "Chatte blanche." Geneviève Massignon, in *Folktales of France*, trans. J. Hyland (Chicago: University of Chicago Press, 1968), classifies a cluster of French oral tales (Stith Thompson Type #402) under the motif of the father promising the marriage of his niece to three sons who then compete in a search for rare items. The "Piece of Cloth" (pp. 89–92) stars a magic cat and is clearly the progeny of "Chatte blanche."
    7. "Chatte blanche," p. 126.
    8. "Chatte blanche," p. 118.
    9. "Chatte blanche," p. 123.
    10. César-Pierre Richelet, "Chat," *Dictionnaire français* (Geneva: Widerhold, 1680).
    11. The request is related to various French customs for disenchanting cats. Closest is the Norman custom to mutilate the cat's tail or ears, thereby preventing its admission to a sabbat.
    12. "Chatte blanche," p. 127.
    13. "Chatte blanche," p. 145.
    14. Bruno Bettelheim, *The Uses of Enchantment: The Meaning and Importance of Fairy Tales* (New York: Alfred A. Knopf, 1975), p. 150.

Bruno Bettelheim and the Fairy Tales

James W. Heisig

One of the most unforgettable things about the storyteller who spreads the marvelous tales which make up Rilke's *Stories of God* is that he believes his stories will better be understood by the children who hear them than by their elders who can only fear the dangers of straining the youngsters' minds with so much imaginative fantasy. The storyteller's favorite audience, though, is a certain cripple named Ewald, whose immobility has made him resemble things with which he fosters many intimacies, but whose familiarity with the art and grammar of silence has made him decidedly superior both to things and to changeable, talkative healthy people. It is Ewald's rare, quiet words and gentle, reverent feelings which the storyteller finds so appealing, in contrast to the crass incredulity of his other peers, who know so little about stories. On one particular day Ewald asks his friend, "Where did you get the story you told me last time?" Despondent, the storyteller has to recount how he found it in a book where the historians buried it some years ago after it had died a slow, painful death. It seems the story was inflicted with heavy words which became too difficult to speak, so that in the end it perished on one last pair of dry lips and was enshrouded with all honors in a book where others of its family lay. Before that, it had lived for four-or five-hundred years as a song, traveling freely from mouth to mouth, only pausing to sleep from time to time in some heart where it was warm and dark. After hearing all of this, Ewald asks, surprised, "But were people once so quiet that songs could sleep in their hearts?"[1]

Rilke's point is well taken—even more so today than in 1899 when he first drafted his collection of stories. Oral folklore traditions in the past one hundred and fifty years have had to accommodate conditions which could only severely imperil their survival. As the highly industrialized societies race toward their apotheosis by means of increased professionalism, specialization, and the general institutionalization of knowledge, the art of storytelling is left behind, replaced by the newer arts of academic autopsy. Rilke's storyteller seems to have sensed that the printing press of itself was not enough to bring this about: it merely provided the most avail-

able graveyard for tales variously slaughtered by the forward rush
of civilization. Like so many folk crafts whose means of production
have been expropriated by technology, the folktale in most of its
traditional genres has become a marketable commodity, ripped un-
timely from the socio-cultural setting in which it once flourished.
And, to complete the process, what is left of the tales returns to
contribute to the epidemic self-depreciation infecting the modern
conscience. Children subjected to the biases of standardized
schooling and mass modes of entertainment no longer want to be
"told" stories that might depart from the "correct" versions
printed in books or on film. And their educators, wary of offending
the complex psychology of the child's development, learn to trust
modernized editions of folktales, if indeed they tell them at all. The
stories grow too heavy to be sung. They lose the right to roam
about from mouth to mouth and be transformed each time they
come to rest in a storyteller's heart.

The amazing thing in all of this is that so much of our traditional
folklore maintains its natural enchantment over children and adults
alike. The fairy tale is a case in point. However much we
bowdlerize, mutilate, moralize, and otherwise bend it to our own
ends, it still seems to move us with a power we have not yet
learned to exorcise or imitate. That fact may well turn out to be
more important that it at first seems. Like the hard-hearted King
Shahryar, charmed for a thousand and one nights by the fantastic
tales of the young Scheherazade, we may find in the end that our
fairy tales contain much of the very wisdom necessary for our
salvation.

It is precisely in this regard that a book like Bruno Bettelheim's
The Uses of Enchantment is so welcome and so timely.[2] For those
who know his earlier books and are familiar with his work at the
University of Chicago's Sonia Shankman Orthogenic School, Bettelheim's name has become synonymous with intelligent and devoted respect for the mysterious world of the child. In this latest
book he carries on these same concerns by turning his attention to
the function of the fairy tale in the development of the consciousness of the child. This is not the first time that Bettelheim has ven-
tured beyond the psychologist's accustomed boundaries. Over
twenty years ago he attempted a psychoanalytic study of puberty
rites among preliterate cultures.[3] The mixture of excitement and
professional criticism which his theories aroused in that work has

no doubt prepared him for similar reactions to the conclusions he arrives at in this full-length study of the fairy tale. Fortunately, it has not deterred him from setting forth his point of view boldly and without compromise—a fact which is all the more to be admired in a man in his seventies, a patriarch among child psychologists who refuses to rest comfortably on his considerable achievements.

Bettelheim is not the first, of course, to apply the principles of psychoanalysis to the fairy tale. Freud himself had suggested in his *Traumdeutung* (1900) that there is an unbroken line to be found between the origins and functions of dreams and of folklore in the psyche; and many since him, from a wide range of psychological persuasions, have carried the suggestion further.[4] But the study of folklore in the past fifty years has become so specialized and so vastly documented a discipline and the distrust of psychological methods so widespread among orthodox ethnologists that it has become exceedingly risky to continue on with such investigations.

On the other hand, we cannot forget the inevitable popular outrage still so easily incited by psychoanalytical ideas. Freud's interpretations of the polymorphous sexual perversity of the child is only beginning to settle into the modern mind, as Bettelheim himself, one of those who has done most to establish and refine the approach, must know only too well. Yet now we find him ordering such dear friends of imagination as Cinderella, Snow White, Rapunzel, Red Riding Hood, and Hansel and Gretel onto the analyst's couch—and the very idea sends a shudder down the spine in spite of ourselves. Surely this is the height of irreverence, the one sacrilege against memory for which psychoanalysis cannot be forgiven!

Indeed, left in the hands of a less sensitive observer of the human personality and a less skillful analyst, the worst might rightly be expected of such a project. Bettelheim's results however are impressive and generally hard to fault, given his stated intentions. Briefly put, the thesis he experiments with in the book is this: Using the psychoanalytic model of the psyche, fairy tales can be seen to communicate to the child an understanding of universal human problems in such a way as to encourage the development of his budding *ego*, give expression to *id* pressures, and suggest ways to relieve them in line with the requirements of the *superego*. The vagueness of the tales, he claims, is pedagogically suited to these tasks in that it engages the child's imagination to fill in the details and to invest his interests on whatever level he finds himself. The message of the tales, the argument goes on, is most critical at puberty, when the tangle of emotions which grip the child is most in need of sorting out and naming; and when the "separation anxiety" is keenest and most in need of some promise of deliverance. And in all of this, Bettelheim concludes, the fairy tale is much more reliable and therapeutic than attempts to educate parents in the arid complexities of child psychology could ever hope to be.

Working within that broad framework, Bettelheim brings to bear years of clinical experience, considerable research into the fairy tale, and a sharp eye for double entendre to uncover the mechanisms and meanings of enchantment in the child. In the end, he may not remove all the offensiveness of a rigorously Freudian perspective, but he probably does more for the respectability of the fairy tale as an interpretative tool than has anyone before him.[5] His awareness of the limitations of his approach, together with occasional references to concrete cases of childhood disorder, ably protect the extreme subtlety which marks his reading of several of the stories from the usual charge of one-sided dogmatism.

In short, Bettelheim succeeds in opening the tales up, in leading us in and out between the lines where they can be made to deliver of their healing secrets. It is not surprising that he directs his strongest criticisms against attempts to detour the fairy tales from their natural functions in favor of other secondary ends and so to close off their power and meaning. Charles Perrault's seventeenth-century moralization of the tales is the object of Bettelheim's most telling complaints. Disney's famous animations (frequently biased in favor of Perrault's versions) are only mentioned twice (pp. 210, 251) as instances of apologic interference with the child's imaginative needs, although a general opposition to this treatment is unmistakable. All such closures remove the story from the genre of the folktale and relocate it amid the great bulk of so-called "children's literature" which he condemns as "emptyminded entertainment," shallow of substance and significance.[6]

By the same token, Bettelheim argues that book versions of the fairy tales, even if accurate, can be counterproductive. Most obviously, the use of collections of these tales to teach reading skills or a love of written literature seriously threatens their effect on the child. Moreover, the use of illustrations bereaves the child of the imaginative freedom he should enjoy, and makes identification with the stories' heroes or heroines more difficult over a long period of time. Similarly, having the story read to one, or reading it oneself, tends to objectify it, to freeze its form and so to eliminate the essential contribution of the listener, who projects himself and significant others in his milieu into the tale. For Bettelheim, the ideal way to transmit the tales is in imitation of their folkloric means of communication: tell them orally and frequently; be faithful to the original without being slavish. Not only does such oral storytelling permit the greatest flexibility of response, but it sets up a valuable interpersonal event between the storyteller and the child. In addition, by separating the fairy tales from tacit interpretations—via the appendage of moral lessons, illustrations, or standardized wordings—their motifs may be taken over spontaneously by the child, Bettleheim suggests, to structure other forms of unconscious activity such as dreams, waking fantasies, and play.

Bettelheim's resistance to premature closure of the manifold of possible meanings contained in any given fairy tale is not simply a result of the same general interpretative principle which governs psychoanalysis' understanding of symptomatic languages. It has to do, he would insist, with the very genesis and structure of the tales themselves. He views the fairy tale as a corporate form of imagination which, so long as it meets the psychic needs of generation after generation of people who preserve it, will survive shifting patterns of reasoning and intellectual trends. Without denying this way of looking at the tales its validity, I think there are certain points in his argument where Bettelheim can be shown to have slipped into interpretative closures of his own which neither the fairy tales nor his own psychoanalytic perspective require. Accordingly, I turn now to a more critical examination of his project, focusing in the main on a number of general hermeneutical questions and adding a few specific remarks on selected tales by way of conclusion. Needless to say, these attempted disclosures will make best sense if read as marginal comments to the text itself and not as a complete substitute argument.[7]

In the course of constructing his argument for the meaning and importance of fairy tales, Bettelheim draws upon a number of assumptions about the psyche of the child. Perhaps the first to strike us is his characterization of childhood modes of thought as essentially similar to those of primitive, preliterate peoples. As the child develops, he learns to replace them with more adult modes of thought which will enable him to live responsibly in our advanced civilization. Once one has understood the structure of this natural generation gap, Bettelheim would assert, it becomes clear that primitive forms of psychological insight—which is how he classifies the fairy tales—are more therapeutic for the child but unnecessary, even regressive, for the adult.[8]

Standing behind this conclusion is the old notion that ontogeny recapitulates phylogeny, that is that the development of an individual organism telescopes and repeats the evolution of the entire species. Its promotion in modern times is associated with the evolutionary biologist, Ernst Haeckel (1834-1919). From there it was taken up for experimentation in theoretical anthropology by Claude Lévy-Bruhl, among others, and eventually found its way into psychology through Freud and Jung. The hypothesis itself fell speedily into disrepute, roughly in the same order, though it is one of those suggestive and stubborn ideas which seem to survive even the strongest contrary evidence and to reappear at the most unexpected times.

Bettelheim's subscription to this principle, implicit though it be here, seems to me unfortunate. [9] First of all, the claim that primitive logics are inferior to and irrational in comparison with scientific views of the world is unnecessary to the claim (which Bettelheim makes, following Piaget) that children begin in a largely animistic world and only slowly learn the art of abstract thinking. Moreover, it has the disadvantage that it intimates a qualitative difference between adult and childhood thinking; and, consistent with that, a depreciation of the role of imagination in abstract thought. Bettelheim comes close to stating this explicitly in passages scattered throughout the book such as: "Every child believes in magic, and he stops doing so when he grows up (with the exception of those who have been too disappointed in reality to be able to trust in its rewards)" (p. 118).

Second, by grounding the comparison of thought-patterns in children and primitive peoples merely on their equidistance from our supposedly unquestionable commonsense world, the possibility of further insight from a study of the social functions of thought-patterns, including those found in the fairy tale, is prematurely closed off.

Third, these two closures combine to encourage further the original bias that fairy tales are really prescientific forms of psychology which are natural to the child's sphere but wholly unnatural to the adult's, which needs more rational means to integrate conscious and unconscious elements in the psyche. In this way, Bettelheim intends to support the usefulness of the fairy tale as a guide to the child's first halting steps in imagination. Yet it is hard to see how anything is gained in denying the tales any role at all in the mature imagination.

At this point the full and final implications of Bettelheim's attraction to the Haeckelian principle become clear. Personal maturity is measured, at least in great part, by one's ability to translate imaginative projections into the language of scientific psychology or some other rational interpretative frame. Enchantment is the necessary business of being a child. Becoming an adult, however, means extensive and deliberate disenchantment. What he calls the "illogic of the unconscious" continues to confront the "rational order" of the "real world" throughout one's life (p. 66). The difference between the integrated and the infantile personality is that the one can *understand* the objective truth about the real world, while the other can only *feel* it subjectively and so must revert to an unreal world. Each frame of reference has its own "truth," Bettelheim says, but there is no doubt that the truth of fantasy is more useful to the child's mind and harmful to the adult's (116ff).

There is a certain immediate appeal about such a point of view. For one thing, it seems to accord with our timeworn folk wisdom about raising children. For another, it supports our modern tendency to charge that wisdom more and more to the care of academic psychology, a tendency which Bettelheim seems to welcome readily enough. Parents are warned against trying to invent their own fairy tales to tell their children for fear of unwitting, but nonetheless dangerous, didactic interpretations. Only the rare individual—Goethe's mother is cited as an example (pp. 153-154)—should extend creativity in storytelling beyond the addition of occasional details. What every parent can do, on the other hand, is grasp the psychological meaning of the fairy tales, and this gives him a decided superiority over the child, which must not be relinquished for the good of both sides. He may never be able to capture the many-leveled meanings of a single one of the tales or understand the varieties of influence involved in its retelling from infancy to adolescence. But "even if a parent should guess correctly why his child has become involved emotionally with a given tale, this is knowledge best kept to oneself." This because, Bettelheim argues, the child *wants* the meaning to be kept on a preconscious level. "Explaining to a child why a fairy tale is so captivating to him destroys the story's enchantment, which depends to a considerable degree on the child's not quite knowing why he is delighted by it. . . . He can gain much better solace from a fairy tale than he can from an effort to comfort him based on adult reasoning and viewpoints" (pp. 18 and 45).

The advice is sound enough, even if the intellectual hubris it appears to cultivate may not be. I stress the point here not in order to take issue at this time with the social function of psychological theory, but because there are hints in Bettelheim's own treatment that he himself is aware of the enchantment which psychoanalysis has over him, not unlike that of the tale for the child in terms of its power and fictions.

To begin with, he sees that the basic charm of the fairy tale is due more to its literary form than to its psychological message. "The fairy tale could not have its psychological impact on the child were it not first and foremost a work of art" (p. 12). He then goes a step further to assert that no other form of literature and art is so "fully comprehensible to the child" as is the fairy tale, by which he means that it is capable of yielding new insights at each return. For this reason he concludes that the exploration of the psychological contribution of these stories to the child's development is more useful to parents than other forms of interpretation might be.[10] The questions which are closed off by *petitio principii,* and which could as easily have been left open, are obvious. Surely educators of all kinds would be interested in seeing a balance between the psychological interpretations of the stories and some investigation of the literary-artistic form which Bettelheim sees as essential. Furthermore, by separating the enchantment of the fairy tale from the world of child psychology, the possibility of its range of relevant meanings to the adult becomes once more deserving of attention.[11]

Likewise, Bettelheim takes pause on one occasion to talk about the limits of his interpretation in such a way as to suggest the inexhaustible intelligibility of the fairy tale. "Today adults use such concepts as id, ego, superego, and ego-ideal to separate our internal experiences and get a better grasp on what they are all about. . . . When we consider the emotional connotations these abstract terms of psychoanalysis have for most people using them, then we begin to see that these abstractions are not all that different from the personifications of the fairy tale'' (p. 75). Except for one later remark about translating a story into ''the pedestrian language of psychoanalysis'' (p. 309), he does not return to the point. If we take the idea as given and add to it Bettelheim's acknowledgement that the fairy tales themselves are interpretations of inner human experiences—which is why they begin in concrete reality and pass into a magical, unreal world (pp. 25, 62)—then their ''illogic'' may be seen as a necessity and not simply as a pedagogic tool for the child who is unable to abstract. Just as the child ''intuitively comprehends that although these stories are *unreal*, they are not *untrue*'' (p. 73), so too the adult may need to see that the same is true about his psychoanalytic stories. The familiarity with the workings of the mind which characterizes the mature personality (p. 97) may appear more true if we use psychoanalytic categories. But as Bettelheim notes: ''Unfortunately, in doing so we have lost something which is inherent in the fairy tale: the realization that these externalizations are fictions, useful for sorting out and comprehending mental processes'' (p. 75). With respect to the general argument of the book, therefore, the tales may yet be useful for adults, even if only to remind us of the inevitable gap between the things of our lives and the talk we use to appropriate them into the story of our life.

One final indication that Bettelheim's commitment to the view that the fairy tale belongs principally to the child is not absolute is his frequent allusion to different ''levels'' of meaning in the tales. Most often he uses the phrase merely to refer to the child's ability to project different psychic states into the stories. He makes brief note of the strata left in the tales by virtue of their long oral history, embracing cultural, religious, and mythical elements, but dismisses it at once from consideration as of little use for our understanding of the child. In this way his closure of the fairy tales in favor of child psychology is supported by his evidence; but it neglects to keep open his own intuition of the benefits of deeper research into their archaeology, whether for his own project or as a way to extend the meaning and importance of the tales into the adult world as well.

We may now consider certain aspects of Bettelheim's interpretation which fall within the general compass of his Freudian standpoint. First among these is his use of the theory of projection;

that is, of the imaginative and largely unconscious transference of
inner psychic states to artificial conditions which distort those
states enough to provide a relaxation of anxiety. While such "externalization" is seen as necessary to relieve inner pressures—and
at no time more necessary than during childhood—it is the very
antithesis of maturation which requires the expansion of consciousness and the dissolution of projections. The benefit of fairy
tales is that they prepare for mature consciousness in offering "figures onto which the child can externalize what goes on in his mind,
in controllable ways. . . . Once this starts, the child will be less and
less engulfed by unmanageable chaos" (pp. 65-66). Bettelheim resists any attempt to specify which tales should be told at which
time in the child's development, insisting that the way in which the
tales teach by "indirection"—camouflaging feelings or displacing
them onto secondary objects—can only be recognized but not organized for pedagogical purposes.

Although some theory of projection is essential for a psychological interpretation of the fairy tale, it is also likely to carry certain
limiting biases with it. In Bettelheim's case, for instance, the concern with dissolving projections into their "real" components
comes close to ignoring the need for criteria to determine what is
real and what is not and overlooking the possibility that certain
very real things of our life cannot but be spoken of in a language of
apparent falsehoods, i.e. of projections. It is not necessary to get
enmeshed in philosophical arguments about the mechanisms of
perception to see these problems in Bettelheim's own method. On
the one hand he allows the unavoidable projections of children and
praises the fairy tales as helpful displacements of feelings too
dangerous to be aimed at their direct referents (pp. 135, 164, 204).
Adults do not need the tales for this, he says, but should remember
enough of their own childhood not to deprive their children of
them. On the other hand, he hints at possible uses of the stories as
meditative devices for adults, only quickly to locate this function in
a preliterate past where, according to his earlier assumption, men
were more like the children of today in their modes of thought.
"Like the patients of Hindu medicine men who were asked to contemplate a fairy tale to find a way out of the inner darkness which
beclouded their minds, the child, too, should be given the opportunity to slowly make a fairy tale his own by bringing his own associations to and into it" (pp. 59 and 25). The possibility of drawing a
continuous line between the child's mind and the methods of the

mystics, modern and ancient—Christian, Hindu, Islamic, Jewish, Buddhist, etc.—is not only sidestepped but directly closed off by Bettelheim's use of the projection theory.[12]

In addition to infantilizing projection, he also tends to privatize it as simply a function of the individual psyche. That established patterns of projection are also used to transmit cultural values and views of the world cannot be dismissed out of hand simply because the individual is capable of casting his own fears and hopes into them. Bettelheim cites Eliade's interpretation of the tales as initiation rites by proxy (p. 35), but only focuses on the person being initiated, overlooking the social context whereby a story relocates an individual in the heroic ideals of a common past.

Finally, some mention should be made of Bettelheim's commitment to the universality and centrality of the Oedipus complex in childhood development. There is some indication that he recognizes how the application of Freud's idea to the subject matter of the fairy tales requires a common social structure based on a common definition of roles. "In the typical nuclear family setting, it is the father's duty to protect the child against the dangers of the outside world and also those that originate in the child's own asocial tendencies. The mother is to provide nurturing care and the general satisfaction of immediate bodily needs required for the child's survival" (p. 206). What we still want to know, or at least see questioned, is whether increasing control of once exclusively parental roles by service institutions might not make the tales so unreal a world as to be an ineffective source of projection for the contemporary child. Further, even if we were to accept with Bettelheim the universality of the Oedipus (or Electra) complex as the major psychic problem from age four until puberty (p. 39), we might still want to distinguish those times at which it is peripheral or negligible to the child's world from those when it is central. This would mean a reevaluation of his discovery of oedipal symbolism as sufficient for understanding the tales he considers. For it is very difficult not to eye with considerable distrust the generalized hermeneutic principle Bettelheim devises to interpret number-symbolism in the fairy tale: one=superego or dominant parent; two=the two parents; three=the child in relation to his parents (p. 106).

These closures brought about by the use of the projection theory point to four other assumptions which I do not believe the fairy tales share with Bettelheim's reading of them. Again, I state them here not to present a detailed alternative, but simply to suggest that the tales may be more open-ended than we often give them credit for.

In the first place, the use of a "growth model" to characterize the unfolding of childhood into adulthood is not to be found in the fairy tales which Bettelheim treats. In addition to using Freud's well known states, he refers favorably to Erikson's epigenetic theory to describe the movement of the children through the tales. The difficulty with such models is that they require a notion of psychic betterment or progress according to some ideal, tacit or overt, of maturity. But the fairy tales seem to operate more simply, speaking only of some aspect or other of experience, some relationship, some insight which has yet to be appropriated by a particular character. The growth model, as Bettelheim uses it, stresses the ideal of a single ego which must gain mastery over the id, the superego and various ego-ideals, by "integrating" them, that is, by subduing them to its supremacy. "Complex as we all are—conflicted, ambivalent, full of contradictions—the human personality is indivisible" (p. 118). The fairy tales, in contrast, speak merely of individuals playing various roles, some of them surprisingly different, which give us an insight into their characters. There is no talk of a central unifying ego, and no assurance that the assumption need be made that each skin-bound individual can house only one personality. The goal of the character seems rather to be finding a place for each of the roles, as if the mature individual were more like a well-organized commune. The benefit of such a reading of the tales is not that it offers reliable criticism of traditional psychological models, but only that it appears to reflect the actual world of the fairy tales whose enchantment over us we have set out to understand.

Second, Bettelheim is ambiguous about male-female differentiation in the fairy tales. He believes that both boys and girls can identify with characters of both sexes in the stories. His lengthy comparison of the stories of "Oedipus the King" and "Snow White" illustrates this well. Elsewhere he claims that the motif of heroine marrying hero at the tales' conclusions in fact indicates the integration of "male and female principles" found in each personality (pp. 126 and 146), the male representing the coming to terms with the outer world, the female with the inner world.[13] Like the apportionment of parental roles in the nuclear family referred to earlier, the symbolism depends on cultural convention, which has proved highly volatile in industrialized societies. Bettelheim does not refer to this level of the problem, but skips over it to point to a mutual envy between the sexes seen on a biological level (p. 266). The only real evidence he draws from the tales themselves is their frequent use of neuter names, as for instance in the heroines of the Grimms' collection: *Das Dornröschen, Das Schneewitchen, Das Aschenputtel*, etc. (pp. 282-283). The idea of a counterbalance to a general male dominance in society by means of an exaggerated attention to female sexual mysteries, which seems a most promising one, is left untouched. In any case, Bettelheim's frequent reference to problems of female psychology reflects correctly the tales he is dealing with and needs an explanation not available within the limits of his chosen method.

A third problematic area has to do with the presence of morality in the fairy tales. While Bettelheim does not treat the stories as fables each with a specific moral—although he would surely have to admit that apologues and *Märchen* do occasionally overlap classifications—he does detect a certain moral world view which they all communicate. "A higher morality," he calls it, asserting that its unique trait is that good and evil are clearly polarized without ambivalence. This he finds helpful to the child who can thus identify without qualification with "good" characters in the stories and project his antipathies on "bad" characters. Where a fairy-tale character is involved in ethically questionable activity—stealing, murder, fornication, deception—the tales are treated by Bettelheim as "amoral" (pp. 9-10). The argument is unconvincing and contrived. It is, after all, not to our interpretation of good and evil that the tales must conform, but rather the reverse. I believe it can easily be shown that good and evil are not so well polarized as Bettelheim supposes. There are numerous cases, and I would even venture to call them the rule in his selection of tales, where good and evil change appearances, where good comes out of evil and vice-versa, and where individual heroes and heroines are curious mixtures of good and evil. Here again, the meaning of the tales may frustrate our pedagogical interests, but in so doing may also lead us to a deeper level of meaning if we are only willing to follow.

In the fourth place, we may note that Bettelheim encourages the child's projection into the fairy tales because in this way the happy ending will promote the hope that adjustment to the real world will offer great rewards, and the fear that maladjustment will bring disgrace. It is not, for him, a matter of false wish-fulfillment as it is an appreciation of the need for wishes to be dramatized. "In the old days, when wishing still did some good . . ." opens the first story of the Grimms' collection. That "good" for Bettelheim is the promise of success which attends responsibility and perseverance. Wishing is then to be encouraged, but contextualized in reality. "Thus, a happy though ordinary existence is projected by fairy tales as the outcome of the trials and tribulations involved in the normal growing-up process" (p. 39). Once more, one wonders about this reading of the stories. The happy ending is not the universal element Bettelheim continually claims it to be. It is sometimes added abruptly, as a concluding device. And it is sometimes outright suspicious. The evident bias at work here is that the characters considered all do in fact mature and so are deserving of happiness. This in turn requires that we see happiness as the natural reward of virtue, a requirement which seems much closer to wishful thinking than to an acceptance of our real world. In the tales happiness is oftentimes given to the undeserving, the naive, or simply the lucky-starred. Bettelheim's argument may well capture the child's simplistic expectations about endings to fairy tales. But that children's interpretative projections in what he calls "true fairy tales" are always correct and always therapeutic is something that needs more critical attention than Bettelheim gives it.[14]

A psychological adaptation of the Haeckelian principle, the sharp separation of the worlds of fantasy and reality, and the full ramifications of his projection theory all circumscribe Bettelheim's analysis of the fairy tale as an aid to the child's natural process of development. The purpose of his method is to understand the effects of the tales and thereby to increase our insight into the mind of the child. If we begin, however, from the fairy tales themselves—even from those which he chooses for examination—and cast ourselves under their spell without any of these particular interests, a further level of meanings comes to light. Hints of this shadow-side to Bettelheim's treatment have come up in the course of our indication of those closures which seemed unnecessary to his overall project. It can now be portrayed more forthrightly, if in bold strokes, by way of introduction to some brief remarks on selected tales.

Bettelheim defines the generic difference of the fairy tale as the presence of magical or supernatural powers which come to the aid of the hero or heroine. I would argue that we need to go further and assert that these powers are not merely *dei ex machina* which highlight the heroism of the protagonists of the tales, but ought themselves to be seen as the prime movers of the plots which underlie these stories. Unbiased identification with the adventures of most all the human characters of the tales, it seems to me, produces less often a sense of heroic strength in adversity than one of victimization, at first in adversity and then often in victory as well. To enter the world of the fairy tale is to enter a world ruled by dark forces, unknown and uncontrollable, alternatively helpful and hostile, which have their own rules and are singularly disrespectful of our efforts to manipulate our own success. In general, they surround such realities as birth, death, suffering, separation, ambition, strife, misunderstanding, and sexuality. Where the main character of a story is a child, these dark forces tend to focus in particular on the despotic superiority of parents, the heartless rivalry of siblings, the accursed onslaught of puberty, or the like. Naming these things as dark forces reminds us that we have here to do with the most universal and deeply felt questions of our nature. It does little to tell us how to answer these questions, other than to promote a simple trust that as these forces interact with one another on the stage of our lives, our own well-being will somehow be served in the end.

Perhaps the best way to characterize the function of the fairy tale would be to adapt the term "superstitious" to that end. Superstition is a relational term. It refers to a mode of though or behavior which stands above (super-stare) and against the current psychological, philosophical, religious, and cultural modes of thought, giving expression to perceptions and needs ignored by other forms of the corporate imagination. Superstitions are not primitive modes of thought (even though we may find in old superstitions of many forms insights later taken up systematically by modern science), but a contrapuntal tradition. The benefit of folkloric forms of superstition is that they have been purified of many particular details of time and space, losing almost all synchronic unity but gaining in diachronic consistency as a picture of the dark side of consciousness. In general they are fragmented and form no total world view, though they may have once belonged to one. This was Hegel's opinion for instance, when he referred to folk superstitions and tales as "the sad and indigent remains of an attempted independence" of the national imagination.[15]

In contrast to Bettelheim's approach, such a view would not make the fairy tale strictly distinct in form and function from myth (pp. 26, 35ff, 199); nor would it focus on the heroic, self-salvific deeds of the protagonists as essential to a true tale (pp. 8, 9, 103f, 127f, 278). Most important, it would not require the restriction of the tales to children, which has been my most common complaint throughout the preceding analysis of Bettelheim's assumptions. This is not to say that many of the fairy tale characters are not easier for the child to identify with than for the adult and therefore of greater interest to the child psychologist, but only that the entire genre of the fairy tale need not be proscribed as pathological or immature for purposes of adult reflection.

Perhaps the most convincing argument for the dis-closure of Bettelheim's method is by way of attention to specific details in the stories themselves. We may begin with the tale of "Rapunzel."

In his cursory and incomplete analysis of the story, Bettelheim sees its central motif as a young girl's achievement of independence from a domineering mother by the use of her own body (the golden tresses). The image of the overly protective mother seems clear enough in the transformation from mother to ogre; but that Rapunzel's freedom is secured, in addition to being ardently desired, is not so clear. The maiden's long hair was hardly her salvation. It was the very source of her imprisonment and of her downfall. It was the point of contact between her and her mother and also between her and the young prince, who mounted it to impregnate her on the spot—apparently with her full consent, even though they hardly knew one another and even though she had never before even seen a man! Rapunzel is punished for her sin by being exiled to a desert, where she gives birth to twins. The prince is blinded by the old woman and only happens on his lover some years later while roaming about the woods eating wild berries after having been exiled from his kingdom. The "happy ending" which Bettelheim draws attention to was not part of the original story set down by Jacob Grimm, but was a later addition of brother Wilhelm.[16] In any case, it is too abrupt to belong to the flow of events in the tale. Like the mother who longs ardently to have a child (a request which God grants) and then longs to keep it (a request which is ultimately refused), Rapunzel and her prince are themselves the unwitting victims of strong desires. In time, all three are punished, not for their desire—which is natural and pre-ethical—but for their blindness to its strength, for committing the original sin against human nature: the denial of consciousness. (Rapunzel, by the way, is named after the European bellflower, whose roots were known for its medicinal value as a cure to jaundice.) It is unlikely that a young child could appreciate much of this material in the tale, beyond some sense of the unfair restraint of the maiden in the tower of her parent's selfishness. Yet the message is there for the finding nonetheless.

In his treatment of "Sleeping Beauty," Bettelheim interprets the "curse" of the thirteenth wise woman fated to befall the young maiden in the fifteenth year of her age as symbolic of the arrival of puberty. Sexual awakening, and the isolation which accompanies it in the natural transition from childhood to adulthood, cannot be avoided, says the story, despite all the efforts made by parents to the contrary. Here Bettelheim comes close to abandoning his strict standpoint towards the "heroism" of the main character when he describes the central message with these words: "Don't worry and don't try to hurry things—when the time is ripe, the impossible problem will be solved, as if all by itself" (p. 233). But he avoids the temptation by insisting on the heroism of a "long, quiet concentration on oneself" as the meaning of the maiden's hundred-year sleep (p. 225). The end result is a transformation of perception which Bettelheim attributes to Sleeping Beauty's personal strength of character, but which the story seems to attribute merely to the passage of time: her world falls asleep and then awakens, finding her richly rewarded for the period of dormancy. Where Bettelheim does renege on his principles is when he notes that the curse turns out to be a "blessing in disguise" (p. 235), thus denying the absolute polarization of good and evil.

The weakest aspect of the analysis, however, may be referring the young child's fascination with the story to preconscious sexuality, a sort of presentiment of pubertal problems just around the corner. It seems more likely that the puberty motif—a common and universal human experience of falling prey to the dark forces of human nature—is being used as an instance of a more encompassing mystery. Even the possibility that Sleeping Beauty can become a model for all turning points in life where transformation requires isolation does not capture the full meaning. The message needs a more mythical and cosmic frame of reference. Something like: death and life are parts of one and the same reality, in whose service they interact in the passage of time. Agriculturally, the image is that of the kiss of the warm spring sun enlivening the cold, sleeping winter earth. In the story's own context, the problem of life and death is introduced at the very outset. A king and a queen long for a child, as a way of insuring the continued life of the crown under their name after they die. And it ends with the statement that the maiden and her prince "live happily until their death." The curse of death by dark forces which marks the birth of the girl is changed into a promise of rebirth, just as the accursed thornbush forest (from which image she gets her original name, "Thorn Blossom") bursts into bloom sympathetically with the rebirth of the maiden. The overall feeling one is left with is that death is but a state of suspended animation. The tale does not argue the reality of life after death. It simply dramatizes the fundamental human desire for immortality.[17] Hence, to read it purely in pubertal terms, or to assign it strictly to childhood problems, would seem a needless limitation on its meaning.

Bettelheim reserves his most extended analysis for the story of "Cinderella," and makes difficult reading of it by dealing simultaneously with a number of variants. This is perhaps the best example in the book of how he needs to overstep his own hermeneutic principle on the absolute polarization of good and evil. Far from seeing her as the wholly good and innocent object of others' derision which we typically see her as, Bettelheim shows how Cinderella is a pubescent young girl caught in the grip of a psychic condition which distorts her perception of her two sisters (sibling rivalry) and of her mother (who becomes like a stepmother and she herself like an unwanted orphan pining for the love of her "dead" mother). Oddly enough, he continues to maintain his position that it was her heroic deeds which saved her. In fact, she runs away from what she most wants (the prince at the ball), clings to a memory of past dependencies (weeping at the grave of her mother), and only yields to change when it is forced on her by magical forces (the birds who announce her presence to the prince). The evidence of the fairy tale itself is that it was dark forces which constellated the problem at home between her and the others in the family, dark forces which provided her with a temporary escape into fantasy, and dark forces which saved her. If anything, Cinderella was uncooperative and dangerously withdrawn, not traits we usually associate with heroism.

I find the most questionable part of Bettelheim's interpretation, however, in his reading of sexual significance into the slipping of Cinderella's foot into the golden slipper and the placing of the ring on her finger. There are sexual overtones to many images in the tales, to be sure. (Indeed, I could go further and point to the sexual symbolism in Cinderella's request for a hazel branch from her father, which she then plants on her mother's grave and ceremoniously waters with her tears until it blossoms into a magical tree fulfilling her every fantasy. The image of her desire that her father "be a man" in the home to save her from her unmerited ill fate, to give her everything she most desires with his magical hazel wand, is one of the most striking images in the Grimms' collection.) My criticism is rather that here, as elsewhere throughout his book, Bettelheim seems to confine sexual signification to *genital* signification, overlooking the more important functions of *phallic* signification. While there are instances in which an image can have both functions, the two should be kept distinct, since they point to distinct levels of meaning. As a genital symbol, the sexual image is a metonymic re-presentation disguised for purposes of good taste or even humor. The phallic symbol, however, is the metaphoric use of a sexual image to represent some deeper psychic reality.

Put in other words, the phallus represents desire—the impulse within which we can neither understand nor master in its entirety, but which is responsible for all human creativity. Desire is necessary (or "instinctual") and never satisfiable. It is premoral, chaotic, and far from always compatible with rational intentions; and for all these reasons, its repression is essential for effective social intercourse. To avoid such intellectual abstraction, the language of sexual metaphor is employed in the fairy tales, as in other mythical idioms. In this way, something is being said which is more than simply a statement about an emotional response to sexual factuality.

For his part, Bettelheim focuses rather on children's interest in genital symbols because of their preconscious sexual curiosity (pp. 128 and 220), and defends the use of symbolic representation over anatomical precision because it accords with the child's natural initial disgust with explicit talk of sexual realities and gradual discovery of their beauty (p. 279). Nowhere is this more clear than in the tale of "The Frog King" of which Bettelheim remarks: "Preconsciously the child connects the tacky, clammy sensations which frogs (or toads) evoke in him with similar feelings he attaches to the sex organs. The frog's ability to blow itself out when excited arouses, again unconsciously, associations to the penis' erectability'' (p. 290). The point is significant, but it may be more important to retrieve the function of the symbol as phallus—as representative of the inevitability and promise of a force which we neither like nor can control. The dark forces are not always pleasant and benevolent, but can be frightening and malicious in the extreme. We can only hope to understand them. (Here we might recall the image of the spirit Mercurius caught in the bottle, who is likened to "a frog jumping up and down.") In short, the genital symbol may be seen as an overtone nuancing a deeper symbolic function. Such possibilities escape Bettelheim's notice, once again, because of his method's limitations; but they are not therefore incompatible with his findings.

The recovery of silence necessary for the life of the fairy tale may seem to many, as it did to Ewald the cripple, a thing of the past. To have plunged deeply into Bruno Bettelheim's *The Uses of Enchantment* can only rekindle the hope that this is not so. There one finds oneself, as it were, on the inside of a magic lantern of images at once so familiar and so unexpectedly unfamiliar. It is hard to resurface without at least a spark of that *amor fatae* which made childhood so enchanting. The fairy tale has not outlived its purpose so long as we need reassurance that there is more to life than our usual heavy words can tell. It is a well-known bit of psychoanalytic folk wisdom that an analysis terminates only when the patient realizes it could go on forever. We could just as well say of the fairy tales: you have invested enough time and imagination in wrestling with their meaning only when you finally come to tell the stories yourself, just as they are, without embarrassment, and to allow them to sleep quietly in your heart.

NOTES

1. Rainer Maria Rilke, *Stories of God* (New York: W. W. Norton, 1963), pp. 47–48.

2. Bruno Bettelheim, *The Uses of Enchantment: The Meaning and Importance of Fairy Tales* (New York: Alfred Knopf, 1976). Selections of the text were published in the *New Yorker*, 51:42, 8 Dec. 1975, pp. 50–114.

3. Bruno Bettelheim, *Symbolic Wounds* (New York: Collier Books, 1954/1971).

4. The best account of the history of psychological approaches to the fairy tales which I know of was done by Paulo de Carvalho Neto, *Folklore and Psychoanalysis* (Coral Gables, Fla.: University of Miami Press, 1972).

5. Bettelheim leaves no doubt about his acceptance of Freud's theory of the structures and development of the personality (*Love is Not Enough* [New York: Avon, 1950/1971], p. 49), although he has described how his personal experiences in the concentration camps of Dachau and Buchenwald led him to appreciate the limitations of psychoanalysis (*The Informed Heart* [The Free Press of Glencoe, 1960], chap. 1).

6. These criticisms remind one of John Ruskin's remarks of over a century ago, appended as an introduction to his 1868 selection of German folk tales designed "to appeal to young people rather than to adults." *The Complete Works of John Ruskin* (New York: T. B. Crowell, n.d.), Vol. 28, pp. 290–296.

7. Part of the wider context of my remarks was developed in a series of lectures delivered in Mexico City in the fall of 1975 and subsequently published as: *El cuento detrás del cuento: Un ensayo sobre psique y mito* (Buenos Aires: Editorial Guadalupe, 1976).

8. In an earlier book Bettelheim had claimed that as late as the seventeenth century the worlds of the child and the adult overlapped so considerably that fairy tales were the favorite literature of both (*The Children of the Dream* [London: Macmillan, 1969], pp. 53–54). The idea is not repeated in the present work, where he prefers the contrast of the primitive mind with that of the child. The influence of Andrew Lang's introductory essay to Margaret Hunt's 1884 English translation of the Grimms' tales, and in particular his comments on the "savage mind," seems to have been particularly formative in this shift of emphasis.

9. The point is made more explicitly, and defended as an argument *ad judicium* for which evidence is said to be lacking, in his earlier *Symbolic Wounds*, pp. 46ff.

10. The missing link in the argument, relating psychoanalysis to art, appears later: "The unconscious is the source of art; . . . the superego's ideas fashion it; . . . and it is the ego forces which enter into the creation of a work of art" (p. 109). In other words, the psychological message is more basic, after all, than the artistic form of the fairy tale.

11. The statement of Jacob Grimm, made in a letter to the folklorist Achim von Arnim, that the reading public he and his brother had in mind were "adults and serious people" is not to be taken lightly.

Jorge Luis Borges, whose success with simplicity of form and plot and fascination for metaphor is unexcelled among modern poets and storytellers, has done much to correct the bias that the fairy tale is the exclusive domain of the child's mind. To cite him in his own medium: "We are as ignorant of the meaning of the dragon as we are of the meaning of the universe, but there is something in the dragon's image that appeals to the human imagination. . . . It is, so to speak, a necessary monster." Jorge Luis Borges, *The Book of Imaginary Beings* (New York: E. P. Dutton, 1961), pp. 16–17.

12. In 1856 Wilhelm Grimm concluded a volume of annotations to the tales with the remark that the remnants of ancient belief are present in the

stories "like little pieces of a splintered jewel that lie on the ground covered by grass and flowers and only to be discovered by very sharp eyes. The meaning of the mystical element is long since lost, but it is still felt and gives the fairy tales their content while at the same time satisfying the natural pleasure in the miraculous. . . ." Cited in Murray Peppard's *Paths Through the Forest: A Biography of the Brothers Grimm* (New York: Holt, Reinhart and Winston, 1971), p. 50.

In this regard, a better balance in a psychological approach to the tales is achieved by Julius Heuscher's *A Psychiatric Study of Fairy Tales* (Springfield, Ill.: Charles C. Thomas, 1963). Bettelheim does not mention the book.

13. This was the basis of his earlier interpretation of male initiation rites in his *Symbolic Wounds*, pp. 19-20.

14. In the matter of morality in the tales, the strongest influence on Bettelheim's argument comes from J. R. R. Tolkien, whose own ventures into fantastic literature reveal such a morphology of good and evil as polar opposites, with evil being punished and good rewarded.

15. Georg Hegel, *On Christianity: Early Theological Writings* (New York: Harper Torchbooks, 1961), p. 147.

16. The story was taken by Jacob from a novelette by Friedrich Schulz, dated 1790; it was one of the few tales which they had not themselves heard narrated.

17. Bettelheim cites a particularly happy phrase of Tolkien's in this regard: "Fairy stories are plainly not primarily concerned with possibility but with desirability" (p. 117). The phrase recalls the position taken by the noted critic and essayist Richard le Gallienne: "Obviously nothing else is so attractive as the impossible; and the power of the fairy tale over the human mind is that, whatever form of the impossible you desire—it gives it to you." Richard le Gallienne, *Attitudes and Avowals* (New York: John Lane, 1910), p. 34.

Arthur Rackham and the Romantic Tradition

The Question of Polarity and Ambiguity*

Christa Kamenetsky

The question of identity has puzzled many critics of Arthur Rackham. Judging by the many contradictory essays written about his work, he still appears to be an artist of various styles that escape a definite classification in the history of the English graphic tradition. Was Rackham a Victorian artist or was he a Romantic visionary? Selma Lanes pointed out Rackham's philistine middle-class tendencies. Although she did not deny his magic in uncovering the fairyland beneath the countryside, she underscored to a greater extent his emotional detachment, his "matter-of-factness," and his affection for detail, texture, and elaborate design in "cozy English interiors replete with rugs, quilts and bric-a-brac."[1] Henry Pitz felt that Rackham's drawings had more "conviction" than those of Caldecott and Greenaway and that he was "English to the very core."[2] This was also Derek Hudson's view, who saw him as close to his British "Cockney origins."[3] Eleanor Farjeon, on the other hand, saw in him an artist capable of transporting the commonplace into a sphere of the imagination, a romantic "wizard" bringing to life a world of fairies, elves, and dwarfs.[4]

How do we reconcile such differing opinions, which emphasize the realistic as well as the imaginative perspectives of Rackham's work? Margery Darrell came to the conclusion that in his "strange mix of magic and materialism" lay the very key to the credibility of his work. "Perhaps it was his very worldliness that made his drawings so believable," she suggested.[5]

Without attempting to minimize the British influences upon his work, we will proceed to view Rackham within the broader perspective of European Romanticism, of which English Romanticism was a definite part. A brief exploration of the nature of European Romanticism, in all its complexity, may throw some light upon the complexity of Rackham's subject choice and on the puzzling ambiguities of his style.

Around 1920, Arthur Lovejoy pointed to the diversity of the

*The author wishes to express her appreciation to the staff of the Clarke Historical Library at Central Michigan University for their kind assistance in making available some of the materials illustrated by Arthur Rackham.

term "Romanticism," suggesting that one should refer to it only in the plural form. He felt that the confusion of terminology had led not only to the present "muddle" of critical thought, but also to the unfortunate ambiguity now associated with the word.[6] Twenty years later, René Wellek contradicted Lovejoy by asserting that there were three unifying principles of Romanticism that could be detected throughout the art and literature of Europe. He identified them as: the role of the imagination as the very basis for poetry and art; the organic view of all natural objects; and the creative use of myths and symbols.[7] In more recent times, Morse Peckham tried to reach a synthesis of Lovejoy's and Wellek's views. He felt it was more important to acknowledge the inherent contradictions of Romanticism as an integral part of the movement than to quarrel about "multiplicity" versus "unity." "Since the logic of Romanticism is that contradictions must be included in a single orientation, but without pseudo-reconciliation," he wrote, "romanticism is a remarkably stable and witful orientation."[8]

Keeping in mind Peckham's observation, we will now move on to examine the seemingly contradictory forces in Rackham's work on the basis that they may correspond to those inherent in European Romanticism as a whole. In this connection, we will give particular attention to his subject choice, his use of the imagination, his organic view of nature, and the ambiguous qualities of his style.

In looking at the wide range of Rackham's illustrations, we notice that he gave considerable attention to folklore and imaginative literature. Among the folk literature of the oral tradition which he illustrated—with a natural feeling for the mood and the cultural uniqueness in the heritage of other lands—were such folk tales as Grimms' *Fairy Tales*, Stephens' *Irish Fairy Tales*, and Aesop's *Fables*. Of the illustrations of his native folklore we may mention Steele's *English Fairy Tales* and *Mother Goose*. Among the literary adaptations of traditional folklore we find his unique illustrations of Wagner's *Rhinegold*, and his *Twilight of the Gods*, Ibsen's *Peer Gynt*, Fouqué's *Undine*, Shakespeare's *Midsummer-Night's Dream*, Irving's *Rip van Winkle*, and Hawthorne's *Wonder Book*.[9]

Rackham's emphasis on universal folklore reflected his romantic interest in the life, language, and literature close to the common folk tradition. As such, it corresponded to the Romantic dream of reviving the folk heritage around the world—a dream echoed also in the so-called color fairy books of Andrew Lang. It was Her-

Rackham, "The Knight took hold of her tightly." From Fouque de la Motte,
Undine (London: William Heinemann, Publishers, 1909). By permission.

der, during the *Sturm und Drang* movement in Germany, who initiated this revival trend by collecting folk songs of many lands. He
was followed by von Arnim and Brentano, Tieck, and later the
Brothers Grimm. The Grimms' *Household Tales* were still widely
read in England at Rackham's time. In 1914, Rackham wrote to
one of his friends: "In many ways, I have more affection for the
Grimm drawings than for the other sets. . . . It was the first book I
did that began to bring success (the little earlier edition, that is)."[10]

Rackham's illustrations of Grimms' fairy tales demonstrate his
fine perception and great skill in getting close to another country's
folk heritage. The universality of folktale motifs may have helped
him in part. Yet it remains a remarkable fact nonetheless that his
illustrations of Grimms' *Märchen* made their way back across the
channel to give many generations of German children a first
glimpse of their own folktales.[11] How well he did capture the spirit
of German folklore may be perceived also from his *Mother Goose*
illustrations, which were later adapted to an edition of German
nursery rhymes. Though some verses in this edition were translated from the English, most of them were of German origin. Yet
Rackham's silhouettes seem to fit the text perfectly.[12] Similarly,
we may notice that his illustrations of *Rip van Winkle* capture the
very essence of the book, and it would not readily enter an observer's mind that in this case a British artist illustrated an American book. Rackham's illustrations fit Irving as they fit American
folklore. We can't well imagine Rip any other way than Rackham
has perceived him.

Viewed from the Romantic perspective, Rackham well demonstrated in his work what Coleridge called "the coloring of the imagination." In Wordsworth's "Preface" to the *Lyrical Ballads* we
read: "The ordinary things should be presented to the mind in an
unusual aspect."[13] Like the Romantic poets, Rackham often chose
to illustrate the commonplace, rendering it colorful in the light of
his imagination. Whether he illustrated scenes from folklore or fantasy, his drawings always reflected a certain mood or atmosphere.
He achieved this partially by using soft pastel colors, in which even
the most meticulously drawn details were blended to an antique
tone, giving the effect of ancient parchment. In his paintings the
soft browns and grey-greens dominate, here and there illuminated
by a warm ivory. His colors vary from light, fluffy tones to rich,
dark ones of the kind one may find in Flemish or Dutch landscape

paintings. The warm hues of Rackham's colors add much to the impression that the imaginary world of fantasy and folk tale is part of the here and now. One is therefore perhaps less surprised than one ought to be at discovering fairy tale creatures amid a world drawn, otherwise, with much attention given to realistic detail.

A second device has helped Rackham in projecting the spirit of imagination into the world of realism, namely, his independent and very peculiar selection of captions for his illustrations. Instead of searching out highlights of plot and action, he would focus upon scenes or lines often overlooked by even the most attentive reader. Selma Lanes observed in this connection: "Thus he often chose to illustrate the unillustrable, or to rescue from oblivion words the reader had most likely never noticed. From Charles Dickens' *A Christmas Carol* he plucked the line: "The air was filled with phantoms, wandering hither and thither in restless haste and moaning as they went.""[14] From *Wind in the Willows,* we may add, he captured the very atmosphere of a golden afternoon, when "the smell of the dust kicked up was rich and satisfying."[15] Rackham thus created a mood that did not leave the observer untouched. He himself felt that the most fascinating form of illustration for the artist was the one in which he expressed "an individual sense of delight or emotion, aroused by the accompanying passage of literature."[16] Again we are reminded of Wordsworth's theory of poetry, in which he expected the poet to arouse the reader's passions and to give him a certain sense of pleasure and delight.

In regard to Rackham's ambiguity of style, we find another striking correspondence with Romanticism, in the element which Morse Peckham called "the illusion of mutability."[17] Peckham had in mind a certain amphibian quality emerging from Romantic art and literature that belonged neither entirely to the world of reality nor entirely to the world of fantasy. By recognizing its kinship to metamorphosis, he reevaluated imaginative ambiguity as a positive force, suggesting that it represented the Romantic striving for unity between the internal and the external world or toward the "perfect identification of matter and form."[18] By tracing certain correspondences in the art of Constable and the poetry of Wordsworth, Peckham tried to establish their similar views of the concept of "organic nature." In Constable's cloud studies, for example, he noticed an attempt to bring together the appearances of landscape and sky through certain parallel lines, movements, and colors—an attempt which he felt corresponded to Wordsworth's view of nature as a creative soul. In "Tintern Abbey," Wordsworth had spoken of the eye and ear in terms of "what they half create, / And what perceive," whereas Constable had said, "It is the business of a painter not to be content with nature, and put such scene, a valley filled with imagery fifty miles long, on a canvas of a few inches, but to make something out of nothing, in attempting which he must almost of necessity become poetical."[19] Both of these quotes also seem to illustrate Arthur Rackham's view of nature. Miss Farjeon well described his landscapes drawings as "delicate webs of leafless branches traced against a wintry sky; . . . pale marbled clouds . . . and strange patterns upon the water."[20] In Rackham's drawings, as much as in Wordworth's poetry, we sense that "there is a spirit in the woods." His illustrations make trees, grass, flowers, and the very fieldstones come alive. In looking at the strangely twisted, gnarled, and knotty trees in his drawings, we can never be quite sure if nature, man, or a creature from the netherworld is speaking to us. What appears to be a knothole turns out to be an eye or a mouth—and yet, it may be a knothole after all.

In the landscapes of Rackham the very concepts of "manhood," "treehood," and "dwarfhood" often become strangely fused and blurred, leaving the observer with a feeling of ambiguity. We recognize in the ambiguity the Romantic world view, according to which the same spirit flowed through all things. Both macrocosm and microcosm, the animate and the inanimate object, were humanized and alive, revealing at their very source the deepest secrets of God and nature.

In some of Rackham's drawings we may witness the very process of a strange metamorphosis at work, gradually fusing natural objects and imaginative perspectives. At times, his illustrations are gloomy and frightening, suggestive of a dark and evil netherworld, and at other times, they are light and gay—or even grotesque. One can never be sure what mood to anticipate. In *Rip van Winkle,* for example, we may feel a bit apprehensive while trying to decide whether some of the roots of an old twisted tree might belong as arms or legs to a withered and misshapen dwarf leaning against its trunk. Another illustration in the same book, no less ambiguous in style, makes us smile, as we discover among some hybrid creatures seated high on top of a branch the plumes of birds and the faces of men. Particularly amusing is a female creature among them, who is busily engaged, of all things, in knitting a sock. Her ball of yarn,

Rackham, "They maintained the gravest faces." From Washington Irving, *Rip van Winkle*, in Margery Darrel, ed., *The Fairy World of Arthur Rackham* (New York: Viking Press, 1972). Reprinted with the kind permission of the publishers.

hanging from her nest in a hopeless tangle, is drawn so realistically that one is tempted to pick it up.

Such opposing moods are very pronounced in Rackham's drawings. Side by side we may observe in them idyllic as well as grotesque elements—moods so contradictory that they do not seem to have been created by the same artist. And yet, it is precisely this sense of contradiction that illustrates the Romantic striving toward unity. Viewed separately, these polarities present such contrasts as those between the contemplative and peaceful mood of Wordsworth, for example, and the grotesque and nightmarish mood of Coleridge. In Germany, the polarities are represented by the "light" bourgeois Romanticism (*bürgerliche Romantik*) of Eichendorff and Brentano on the one hand and the "Dark" or "night side" of horror Romanticism (*Schauerromantik*) of Tieck, Novalis, and E. T. A. Hoffman on the other.[21] Oscar Walzel commented on these seemingly contradictory forces of European Romanticism: "I maintain that two antithetical methods of forming a work of art may be distinguished from each other. . . . The first is rather calm and simple and lays no claim on emotional intensity. The other is more roaring and pathetical and at times grotesque, and even inclined to hyperbolic expression. The current conception of baroque, or as Wörringer terms it, "Gothic," is applicable only to the latter."[22] In some of Rackham's illustrations we find an echo of the idyllic world of the *bürgerliche Romantik,* as seen in the engravings of Ludwig Richter (first German illustrator of the Grimms' *Household Tales*), the paintings of Moritz von Schwindt (well known for his enchanted forest scenes), and later in the works of Karl Spitzweg, master painter of the small town atmosphere. In both Spitzweg and Rackham we discover a similar fondness for crumbling medieval walls bathed in late afternoon sunlight, rooftop scenes, and quaint characters. In some other Rackham drawings we perceive the dark world of the *Schauerromantik* and certain moods reminiscent of E. T. A. Hoffmann. In visual terms, Rackham expressed the dark sphere of Romanticism by means of bizarre line movements and tensions in forms. By using a fairly dark tint of raw umber, he would create the atmosphere of the netherworld, in which the real and the unreal lived together side by side in an ambiguous relationship.[23]

Rackham's dual vision of life comes out well in a work not meant for children. His illustrations for Walton's *The Compleat Angler* show well fascination with both the idyllic and the grotesque. And yet, there are drawings, interspersed with contemplative fishing and village scenes, that seem to have lost their way from the children's bookshelf: insects with spectacles are scribbling something into books; dwarfs are engaged in frog hunts; and fish skeletons, equipped with crutches, are contemplating their future fate in the angler's frying pan. The last drawing, ironically, is accompanied by a delicious fish recipe in the text, which reads: ". . . and pour upon it a quarter of a pound of the best fresh butter, melted and beaten with half-a-dozen spoonfuls of the broth. . . ."[24]

Although we smile at these drawings, we perceive quite a different mood in another one, which is reminiscent of a tale by Edgar Allan Poe or E. T. A. Hoffmann. An odd old couple is bent over what appears to be a huge book of knowledge. Their wrinkled, grinning faces seem out of place in the museumlike surroundings of skeletons and weird-looking stuffed fish and birds. There is a striking incongruity between the rich folds of the neatly arrayed silk and brocade clothing of the couple and the bare spiny bones hanging overhead. The open book may suggest a Romantic symbol of the hieroglyphics of life, yet the facial expressions are far remote from radiating a sense of wonder. Instead, they suggest something resembling more closely the features of the grotesque.

The Romantic grotesque may be translated as ungraceful, out-of-harmony, or incongruous. It was capable of taking on a humorous as well as a horrifying quality, depending upon the emphasis of the writer or artist. Paul Ilie characterized it as "a low keyed disquietude."[25] In analyzing the fantasies of Bécquier, Ilie called attention to the hybrid and ambiguous nature of his portrayals of transformation that showed but little resemblance to Ovid's portrayal of metamorphosis. Whereas Ovid had clearly indicated changes from one form to another, the Romantic grotesque remained ambiguous and hybrid in nature, thus transmitting the eerie feeling of metamorphosis still in process. It is just such a feeling which emerges from many of Rackham's drawings. We are never quite sure about his portrayal of nature as nature, of man as man, or of a symbol as a symbol.

It may well have been Beardsley who inspired Rackham with the element of the grotesque. Hudson noted a strong influence, especially with respect to some nightmarish scenes, one of which in fact is entitled: *A nightmare: horrible result of contemplating Aubrey Beardsley after supper.*[26] Further, Hudson noted the influences of Gothic and Italian primitives and also of "Cruikshank, Caldecott,

Dickey Doyle, Arthur Boyd Houghton, [and] the artists of Germany and Japan.''[27] It is also possible, however, that Rackham received inspiration along these lines from the very writers of the German *Schauerromantik*, not to mention, of course, Edgar Allen Poe, whose works he illustrated. We know that Rackham frequently spent his holidays on the continent, usually in Germany and also that his wife, Edythe, studied art there prior to her marriage.[28] One of Rackham's admirers pointedly commented in 1905 ''I have at last been able to get to your exhibition which I enjoyed immensely. Hitherto one had to go to the Continent for so much mingled grace & grotesque as you have given us. . . .''[29]

A study of all of the influences on Rackham will lead us to a complex and varied pattern that easily might distract our attention from his own original contributions to the art of illustration. And yet, a study of some affinities of mind may give us a clue as to the direction of his thoughts—particularly since Rackham himself acknowledged above all other influences his affection for the spirit of the Germanic North. When once asked by a friend how he would explain a peculiar Indian flavor in his drawings, Rackham responded: ''I think I myself am more conscious of Teutonic influence.''[30] Indeed, Rackham visited Wagner's Bayreuth several times while traveling in Europe, and he was as fond of Wagner's Nordic operas as he was of Norse mythology.[31] It is possibly from here that he drew his inspirations for the thievish, gray, and grotesque dwarfs who appear in his various fairy-tale illustrations. The Nordic *alb* (later Elberich or Oberon) had nothing whatever in common with the dainty dwarfs of Disney. Jacob Grimm in his monumental work *Teutonic Mythology* also commented on the dark or gray complexion of the ''dark elves,'' as he called them.[32] According to the Edda they had emerged originally as maggots from the rotten flesh of the slain frost giant Ymir.[33] It may be noted that Norse or Teutonic mythology represents a common heritage for both the English nation and the German nation alike—a fact which may explain why Rackham's illustrations are so very much at home in the Nordic folk heritage of both countries.

From the perspective of European Romanticism, the double nature of the netherworld of dwarfs and elves held a special interest for writers and artists because it seemed to correspond to their own view of the world. Ricarda Huch characterized the Romantic movement as one that upheld the contrast between spirit and nature, light and darkness, force and materialism. Swaying back and forth between these opposites, the poets of the time hoped to achieve a synthesis of mind and spirit.[34] Walzel saw in this polarity a reflection of the Romantic dream of harmony. By oscillating between thesis and antithesis, he said, one hoped to recover the "golden age" of the ancient past. This oscillation, in turn, gave birth to Romantic irony, as the inherent contradictions were not resolved but kept alive.[35]

By never committing himself completely either to the one world or the other, Arthur Rackham developed a certain spirit of ironic detachment in his illustrations, which we recognize as his peculiar sense of humor. It was his special gift to create an illusion of reality by giving minute attention to realistic detail. Unnoticeably, he would then introduce, by means of color or ambiguous forms, the spirit of the imagination. It seems that he very much enjoyed the freedom of belonging to both worlds and to neither, thus asserting the very freedom of his creative mind.

There is an odd little drawing among his letters and notes that served as a wedding announcement for his daughter Barbara.[36] It shows an old, twisted, knotty, and leafless willow tree with grotesque branches sticking out like sinewy arms at the sides and like windblown hair on the top. Strangely enough, this tree bears the very features of Arthur Rackham—glasses, long nose, and all. On one of the "branches" sit two little birds ready, it seems, to build their nest. Who was Rackham, we may wonder—a man, a dwarf, or a tree; a "realist" or a "fantasist"?

If we have viewed Rackham's work within the context of European Romanticism, it should be remembered that there is nothing rigid about this attempt. Classifications remain constructs of the mind and, like metaphors, can only be carried so far in bringing out certain affinities of thought. In his work *Beyond the Tragic Vision,* Morse Peckham wrote: "Thus even a single work of art must not be regarded as culturally coherent, as reflecting one and only one aspect of a construct model."[37] Periods or movements were "constructs" or "operational fiction," he warned, and they should be used with caution. In the case of Romanticism however, as both Peckham and Walzel agreed, we have to do not with a single coherent construct but with a multiplicity of patterns characterized by polarity and imaginative ambiguity. For this reason alone, there is little danger that an application of Romantic theories to

Philip Soper &
Barbara Rackham
were married on
27th July 1935!

And they live at
6 Regent Square
London W.C.1

Rackham, "Marriage Announcement of Daughter Barbara." From Derek Hudson, *The Life and Work of Arthur Rackham* (New York: Charles Scribner's Sons, 1960); originally published in London by William Heinemann. By permission.

Rackham's work might lead to a rigid interpretation of his art.

The perspectives of European Romanticism open up new possibilities of viewing the seeming contradictions in Rackham's illustrations as complementary forces arising from a dialectical approach to nature. To Rackham and the Romantics, nature was humanized and alive. By swaying back and forth between the worlds of fantasy and reality, he imparted to both the spirit of his creative imagination.

Like the European Romantics, Rackham felt at home in the folklore and fantasy of many nations. His interpretation of both reflects his capacity to perceive a living creature behind every bush and tree, in the ripples on the water, or in the movement of the clouds. Ambiguity and metamorphosis to him became a way of seeing which corresponded to the Romantic search for a mythopoeic vision of life. As if he were holding up a mirror to the complexity of our souls, Rackham cunningly revealed to us our dreams of beauty as well as the distorted features of our nightmares and secret fears. In that sense, polarity and ambiguity not only mark his poetic vision, but also the special sense of humor that places him, beyond doubt into a class of his own.

NOTES

1. Selma Lanes, *Down the Rabbit Hole: Adventures and Misadventures in the Realm of Children's Literature* (New York: Atheneum, 1972), pp. 67–79.

2. Henry Pitz, *Illustrating Children's Books: History–Technique–Production* (New York: Watson-Guptill Publ., 1963), pp. 42 and 86.

3. Derek Hudson, *Arthur Rackham: His Life and Work* (New York: Scribner, 1960), p. 156.

4. Eleanor Farjeon, "Arthur Rackham: The Wizard at Home," *St. Nicholas, XL* (March, 1913), 391.

5. Margery Darrell, ed. *Once Upon a Time: The Fairy World of Arthur Rackham* (New York: Viking Press, 1972), p. 12.

6. Arthur O. Lovejoy, "On the Discrimination of Romanticisms," *Publications of the Modern Language Association*, XXXIX (1924), 229–253.

7. René Wellek, "The Concept of Romanticism in Literary History," *Comparative Literature*, I (1949), 1–23, 147–172.

8. Morse Peckham, "Toward a Theory of Romanticism." *Publications of the Modern Language Association*, LXVI (1951), 5–23. See also: *Studies in Romanticism*, I (1961) 1–8.

9. For more detailed information on Rackham's various illustrations, consult Sarah Briggs Latimore and Grace Clare Haskall, *Arthur Rackham: A Bibliography* (Los Angeles: Suttonhouse, 1937). Also Hudson, Appendix.

10. Hudson, pp. 46–57. For the reception of Grimms' *Household Tales* in England, see Iona and Peter Opie, *The Classic Fairy Tales* (New York: Oxford University Press, 1974), pp. 25–28.

11. See: Ethel M. Chadwick, "Arthur Rackham," *Dekorative Kunst*, II (Munich, Dec., 1909), 23–34.

12. George Dietrich, ed., *Mein Kinderhimmel: Gesammelte Kinderlieder und -Reime*, ill. by Arthur Rackham (Munich: Mohn Verlag, 1919).

13. William Wordsworth, "Preface to the Second Edition of Lyrical Ballads (1800)" in *Selected Poems and Prefaces of William Wordsworth*, ed. Jack Stillinger (Boston: Houghton Mifflin Co., 1965), pp. 446-447.

14. Lanes, p. 68.

15. Darrell, p. 7.

16. *Ibid.*

17. Morse Peckham, p. 11. See also: Robert F. Gleckner and Gerald E. Enscoe, eds., *Romanticism: Points of View*, 2nd ed. (Englewood Cliffs: Prentice Hall, 1970), pp. 231–258.

18. *Ibid.*

19. Morse Peckham, *The Triumph of Romanticism* (Columbia, S.C.: University of South Carolina Press, 1970), pp. 105–122.

20. Farjeon, p. 391.

21. See Marianne Thalmann, *The Romantic Fairy Tale: Seeds of Surrealism* (Ann Arbor: University of Michigan Press, 1964). Also: Ricarda Huch, *Die Romantik: Blütezeit–Ausbreitung-Verfall* (Tübingen: Rainer Wunderlich Verlag, 1951), p. 397.

22. Oscar Walzel, *German Romanticism* (New York: Ungar Publ. Co., 1965), pp. 51–78.

23. Robert Lawson, "The Genius of Arthur Rackham," *Hornbook* (May–June, 1940) p. 150.

24. Izaak Walton, *The Compleat Angler, or the Contemplative Man's Recreation*, ill. by Arthur Rackham (Philadelphia: D. McKay, 1931). The book was orginally published in 1653. It includes not only instructions on angling but also proverbs, superstitions, legends, and popular rhymes. Obviously, it was the folklore that inspired Rackham to illustrate this work.

25. Paul Ilie, "Bécquier and the Romantic Grotesque," *Publications of the Modern Language Association* LXXXIII (1968) 319–322.

26. Hudson, p. 45. Hudson thought that Rackham's subject choice was healthier than Beardsley's and wider than Tenniel's. He accordingly called him "a loveable grotesque."

27. *Ibid.*, p. 44.

28. *Ibid.*, pp. 54–55.

29. *Ibid.*, p. 58.

30. *Ibid.*, p. 46.

31. *Ibid.*, p. 92.

32. Jacob Grimm, *Teutonic Mythology* II (New York: Dover Publications, 1966), pp. 439–517. See also Reidar T. Christiansen, ed., *Folktales of Norway* (Chicago: Delacorte Press, 1966), Introduction.

33. Jean Young, ed., *The Prose Edda of Snorri Sturluson* (Berkeley: University of California Press, 1960), p. 41.

34. Huch, p. 512
35. Walzel, pp. 45–67.
36. Hudson, p. 138.
37. Peckham, cited in *Triumph*, pp. 151–152.

Maurice Sendak and the Blakean Vision of Childhood

Jennifer R. Waller

In his studio, to the right of his desk amid reproductions of the works of Watteau, Goya, and Winslow Homer, Maurice Sendak has a reproduction of one of William Blake's works.[1] In an interview, Sendak describes Blake as "from the first, my great and abiding love . . . my teacher in all things."[2] While the influence of George MacDonald, Andrew Caldecott, Attilio Massiono, and the tradition of the American comic book are all much more immediately definable in Sendak's work, the strength of his emotional response to William Blake is undeniable. In the same interview, he asserts Blake to be his favorite artist and goes on to explain that "of course, the *Songs of Innocence* and the *Songs of Experience* tell you all about this: what it is to be a child—not childish, but a child inside your adult self—and how much better a person you are for being such."[3]

In this paper I want to suggest the usefulness of comparing Sendak's insights into childhood with Blake's and, as well, to compare their responses to the challenge of combining artistic vision and entertainment in a composite medium. For Blake, the state of childhood, with its innocent ignorance of destructive reason and of the processes of the adult's self-conscious rationalization and self-justification, represented a time when the human imagination was most potent. Adulthood too often brought the destruction of the powers of the imagination. Blake's reassertion of the power of the imagination was, of course, part of his rebellion against the reasonableness and moderation of eighteenth-and nineteenth-century classicism. Imagination became a "Divine Vision" which allowed the poet to achieve by his own art what the child could do spontaneously—transcend the limitations of the senses and the restrictions of rational categorization. The child of the *Songs of Innocence* seeking to find out "Little Lamb who made thee / Dost thou know who made thee?" perceives an answer not by his powers of reasoning but by the strength of his love. The child's powers of perception, enjoyment, and responsiveness represent imagination unfettered by the constricting demands of rationalist philosophy, whether in Lockean reason or established theology. That such childhood perception could be re-created was, in a sense, evidence enough for Blake that the Divine existed in man.

Like Blake, Sendak draws unusual strength from the vision of imagination. Like Blake too, he uses the image of childhood to represent the liberation of his creativity: "An essential part of myself—my dreaming life—still lives in the potent urgent light of childhood."[4] Commenting directly on his own work, he defines the relationship he has with "the kid I was"—an interesting phrase—who did not grow "up into me" but "still exists somewhere in the most graphic, plastic, physical way."[5] The presence of this child is indispensable to his work, for as he asserts, "one of my worst fears is losing contact with him."[6] To lose contact with this vision of childhood would be to destroy the substance of Sendak's creative talent—his extraordinary powers of evocative imagination and his sensitivity to the experience of childhood.

Both artists, as illustrators *and* authors, seek to use their composite form to express their vision through structural tension. Often their words may rationalize experience which may be either elaborated, or sometimes, contradicted by the illustrations, which bring out more fully the dreamlike, wordless level of the unconscious. Since Blake was obsessed with the intention of destroying the dualistic world of mind and body, time and space, he saw in the composite medium the possibilities of dramatizing "the interaction of the apparent dualities in experiences."[7] Sendak on the other hand, because he was writing and illustrating children's books, was forced to the realization that a child's book is not simply read or rationally understood: "There's so much more to a book than just the reading; there is a sensuousness. I've seen children touch books, fondle books, smell books."[8] Sendak is similarly conscious of certain contraries in human experience, which he attempts to assimilate in his composite form. He describes his desire to combine the disparate elements in his own experience of his "weird old-country, new country childhood." He speaks of his "obsession of *shtetel* life," and "the illuminating visions especially loved artists" have shown him in "words and pictures."[9]

Any artist working in a composite medium clearly faces special problems. Sendak has developed a style of illustration which can initially be explained by reference to the *Little Bear* books. Here the text and Sendak's illustration are both enclosed within a formal decorative border. Like Blake, Sendak is not merely aiming for some kind of aesthetically satisfying unit. Neither does he want to make the pictures express only the fabric of the text. This would in Sendak's estimation be a "serious pitfall".[10] He hopes to allow "the story to speak for itself, with my picture as a kind of background music—music in the right style and always in tune with the words."[11] Background music such as that which accompanies film, it should be noted, is an essential element of the dramatic structure, making the listener only partially aware of feelings which he may be unwilling or unable to verbalize. Sendak's concern in this way to assimilate divergent art forms into a harmonious unity seems to be becoming more insistent recently as he establishes his reputation in the no-man's land where he is both author and artist. With Sendak's own works, *Where the Wild Things Are* and *In the Night Kitchen,* we can go a step further and put him in an explicitly Blakean context. He seems to be responding to the challenge presented by such a poem as Blake's "Infant Joy":

> I have no name
> I am but two days old.—
> What shall I call thee?
> I happy am
> Joy is my name,—
> Sweet joy befall thee!
>
> Pretty joy!
> Sweet joy but two days old.
> Sweet joy I call thee:
> Thou dost smile.
> I sing the while
> Sweet joy befall thee.
>
> —*Works*, p. 16

Encircling the words of the poem and the ostensibly simple domestic scene of mother and child it describes, is a twining vine bearing flamboyant flowers, suggesting passion and sexuality. The lower leaves of the plant are angular and strained and suggest a hint of impending experience—experience which may transform the simplicity of domestic love through the expressions of frank sexuality and are, of course, the origins of the scene. The eventual complexity of human love is suggested in this encircling illustration. It thus provides a portent, as well as the orchestration for pain and sorrow evoked in the equivalent poem in the *Songs of Experience:*

> My mother groaned! My father wept.
> Into the dangerous world I leapt:
> Helpless, naked, piping loud;
> Like a friend hid in a cloud.
> Struggling in my father's hands:
> Striving against my swadling bands:
> Bound and weary I thought best
> To sulk upon my mother's breast.

—*Works,* p. 28

Some of the same intention is apparent in *Where the Wild Things Are.* Max's rebellion and frustration at his punishment spread over four pages and are described in the text:

> That very night in Max's room a forest grew / and grew— / and grew until his ceiling hung with vines and the walls became the world all around / and an ocean tumbled by with a private boat for Max and he sailed off through night and day.

As the bedroom is transformed into the land "where the wild things are," the phrases become longer and more unwieldy until the reader must gasp for breath. Each stage in the transition is marked by the physical act of turning a page, and by the time the rumpus commences the visual images have taken over entirely from the words. The illustrations, which initially remained neatly contained within a white border on one side of the centerfold, have now swamped the page. The tensions between the competing mediums of prose and picture illustrate the transformation from Max's initial reasoned reaction, described in words, to his wild frenzy and cathartic rage, which can only be illustrated in wordless pictures. Inside the space of one children's picture book, the illustrations, comparable in function to the border of Blake's "Infant Joy," have conquered the page leaving the child in the midst of Experience like Blake's child in "The Garden of Love":

> So I turn'd to the Garden of Love
> That so many sweet Flowers bore,
> And I saw it was filled with graves,
> And tombstones where flowers should be:
> And priests in black gowns, were walking their rounds,
> And binding with briars my joys and desires.

—*Works,* p. 26

Where the Wild Things Are, surely one of the best children's books of our time, presents a responsiveness to childhood strikingly akin to Blake's in which childhood is not a world of idyllic escapism but of combined vulnerability and creativity. One of Blake's most important contributions to the development of nineteenth-century Romanticism was the recognition of the experience of childhood as the subject and inspiration of serious poetry. The child was no longer just the passive recipient of moral commonplaces, though Blake did not neglect this notion. His small emblem book *The Gates of Paradise,* written and illustrated for children, was a powerful and pessimistic exemplum of the vanity of human existence. But the thrust of his work was to express, for the first time in English literature, such spontaneous experiences of childhood and such assertions of the independence and integrity of childhood experience as the children's reply in "Nurse's Song":

> No no let us play, for it is yet day
> And we cannot go to sleep
> Besides in the sky, the little birds fly
> And the hills are all covered with sheep
> Well well go & play till the light fades way
> And then go home to bed
> The little ones leaped & shouted & laugh'd
> And all the hills ecchoed
>
> —*Works,* p. 15

The *Songs of Innocence,* in particular, asserts that childhood is a time of freedom from the constricting demands that lie behind the adult's acceptance of established theology and philosophy. Freed of these demands, even the child in "The Chimney Sweeper" is open, sensitive, and responsive to human delight and sorrow. It was not a totally idyllic world, for the world of innocence is full of the portents of experience. The predominant tone of the poems is still one of vulnerability, weeping, and lamentation—even if this sorrow is ultimately controlled as in "The Little Boy Found":

> The little boy lost in the lonely fen,
> Led by the wand'ring light,
> Began to cry, but God ever nigh,
> Appeard like his father in white.
>
> He kissed the child & by the hand led
> And to his mother brought,

> Who in sorrow pale, thro' the lonely dale
> Her little boy weeping sought.
>
> —*Works*, p. 11

This awareness of the ambivalence of childhood experience separates Blake's responses to the child from later Romantic exploitations of the symbol of childhood. Blake's child, like Wordworth's, possesses an intuitive power of responding and knowing. But Blake does not contemplate the state of childhood nostalgically. Wordsworth looks at childhood through the eyes of an adult awakening to his lost innocence and attempting to recapture it simply because he is adult and aware of his lost security. Blake, rather, leaps into a state of childhood and re-creates the moment when pain and vulnerability mingle with joy, perception, and lack of cynicism. Blake's child is not observed coming from heaven "trailing clouds of glory"; rather he *is* that glory for a brief and vulnerable moment. We see feelingly through his liberated responsiveness.

Generations of post-Romantic children's writers have wallowed in their own sense of nostalgia for their younger selves, so that childhood is usually portrayed as a time of innocence and only fleeting pain. But for Blake, and I would argue, Sendak, the approach is different. Sendak's evocation of childhood separates him from most contemporary children's writers in much the same way as Blake's creation of childhood separated him from Wordsworth's contemplation of the state. This is not to deny that Sendak is in the Romantic tradition. He is extremely conscious that elements of subjective biographical experience and responsiveness are the substance of his art. His description of the genesis of his books—"if something strikes me and I get excited, then I want it to be a book"[12]—sounds like a vaguely expressed Wordsworthian "overflow of powerful feelings." But in describing the impact of childhood experience on his work, he makes an important distinction between the act of remembering childhood or "pretending that I'm a child" and the action of a "creative artist who also gets freer and freer with each book and opens up more and more."[13] In another instance he insists on the continued existence of the "kid I was" continuing "somewhere, in the most graphic, plastic, physical way." Perhaps most significantly, he destroys the connection between himself as adult and the child when he speculates that "the kid I was never grew up into me."[14] Thus, like Blake, he does not use the child to comment upon himself as the adult. The connection implicit in Wordsworth's phrase, "The child is father of the man," does not exist for Sendak in the context of his imaginative creation.[15] Like Blake, he seems to be asserting that "Imagination has nothing to do with Memory," rather it is "Divine Vision."[16] Thus he attempts to shear off the partisan preoccupations which invade our own memories of childhood now that we are adult—our nostalgia, our obsessions with the lost opportunities and pastimes of childhood.

His assault on our more conventional responses to childhood is revealing. Some reviewers agonized over the disturbing evocations of *Where the Wild Things Are* or the unveiling of a small boy's penis in *The Night Kitchen*. Psychologists and librarians have reacted with their own understanding of childhood—or rather their own need to believe that some part of human existence can be, and therefore should be, protected from pain, fear, and the menace of chaos. For such readers, Max in *Where the Wild Things Are* may be a disturbing creation; his imagination makes him as vulnerable as the playful children in the pastures of Innocence. His world of mischievous make-believe is so fragile that his mother's anger can shatter it and thrust him into the expanding world of his own rage and fear, the world of Experience. In this state he creates from within himself demons which are really reflections of his own aggression. Eventually these menaces will be overcome and controlled and the child will return to bed and thus to what may be read as analogous to Blake's state of further or mature innocence, where the lamb and the tiger are reconciled. The book's ending is not merely a happy conclusion. There is a real sense of "look we have come through"—as Sendak has explained, he risked his own imagination in writing the tale: "When I write and draw I'm experiencing what the child in the book is going through. I was as relieved to get back from Max's journey as he was. Or rather, I like to think I got back."[17]

Like Blake, Sendak has taken seriously the horror and the largely helpless frustration of childhood that have to be sublimated into fantasies. Wordsworth's child meditates and broods on the beauty and challenge of nature. Self-consciously he appears to be preparing himself for the time when he will be a man. Blake's children are laughing, playing, weeping, and above all asking questions or arguing with others: "Little Lamb who made thee. . . ?"; "Fa-

ther, father, where are you going?''; ''Can I see anothers woe.
. . ?'' (*Works*, pp. 8, 11, 17). One of the most striking characteristics about Sendak's recurring prototypal figure of Max in each
of his forms—human or canine—is his assertiveness and his
astonishing curiosity. Kenny in *Kenny's Window* dares loneliness
and despair on his mission to find answers for his questions:
''What is an only goat?''; ''Can you fix a broken promise?'';
''What is a Very Narrow Escape?''. Maybe he would even dare to
ask: ''Tyger, did he who made the Lamb make thee?'' (*Works*, p.
25). Moreover, like the questioner in *Innocence and Experience*,
Kenny sometimes receives only half-answers or answers which are
truer to feeling than they are to logic.

Generations of critics have argued about the nature of Blake's
states of Innocence and Experience. Certainly in the *Songs of Experience*, cynicism and self-consciousness creep into the imagined
world making previous situations suddenly seem unendurable and
tragic. The change is not one from happiness to sadness, for sadness has already been present in *Innocence*. Rather, the world of
Urizen—of definition and order—has destroyed freedom and sensitivity. When children are observed at play, jealous nostalgia in-
vades the ''Nurse's Song'':

> When the voices of children, are heard on the green
> And whisprings are in the dale:
> The days of my youth rise fresh in my mind,
> My face turns green and pale.

> Then come home my children, the sun is gone down
> And the dews of the night arise
> Your spring & your day, are wasted in play
> And your winter and night in disguise.
>
> —*Works*, p. 23

Sexuality becomes corrupt as man's intellect reasons that:

> The Sexes sprung from Shame & Pride
> Blow'd in the morn: in evening died. . . .
>
> —*Works*, p. 30

It is in this context that Mickey's penis is clothed and the fears of
Jenny's search for ''experience'' in *Higglety Pigglety Pop!* become
unendurable. It is also in this context that criticism of Sendak's
frank approach to the ambivalence of childhood grows. Defending
himself against the charge that he frightens our little ones, Sendak

describes what he sees as the experience of childhood in terms which significantly parallel Blake's creation of joy and love, of curiosity and knowledge, intermingled with vulnerability and pain. Children are not, he claims, "drab, but they're not innocent of experience either. Too many parents and too many writers of children's books don't respect the fact that kids know a great deal of pleasure, but often they look defenceless too. Being defenceless is a primary element of childhood."[18]

Sendak's approach to childhood is as unsentimental as Blake's. Like Blake, he regards the material of his childhood experience as the substance of his imaginative powers. His childhood world is invaded by fears which may be unendurable if perceived wholly by an adult but which may eventually be controlled by the courage of a child's imagination.

An examination of *In the Night Kitchen* may illustrate his Blakean view of childhood a little further. The dream world presented is a bewildering one, and tumbling through it is Mickey, full of rage and frustration at his exclusion from the adult world. While lying in his bedroom, his rage wells up and his shout swamps the page. Instantly his adventures begin as he tumbles into dreamland, shedding his clothes as he passes the chandelier. Suddenly he appears as round and chubby, and somehow his naked body emphasizes his vulnerability. Just why he is so helpless becomes apparent on the next page when the bakers, whose eyes are closed and sightless, loom up obviously intending to bake Mickey (the blind forces of Urizen?). Throughout the tale, those closed eyes of the bakers and Mickey's own dreaming eyes seem to reinforce the absence of communication between the opposing characters. The bakers' activities swamp the next few pages; their self-satisfied grins dominate the pages. Eventually Mickey is able to again take control of the action and his bewildering environment by the power of his own imagination. The pictures become smaller as he creates an escape plan from the dough, suggesting quick, purposeful action. But when he is threatened by nonexistence, the bakers again loom up across the page as figures in a nightmare.

Mickey secures himself inside a milk bottle, floating like a baby in the womb. From here Mickey is able to provide the bakers with their milk, and he is free to leave—falling out of the dream in rather the same bewildering fashion that he fell into it. In sleep looking back on the experience, the "oh" of terror becomes the "ho" of recognized victory, then the "hum" of weariness and finally the "yum" of reaping his imaginative reward. On the final page he becomes, in his own mind at least, the victorious provisioner of our needs. But the battle has been an arduous one. Mickey's courage, and finally the superior powers of his imagination as he conjures up his methods of escape, have allowed him to foil the menaces that surround him. But they have been very extreme. He has been surrounded by menacing portents like jars that are labeled "Baby Syrup" and "Infant Food" with pictures of plaintive children on the outside. The terror of the experience seems to be aggravated by Mickey's failure to communicate with these smug self-satisfied adults. Mickey must always act independently in order to protect himself. The fat gnomes bear little resemblance to real adults. But then, perhaps, the child's perception of an adult has similarly little relation to the adult's perception of himself.

Like Blake's children, Sendak's Mickey lives in a separate world of ingenuity, sensitivity, and sometimes delight. He is often vulnerable, subjected to fear and pain, but his courage and his persistent imagination finally defeat the self-obsessed adult world. For all the terrors Mickey encounters, the book remains amusing and ingenious; just as the world of Innocence, for all its portents of sorrow, is one of peace and love. Sendak's trust in the ability of the childhood imagination to ultimately accommodate the terrors of experience is obvious.

Sendak's books, unlike many contemporary works for children, are not therapeutic in intent. They do not explain to the child how to imagine, what to imagine, how to reinterpret the adult world. They simply attempt to reflect and evoke the child's imaginative experience. Perhaps for this reason, children quickly identify with the protagonists and can easily act out plays about *Where the Wild Things Are* or what it is like to be Max or Mickey or Hector. Like Blake, Sendak has preferred to leap into the middle of the experience of childhood rather than to contemplate it from a nostalgic viewpoint. To place Sendak alongside Blake in the manner I have sketched in this paper is necessarily to ignore many of the evident influences upon his work. But it does, I believe, illuminate a central part of his genius. When we compare their visions of childhood in particular, we understand something of how Sendak's Max is a totally believable and fascinating child in his own right, in a way in which probably no other book child is. It demonstrates how, despite the brevity of the text in most of his books, so many complicated human experiences and emotions are evoked. It shows also that it is not simply technical superiority and slick promotion that make Sendak the most popular children's writer-illustrator of the 1960s and 1970s. Rather, it is the singular depth of perception of the nature of childhood experience which he possesses. In a very real sense he has emancipated the children's picture book. He has demonstrated that it may actually be about children, not just about loveable steam shovels or cute dogs or shapes—or even about the children we as adults want to remember or imagine. He presents the child as the Human Force Divine, in a very real Blakean sense.

NOTES

1. N. Hentoff, "Among the wild things," in *Only Connect,* ed. S. Egoff et. al. (Oxford: Oxford University Press, 1969), p. 327. Quotations from Blake are taken from *The Poetry and Prose of William Blake,* ed. David V. Erdman (New York: Doubleday, 1970). References to the "Songs of Innocence and Experience" are incorporated in the text and referred to as *Works*.

2. "On Receiving the Hans Christian Andersen Illustrator's Medal," *Top of the News,* XXVI (1970), 368. Hereafter cited as "Andersen."

3. "Questions to an Artist Who is Also an Author: a conversation between Maurice Sendak and Virginia Haviland," *US Lib. of Cong. Quart. J.,* XXVIII (1971), 273.

4. "Andersen," p. 366.

5. Hentoff, p. 329

6. *Ibid.*

7. W. J. T. Mitchell, "Blake's Composite Art," in *Blake's Visionary Forms Dramatic,* ed. by David Erdman and J. E. Grant (Princeton, N.J.: Princeton University Press, 1970), p. 62.

8. "Questions to an Artist," p. 264.

9. "Andersen," p. 368.

10. Hentoff, p. 339.

11. *Ibid.*

12. "Questions to an Artist," p. 266.

13. *Ibid.,* p. 268.

14. Hentoff, p. 329.

15. *W. Wordsworth: Poetry and Prose,* ed. W.M. Merchant (London: Hart-Davis 1955), p. 551.

16. "Annotations to Wordsworth's *Poems,*" *Works,* p. 655.

17. Hentoff, p. 344.

18. *Ibid.,* p. 329.

The Good Life, Prairie Style

The Art and Artistry of William Kurelek

Patricia Morley

In his autobiography, William Kurelek has written that people are more important than art.[1] The choice is not an either / or, but the emphasis is indicative. For people are the most distinctive feature of Kurelek's art, and the simple tales which accompany his paintings focus on the way in which people work and play and live.

It is only in the last few years that the paintings of this Canadian artist have been widely reproduced in book form, and in the same period Kurelek has entered the field of children's literature with three highly acclaimed books: *A Prairie Boy's Winter* (1973); *Lumberjack* (1974); and *A Prairie Boy's Summer* (1975). Kurelek is one of the very few artists to have books chosen for two consecutive years by the *New York Times* as Best Illustrated Book of the Year for Children.

The text which the artist has written to accompany his paintings for children in each of his three books has received little comment to date. Kurelek writes in plain, stripped prose with an engaging honesty and simplicity.[2] The elaborate symbolism which one finds in some of his religious paintings has no parallel in his prose. A wry sense of humor is one of the distinctive features of text and paintings alike. His memory for homely detail is extremely keen.

The anecdotes of farm and bush life are connected not only by time and place but also by the engaging personality of the narrator. *Lumberjack* is told in the first person, while the two prairie books are told in the third person and feature a farm boy, William, and his brother and sister. In each, the central personality is shy, sensitive, idealistic, gawky, and mechanically awkward—a child with whom many children would empathize.[3] To William, the annual field day is an embarrassment; June softball is a torment. One painting in *Summer* shows William daydreaming about a sensational catch which will earn him the respect and admiration of the other children. But the text reads: "The sun was in his eyes. So do you think he caught it?"

Kurelek's father came to Canada from the Ukraine. The artist, born in 1927, grew up in the prairies during the Depression—first on a grain farm in Alberta, later on a dairy farm in Manitoba. He

describes his Manitoba boyhood as "much more vivid and cre-
atively pressing" than his previous years, contrary to the idea that
the first six years of a child's life make the biggest impression on
his character. William was early seen to be different—a
dreamer—and suffered from the isolation which such difference
always entails. His relationship to his father was particularly
difficult. The fascinating story of how the artist grew from an
introverted, depressed, and repressed neurotic into a strong,
happy, and creative individual is told in his autobiography. The
journey involved his discovery of a religious faith which is as central to his art as to his life.

The epigraph to *A Prairie Boy's Summer* catches this vision.
Kurelek dedicates the book to his sister Nancy, "who more than
anyone else shared with me the surprise and wonder of prairie seasons as a child, who has added to that surprise and wonder a sense
of awe and love for the Creator of those wonders. Many call it the
Living Whole—Ultimate Cause—Nature. We two call it: God."

Kurelek has often declared that his paintings fall into two
basically different types. He calls them "the nostalgic-pastoral and
the religious commentary."[4] The twelve paintings in his 1976
Fields series (a treatment of boyhood scenes viewed through the
eyes of the adult philospher-artist) suggest a fusion of these two
categories. The natural world whose smells and sounds and sights
evoke nostalgic memories of childhood is also a spirit-filled place
witnessing to God's presence.[5] The religious quality of Kurelek's
vision adds strength and depth to the homely subjects around
which he builds his stories for children.[6]

Kurelek remembers his father as a natural storyteller. His
protagonist, young William, dreams of being surrounded by city
high-school students who listen in admiration to his stories of farm
adventures: "How mistaken his daydreams turned out to be! . . .
Many years would pass before William found a way to get people
interested."[7] But find it he did. Most of his paintings, especially
those for children, depict action and suggest stories in themselves.

Lumberjack comes out of two summers spent in the bush in
order to earn college fees (1946) and a stake to study art in Europe
(1951). It was a hard job, possible only for the physically strong
and the psychologically determined. Kurelek records here a way of
life that, with the invention of the mechanical tree harvester, has
largely ceased to exist. The artist notes the modern changes in an

epilogue, which likens the huge mechanical monsters to giant insects from another planet.[8] The accompanying painting shows the driver of the machine behind the bars of his cab, doubly imprisoned by the placement of two giant trees. A recurring theme in Kurelek's work is freedom or its lack. He is evidently not optimistic about a technological world. He concludes: "Was our old way of life, for all its hardships, more romantic, more humane, more socially satisfying? I leave the answers to others. I only know I am glad to have been a part of that good life before it passed into history."[9]

The first episode in *Lumberjack* promises adventure and sets the drama in the incredible country north of Lake Superior: "The forest behind us stood tall, lush and bold on the round-shouldered mountains that seemed to march upward and backward from the water's edge." Mountains are a new experience for a boy from the prairies. The sense of a vast wilderness land underlies this book, even in the homely camp scenes of washing up, preparing lunch, or using an outdoor privy.

In the midst of the wilderness stands the bush camp. Kurelek's strong sense of society, of community, reflects both his Ukrainian heritage and his Catholic faith. *Lumberjack's Breakfast* depicts some two dozen men at two tables laden with food: mountains of flapjacks, big bowls of porridge, stacks of camp-baked bread, and tin dishes of bacon, potatoes and beans. Steam rises from the platters and jugs, and the men look happy. In *Relaxation,* some of the men are stretched on bunkhouse cots while others play cards. Shades of green predominate along with reds and yellows. A large circular coil of wire on the back wall suggests a unity of spirit. Ralph Connor has written of drunken fights in lumber camps because the men had nothing to do during their time off, but there is nothing of this in Kurelek's portrait of the life.[10] In the last episode, "Bunkhouse—After Midnight," the painting shows a double row of filled cots in brownish gloom, with the lines of the central aisle converging towards an infinite point—a favorite Kurelek trick of perspective. In the center, the grill of a circular woodburning stove grins merrily. The vignette concludes: "The windows were frosted over with a half-inch of artwork by a better artist than I—He who gave me such talent as I have."

By contrast, the isolation of a lone worker is often poignant. In *Working in the Rain,* the narrator continues to cut wood, wearing a fisherman's black rubber outfit, because he needs the money. He is thinking of the others back at camp playing cards. The black-clad sawyer, encircled by forest under a steady downpour, could be the only man in the world. The return to camp in winter, at the end of the day's work, dramatizes the rhythm of penetrating the wilderness and returning to society, a rhythm which has been an integral part of the Canadian experience. In the background looms the forest, dark and threatening. The text concludes: "The darkness of the forest closing in behind seemed to be driving us back to the tiny nucleus of human habitation that was our camp" (Episode 24).

One thinks of Northrop Frye's comments on Canadian art concerning the impact of the wilderness upon the imagination. Canadian literature indicates that the northern land has engendered a sense of mystery, of awe. The two themes which Frye finds central to Canadian poetry—a comic theme of satire and exuberance and a tragic theme of loneliness and terror—may also be found in Kurelek's work. His tragic theme belongs primarily to the paintings of his depressed period (*The Maze,* for example, painted during his hospitalization in England) and to some of his religious paintings which express his "doomsday" vision. His children's books reflect his comic mood. Now and again, however, as in *Working in the Rain,* the loneliness surfaces. Frye sees the poet's vision of Canada, that of a pioneer country in which man confronts the wilderness, being superseded "by a vision of Canada as a settled and civilized country, part of an international order, in which men confront the social and spiritual problems of men."[11] Kurelek's work has followed this path. His experience is archetypally Canadian in many ways.

The two prairie books are beautifully complementary. They show the chores, the games, the activities of children on a small prairie farm in the first-half of our century. An entire life is caught in microcosm in twenty pictures, each with its companion story. *A Prairie Boy's Winter* is framed by the departure and return of crows, to young William the surest sign of the onset of winter and its imminent end. My own feeling as a child in Ontario was the same, despite the popular robin mythology. Not the sight so much as the sound of the crow spelled late autumn, early spring. The first painting shows five children by a bare birch grove while dozens of crows fly overhead; the second depicts a lone crow in a brilliant winter sky beneath which pointing children dance for joy. *A Prairie*

Boy's Summer lacks this overt circular structure but, like the earlier book, progresses from the beginning of the season toward its end. Where the dominating colors of *Winter* are white and the blue of a winter sky, *Summer* is dominated by greens. Even the cloth bindings of the two books match their predominant colors.

Winter stresses the endurance necessary for surviving in a northern climate. Watering the cows in midwinter is a fearsome task, an ordeal for man and beast. While his brother chases the reluctant herd out and his mother pours hot water over the pump, William uses an axe to hack away the ice from the trough: "The water was so cold that now and then as the cows drank they had to lift their teeth out of it when the chill became too painful." *The Blizzard* shows William leaning hard into the wind as he heads for the half-obliterated barn. The children hope, of course, for an extra holiday from school. After the two day blow they venture out to examine the snow sculptures. *Snowdrift Fun* shows them honeycombing an enormous drift with tunnels and caves. It was in Frederick Philip Grove's *Over Prairie Trails* that I first read of snowdrifts as high as tree tops. Being a city child, I felt that Grove must be exaggerating. But Kurelek's *Milk Truck on Snowploughed Road* shows drifts nearly up to the tops of telephone wires, while the truck rolls between plowed walls much higher than itself.

Henry Kreisel has written of the paradoxical sense of freedom and entrapment, of vastnesses and isolated enclosures, which prairie literature reflects.[12] Kurelek's *Skating on the Bog Ditch* shows three boys speeding down a frozen strip which heads towards an endless sky. A patch of snow has tripped one boy. *Mending Pig's Fence,* in the *Summer* volume, treats the pigs' yearning for freedom with quiet humor. Most of the "escapees" come back to be fed. If one pig is available, the others can be lured back to captivity by tormenting their comrade, whose squeals will bring them rushing back. Describing the milking scene in *Summer,* Kurelek emphasizes the discomforts of heat and flies: "The little patch of outside in the picture is like the promise of freedom a convict sees through the bars of his window. The rows of stantions and support pillars are like the bars."[13] In many of his paintings, the dominant lines head towards the horizon or a patch of sky seen through an opening suggests freedom craved and sought.

Kreisel has also noted the dominant part played by puritanism in prairie literature. He sees it as "one result of the conquest of the land, part of the price exacted for the conquest.''[14] Kurelek's father was a man hardened by his upbringing and by adversity, a man whose puritan ethic of work, self-denial, and emotional repression has been portrayed by many a Canadian novelist. In his autobiography, Kurelek relates how his paternal grandfather tried, by hacking up a favorite piece of ice beside the house, to keep his grandchildren from wearing out their boots sliding on the ice.[15] Both parents were severe disciplinarians:

> This parental attitude—that children were to be punished not only for being bad—but also for making mistakes, for being afraid, for being ill, for being careless, for lacking vigilance, took some swallowing. But eventually the message got across; the Kureleks rarely bare their personal troubles or failures even to this day.''[16]

To work, and to feel guilty about not working, was bred in the bone.[17]

Kurelek still works extremely hard, sometimes painting seventeen hours a day. But he no longer works compulsively. He paints in order to glorify God, to lead men to Him, and to celebrate beauty. The farm chores in the two prairie books, some of which were doubtless bitter at the time, are described with an underlying humor which transforms hardship, without idealizing it, into an acceptable and even an enjoyable part of life. Happiness is the prevailing mood in his books for children. Milking hazards such as flies and heat are somewhat alleviated by William's little sister, Nancy, holding the cow's tail: "As relief from the milking ordeal, William amused himself by squirting one of the barn cats that waited nearby, meowing for its evening ration. It would jump away as if upset, but really it liked the white shower; for it sat down further off and set about licking away the milk" (*Summer,* p. 12). The chore of driving the cows into the barn also has its lighter moments. William is amused to observe the warfare carried on between the barn swallows and the cat, who pretends to ignore the screamed insults and the dive-bombing attacks while plotting retaliation. "Pasturing Cows" describes the cows' escape to greener pastures while their young cowherd is absorbed in a frontier adventure story.[18]

But prairie life is not all work. The games of farm children, the narrator tells us, are handed down from generation to generation. "Fox and Geese" is a variant of tag played by trampling the pattern of a large spoked wheel into fresh snow. Rinks and hockey sticks are made by the boys themselves, who probably enjoyed them more than the costly stadiums and equipment expected by children today. The swimming hole is a widened portion of the bog ditch, with a sod dam and a rough diving platform. William disliked the hole's local inhabitants: whiskered black catfish and crayfish for whom the sod dam served as an apartment. In a painting on this theme the boy, fearful but fascinated, raises a sod to stare at a crayfish, while nearby youths are stuffing another one into his running shoes. The last *Summer* scene shows older children practicing archery at recess with homemade bows and arrows. The arrows sail far beyond the schoolyard in the same way William thinks of leaving in a few years for a city high school: "It seemed the boys were conquering the awesomeness of the prairie expanses at last."

Some of the charm of the two prairie books lies in their "how-to" quality. Descriptions of farm chores are simple but detailed to the point where the young reader can say to himself, "So that's how it's done!" Details also bring the scene to life imaginatively: frogs in the new mown hay, horses bullying the cows out of the best places in the smudge screen, gulls following the plow to gobble the turned-up worms and bugs, a dog driving a rabbit out of the last stand of grain, and the mischievous glint in the little eyes of pigs.

In the final analysis, the prairie books represent two things—a boy and a place—a land and a people formed on it and by it. Kurelek loves both. The intimate relationship between land and people suffuses the work and leads the child reader into a deeper appreciation of our place in planet earth. In a recent celebration of the landscape of Canada's ten provinces, Kurelek describes the prairies thus:

> From the scenic viewpoint, by far the most magnificent feature of the prairies is the panorama of sky, awesomely grand and varied. When the weather forecast says scattered showers, you can actually see several showers taking place within the full circle of your vision. Even the wind is visible, as in W. O. Mitchell's wonderfully evocative book, *Who Has Seen the Wind?*[19]

Even the wind is visible in some of Kurelek's paintings. And the blades of grass. These are books for children and adults alike, books full of humanity, humor, vitality, and joy. Kurelek is an artist, as Joy Carroll says, "with spaces and silences inside him."[20] His inner peace is contagious.

NOTES

1. William Kurelek, *Someone With Me* (Ithaca: Cornell University Press, 1973), p. 501: "I don't think art is the most important thing in life. People are."

2. Referring to *Kurelek's Canada* (1975), Phil Lanthier writes: ". . . . the land itself provides the elemental pleasures which Kurelek is willing to endorse: square dancing, ice-skating, fishing, talking, homecoming, the first snow fall, and clean jokes," "The Artist as Piers Plowman," *Matrix* (Fall, 1975), p. 4. Cf. Joy Carroll, "Kurelek sees us better than we see ourselves," *Maclean's* (Aug. 1975), p. 70: "Kurelek's prose accompanying the paintings is often awkward but scores on simplicity."

3. In the Artist's Notes of a brochure put out by the Art Gallery of Windsor when it acquired the collection of paintings which compose *A Prairie Boy's Summer,* Kurelek writes: "These are my remembered stories of farm adventure. 'William,' the boy hero of the book, is of course myself. I deliberately dress my stock characters alike throughout the series. William wears a white shirt, blue trousers and sneakers or work boots and my sister Nancy is in a simple red dress."

4. Judith Sandiford, "Painting Beauty. Kurelek's Miracle," *Ottawa Citizen* (Mar. 6, 1976), p. 72.

5. William Kurelek, *Fields* (Montreal: Tundra Books, 1976).

6. Kurelek has painted many series of paintings on a religious theme to help teach and share his Christian faith. He purposely alternates such didactic paintings with homelier ones of everyday life and farm childhood. In *Someone with Me* he writes: "Now to my religious works, which are didactic or moralizing. The subject is not dictated to me as it often was to medieval artists. I choose it myself and paint a theme that I strongly feel needs to be made public, and I deliberately use the popularity of my other more pleasant, memory-recording type painting so that I can attract the public. I've worked it out so that every second major exhibit of mine is moralizing, and every other one is merely story telling. Eventually, perhaps these two main overall themes will become married, completely merged" (p. 507). I suggest that they have already merged to a greater extent than the artist realizes.

7. William Kurelek, *A Prairie Boy's Summer* (Montreal: Tundra Books, 1975), p. 11.

8. As noted above, metaphors are relatively exceptional in Kurelek's text for children.

9. William Kurelek, *Lumberjack* (Montreal: Tundra Books, 1974), Epilogue.

10. Ralph Connor, *The Man from Glengarry* (Toronto: McClelland and Stewart, 1969), pp. 253–255. Peter Sypnowich describes Kurelek's bush experience as follows: "In bush camps and on construction jobs, the other workers called him 'Bozo' or ignored him, while he was repelled by their constant talk of drink, women and cars" ("The Easter Story," *Star Weekly,* Apr. 13, 1963). This suggests that the material has been idealized to a certain extent.

11. Northrop Frye, "Preface to an Uncollected Anthology," *Canadian Anthology* (Toronto: Gage, 1966), p. 528.

12. Henry Kreisel, "The Prairie: A State of Mind," *Canadian Anthology* 3rd ed. (Toronto: Gage, 1974), p. 623. See also: "The prairie, like the sea, thus often produces an extraordinary sensation of confinement within a vast and seemingly unlimited space" (and *passim*).

13. Letter of Mar. 28, 1976 from the artist to author.

14. Henry Kreisel, "The Prairie: A State of Mind," p. 626: "Like the theme of conquest of the land, the theme of the imprisoned spirit dominates serious prairie writing and is connected with it."

15. William Kurelek, *Someone With Me*, p. 4.

16. *Ibid.*, p. 18.

17. See *ibid.*, p. 175: "I had worked myself into a guilt complex about wasting a single moment."

18. Cf. *Someone With Me*, pp. 63–64: "I hated farm work—I guess because there was so much of it. It was a bottomless bucket, and it interfered with my creative play."

19. William Kurelek, *Kurelek's Canada* (Toronto: Pagurian Press, 1975), p. 88.

20. Joy Carroll, "Kurelek sees us better than we see ourselves," *Maclean's* (Aug., 1975), p. 70.

Donald Duck

*How Children (Mainly Boys) Viewed Their Parents (Mainly Fathers), 1943-1960**

James A. Freeman

> Children show no trace of the arrogance which urges adult civilized men to draw a hard-and-fast line between their own nature and that of all other animals. Children have no scruples over allowing animals to rank as their full equals. Uninhibited as they are in the avowal of their bodily needs, they no doubt feel themselves more akin to animals than to their elders, who well may be a puzzle to them.[1]

It seems ungrateful to seriously analyze the Donald Duck adventures which I read in *Walt Disney's Comics & Stories* from 1943 until the early 1960s. As uncounted millions of other young Americans, I turned to them, the first stories in each issue, for the simple pleasure of watching hapless Donald as he pursued impossible dreams. Although fame, fortune, and triumph usually eluded him, his perfervid struggles elated me. I don't think I was any crueler than any of my preadolescent pals. Indeed we all were pleased as we read and reread how Donald's nephews, Huey, Dewey, and Louie, tried to save him from disaster. Month after month he was nearly overwhelmed by a gorgeous gallery of opponents: Scrooge McDuck, Gladstone Gander, neighbor Jones, cavemen, spies, smugglers, irate employers, intractable animals, and, consistently, his own rash enthusiasms. Yet he emerged at the end of each story in roughly the same condition as he had entered it, battered perhaps but not much more sunk into the world he only dimly comprehended. Whatever our reasons for appreciating Donald then, they were largely unarticulated. He was ours for ten cents, a friend and a clown whom we all understood.

Recently, however, after years of studying books without pictures, I reread my collection of Disney *Comics*. Carefully preserved for this later, more analytical age, the Duck stories resemble those Egyptian statues that were to spring to life when the revived pharaoh needed them. While the adventures are still entertaining, I experienced a shock that few kings would have welcomed. The overt situations that engaged us so many years ago

*An earlier version of this paper was delivered to the Children's Literature Section of MLA, December 27, 1975.

spring, oddly, not from the supposed preoccupations of children. Rather they deal almost exclusively with activities that we usually label "For Adults Only": Donald is swindled in real estate; Donald loses job after job; Donald wants only a pedigreed dog (unthinkable snobbery for a kid!); Donald is pestered on his vacation by salesmen; Donald tries to impress Duckburg society by giving a lavish jungle party; and so on.[2] Skillfully, but curiously, these plots deal mainly with the ambitions and perils of adults, not children. Even when the three nephews act and thus provide young readers with surrogates, their deeds are almost always responses to some crisis in Donald's career or value in his imagination. Whatever the outcome of their efforts, it has been precipitated by a grownup concern: They try to help him woo Daisy by faking feats of strength; they try to warn him against buying a salted mine; and they urge him to campaign for marshal of the Easter parade. In almost every tale the central *donnée* is some obsession of the adult world. Now that I was older I was at a loss to explain why the enormous audience for *WDC&S* was composed of readers who would not shave or vote for many years. The one extended critique on Disney comics which I could find was not really about our American experience with these magazines. (Richard Schickel's *The Disney Version* is mainly about films and fan journals are mostly nostalgic, not evaluative.) The commentary had been penned, with vigor and outrage, by two Marxists from Chile who blame the Latin-American "Pato Donald" for indoctrinating their countrymen with the imperialist ideology that eventually toppled Allende.[3] True or not, their analysis does not reveal what got to us as we sat on our beds, barricaded (we thought) from the world by a rampart of Disneys.

The lure of Donald in those years does not seem to be based upon the same grade-school fantasies that attracted us to, say, Tarzan, Superman, Plastic Man, or the Blackhawks. (I speak only for boys, of course. We never knew what girls thought of.) Donald's world includes people of all ages and professions (unlike Burrough's jungle), characters who are what they seem to be (unlike those in Metropolis), stable physical dimensions (unlike "Plas"), and few references to specific causes (unlike the patriotism of the Blackhawks). When Carl Barks, the brilliant artist who drew the Duck strips, says, "I was writing for about age 12 or 13," he verbalizes a truth which the older generation misinterpreted.[4] Evidently they considered *WDC&S* to be mental farina that would not overstimulate pubescent psyches. Dr. Fredric Wertham, the psychiatrist whose polemic against comics, *Seduction of the Innocent,* nearly ruined the comic-book industry, quotes a parent-wise child who concealed his beloved crime stories under copies of Walt Disney.[5] To the credit of parental perception, it does not seem as if pictures and words about a talking duck threaten traditional authority. Pictures of animals have been with us since prehistory in the caves at Altamira, some 20,000 years. Talking animals appeared centuries before Uncle Remus in the Sanskrit *Panchatantra,* Aesop's *Fables,* and the legend of Balaam's Ass. And Krazy Kat kept company with our earliest comic humans such as The Yellow Kid, Little Nemo in Slumberland, and The Katzenjammer Kids. Not only are Donald's roots deep in our collective memory, but his stories contain few of the Grand Guignol pastimes which gorged other monthlies with scenes of torture and slaughter. If adults saw him at all, it was as the movie-cartoon squawker, irate and incoherent. Yet, despite the lineage and appearance of the Duckburg annals, only a superficial reading can for long suppose that the comic books are innocuous. I would even suggest that they titillate the same anarchic cravings in children to which the forbidden crime-and-horror magazines appealed.

Whatever else Donald may be, he is a parent. Far from being a fey creature unlinked to the child's everyday experience, some placidly irrelevant "Teenie Weenie" who can easily be dismissed, Donald consistently exhibits traits which any schoolboy recognizes as defining a parent. The only father figure available to Huey, Dewey, and Louie, he wants them to bathe, do chores, bank their money, go to school and do homework, practice classical music, stop reading comics and old love letters, and generally stay out of trouble. He clearly stands for antikid values such as cleanliness, culture, profitable work, and meaningful play. His sponsorship of these child-squelching dicta leaves no question as to which group, oppressor or oppressed, Donald belongs. A web-footed Apollo, he tries to stand in the way of his nephews' Dionysian scamper to pleasure. As in real life, his adherence to conventional dictates often puts him in conflict with the young. Not only does Donald try to impose adult values upon the kids, but he sometimes also competes with them. Ferocious energy ignites him when he attempts to beat them at such varied enterprises as walking the tightrope, skating, performing magic tricks, or running an ice taxi. The importance of molding the kids looms so large in Donald's mind that he himself breaks rules, lies, and sabotages with ingenious virtuosity. He illustrates, in his way, that obsession of adults to control everything. Frustrated as they must inevitably be in such a megalomaniacal endeavor, they settle instead for conquering their young. One grim restatement of this parent-child connection is in James Joyce's story "Counterparts": An unhappy Dublin clerk, scolded by his employer, returns home—to beat his son.

If Donald were no more than a metamorphic parent, then I doubt he would appeal to many children. What gains their interest, I think, is the way Barks allows him to simultaneously resemble and parody our demanding, combative sires. Like Huck's Aunt Sally, Donald aims to "adopt" the nephews and "sivilize" them. But unlike Sally, he is seldom a real threat. We can (to use Huck's word) "stand" his maxims about cleanliness because he is so often dumped into the mud. The aphorisms which advocate education are bearable because Donald himself so seldom knows what's happening. The first complete story in April 1943, while simple by later standards, predicts the split between Donald's ideals and his performance: Having planted a secret garden that the kids won't destroy, he is lured into a football game and he himself tramples his own vegetables. With complete psychological validity, Donald brags most about the affairs he knows least. "I know all about falcons," he burbles, "I saw one in a movie once." This bumptious ignorance appears in many other episodes from fishing ("I know all the angles") to flower raising (about which Donald knows "everything, kids, everything"). As with cleanliness, so with knowledge: Donald himself calls our attention to the abstract desirability of a trait and then, mercifully for kids, fails to exemplify it.

Another area in which Donald assaults our joyous id, thus resembling a tyrannic parent, and simultaneously fails, thus encouraging a child's fantasy, is in that of work and play. At both he is a flop. The ethic of strive and succeed while facing the world, trying to do and dare while struggling upward (all titles from Horatio Alger) is a staple of adult propaganda. It justifies the other nemeses of childhood, washing and going to school. That simple Deuteronomic formula, "Be good and prosper," adopted by capitalism, pictured by Hogarth, and touted by Scrooge, is swallowed by Donald. It proves to be bitter medicine, however, since he is constitutionally incapable of translating dream into fact. "There are jobs," begins one tale in which he fails as night watchman at a waxworks, "but Donald never seems to find one that he can do." In this case the trouble is Donald's need for at least sixteen hours' sleep. In other episodes we are treated to variations upon the theme of making a place in the world that is both recognizable and predictable. In fact, Donald cannot really do more than mash dirt clods on a race track, "tromp" potato peelings, or "skim the scum off the vats at the vinegar works." In his dreams however he has ambitions to be a successful chemist, bill collector, pearl fisher, postman, appliance repairman, actor, and dog catcher. The long list of Donald's temporary vocations almost exhausts the range of normal occupations that children know their fathers to be involved with. He does not attempt jobs that require formal training: doctor, lawyer, or teacher. But he attacks the most disparate enterprises, from cargo-boat captain to quiz-show contestant, with heedless confidence. Donald's economic disasters present a suspicious preadolescent with a barnyard Doppelgänger for his own father— that Willy Loman whom the child sees trudge wearily home each night drained of illusion or reward.

Donald's hobbies are as mismanaged as his professions. He fights with neighbor Jones and thus cannot enjoy his rare-book collection; he gives away a prize dime from his coin collection and has a mental breakdown when it mysteriously reappears; he boasts to the kids, "Ice fishing is for experts like me," yet bungles it so badly that he is nearly swept over a waterfall; he practices so energetically for a dance contest that he exhausts himself. The specific interests change, but Donald never does. Like Ovid, St. Paul and, ultimately, all humans, Donald claims to know what's right, but usually does what's wrong. Between the idea of father as a take-charge success at work or play and the reality observed by most children falls the shadow of failure which Donald fleshes out. World literature is full of losers, of course. Behind Portnoy stands a bedraggled column of one-downers which reaches at least to Jason in Apollonius of Rhodes, the unspectacular captain who is ever *amēchanos*, "at a loss, awkward." But Donald is, after all, almost a father. The gap we observe between his aims and his accomplishments is particularly poignant to me now that I am a parent. But I suspect that his failures reassured us as children. They supplied confirmation to our developing egos that adults were not perfect after all.

Barks wisely tempers his otherwise dank picture of a failed father by several devices. In the first place, Donald is the kids' uncle, not their (unknown) father. Thus in the family romance which the young reader entertains, "unca" Donald is analogous to the humble stepparent who superintends his wards until their rightful parent, always rich and skillful, reclaims them. At one point Scrooge McDuck ponders whether Donald, Gladstone, or the nephews should inherit his fortune. He elevates the kids, in imagination at least, to an importance which has nothing to do with Donald. Repeatedly they complain that Donald is inadequate when compared to the parents of other children. Even when he is most ebullient about his abilities, Huey, Dewey, and Louie disbelieve him. For instance, Donald vows to win money by photographing a rare bird: "No woodpecker can make a cuckoo out of me." But, taught by long experience, they lament that whatever he plans "will be a flop." Their low estimate of his capabilities often torments him. After pooh-poohing the nephews' interest in science fiction, Donald finds that Gyro Gearloose has built a working machine from plans in their magazine: "When the kids hear of Gyro's invention," he mopes, "my name will be Caveman Duck." Donald's questionable status in his own family, at the same time potentate and patsy, gives added significance to the start of a misadventure in the desert. The captain says, "If this were a fairy story, it would begin: 'Once there was a great king of luck [i.e. Gladstone]. . . . Among the great king's fellow mortals was a lowly cousin. . . ' " Despite the closeness of their relationship, the kids can always escape from any ultimate connection to Unca Donald.

Another mechanism which Barks employs to ease juvenile anxiety in the presence of a father is denial, not of Donald's paternity, but of his dignity. Just as *Unca* is not *father,* so triumph on Donald's part is usually negated by making him laughable. The strategy of rendering innocuous whatever may harm the perceiver is, like the fiction of an absent parent, a defense mechanism shared by psychology and literature.[6] Freudian dream theory postulates a censor which transmutes images of the fearful into objects that are merely absurd. In literature, some of the terror inspired by the hunlike Snopes family is undercut by Faulkner in *The Hamlet* by having Ike Snopes fall in love with a cow. In Donald's adventures,

Barks often makes him grotesque at the very moment of victory.
The initial characterization of a guardian as a lowly duck is the first
step in this process of belittling the power of parenthood. He is,
after all, "that dumpy duck in the sailor suit." No sinister Long
John Silver, Donald in his nautical togs has ludicrous associations
for observant children. Often garbed themselves in cutdown versions of adult attire (cowboy outfits or farmer's overalls), kids
know deep down that they may look cute but they are incapable of
doing more than "helping" real cowboys or farmers. When an
adult who isn't a sailor wears a sailor's costume, there is a note of
pointless regression. And as Booth Tarkington shows in *Penrod,*
those who wear sailor suits are often pampered, effeminate, and
ineffectual.[7]

Even when Donald is not totally ineffectual, the stories teach
several ways in which even a successful father may be dealt with.
One tale has Donald bump his head and metamorphose into "Professor Donald Duck, mightiest chemist in the universe." Although
he makes good his claim by inventing "Duckmite," a powerful
explosive, he cannot control it. The great scientist lights a match to
check fluid level ("BOOM"), is blown into a pond ("SPLOSH"),
and emerges with a whoop of "SUCCESS! SUCCESS!"—but also
with a frog perched on his head. He eventually flies to the moon,
but the knowledge-inspiring bump subsides and no one believes his
adventure. These ludicrous juxtapositions eliminate any tragic
potentiality which might lie in an account of fall from high estate.
Far from being a feathered avatar of Victor Frankenstein, Donald's
rise and fall, both literal and figurative, invite us to savor his silliness, not his pathos. No matter how decent we may be, it is difficult to expend much sympathy when the potential receiver has
been swallowed by a clam or so bloated by gassy water that he
floats aloft, tied by one leg to his horse.

The assault on Donald's dignity is bearable since it does not bat-
ter everyone in Duckburg. He alone has his energies checked by a
form of personal bad luck. Like Odysseus frustrated by Poseidon,
Encolpius by Priapus in *The Satyricon,* or Valjean by Javert, Donald experiences *mala fortuna*. But, unlike these beleaguered victims, Donald is his own adversary. His own clumsiness, for example, alienates a client on his fishing boat. Donald hits him with a
fish, pricks him with a sticklefish, and gets him lost, drenched with
rain, and whirled about by a water spout. After this series of self-

generated disasters, Donald has the gall to sneer at his prudent nephews while they save him, "Some people have all the LUCK!" There is some flaw in his nature which encourages disaster. As Henry Fielding knowingly says in the preface to *Joseph Andrews,* "Affectation proceeds from one of these two causes, vanity or hypocrisy: for as vanity puts us on affecting false characters, in order to purchase applause, so hypocrisy sets us on an endeavour to avoid censure, by concealing our vices under an appearance of their opposite virtues." Donald's conceit alternates with his fear to force him into ludicrous predicaments.

Two of Donald's relatives display good fortune and prove that his lack of nobility is special, not general. Gladstone Gander, his brash cousin, is the first minion of *bona fortuna*. For him, success is an aspect of his character as unalterable as his feathers. Statements that would be foolhardy in another's mouth are correct when uttered by Gladstone. "It is true that I am lucky" and "I'm the luckiest guy in the world" arouse the jealous envy of no deity. Only Donald is perturbed that the allegations are demonstrably true. Gladstone wins all the turkies in a raffle: "You just can't beat the Gladstone luck," he chortles. He gets all the items on a list and "make[s] the rest of us feel so futile." Gladstone's faculty frustrates almost every shift of Donald to outdo him: Donald flees to Florida but cannot escape treating Gladstone to dinner; Donald buys a plastic rabbit's foot but still is conned into digging up pearls for his lucky cousin; Donald and Scrooge McDuck win the contest for a uranium mine—while Gladstone has found ten mines by himself. Donald's mightiest exertions raise him only to a controlled height which is always topped by Gladstone's. Like some unfortunate creature assigned to a low rung on the ladder of being, but in teasing view of higher rungs, Donald can only lament, "I'll always be unlucky."

A second relative who reminds us that Unca Donald has some defect is Scrooge McDuck.[8] Although Donald's rich uncle does not appear until November 1948, he, like Gladstone, pinpoints what readers and children often feel about parents and about Donald: both are star-crossed. Scrooge's name connotes unfeeling miserliness. His tcp hat, spats, and mutton-chop whiskers represent "Plutocrat," and his activities show him absorbed in finance. He "dives around in [money] like a porpoise," gleefully enjoying his "nine fantasticillion dollars" that need "three cubic acres" of stor-

age space. Unlike Gladstone, who only holds out his hand for
money to drop into it, Scrooge has amassed his wealth by the usual
means of mercantile enterprise. He owns, ultimately, all means of
production. For instance, Donald is hired to spend some of
Scrooge's extra cash but fails since everything he buys comes from
a Scrooge industry and thus makes the irate uncle worth even more
than "500 triplicatillion" dollars. Despite Scrooge's omnipresence
whenever economics is concerned, he is a humorous creation and
serves to emphasize the same point as Gladstone: Donald has no
resources to combat the former's luck or the latter's financial expertise. Even after raising a sunken ship by means of ping-pong
balls, Donald earns nothing since the equipment he bought for his
ingenious salvage operation was all owned by Scrooge.[9] The
supernatural element of fate personified by Gladstone is restated
by the prosaic element of free capitalism in the character of
Scrooge and both show how unimpressive Donald is when judged
by any standard.

There is, in addition to the assertions that Donald is neither a
true parent nor a dignified adult, a third device by which Barks
soothes us while presenting a kind of father. Unlike most adults
and all parents, Donald has no sexual victories. We were boys yet
but nervously edging toward puberty. Daisy is pursued but not
won. In fact, her elusiveness marks one significant difference between her and Minnie Mouse, who is often Mickey's companion on
extended adventures. Even the nephews outdo Donald for Daisy's
favor: They win a beachcombing contest and the privilege of sharing her lunch. Kindly but humiliatingly, they pass food to the defeated Donald. When Donald manages to be in any romantic situation, his inadequacy prevents satisfactory union. Once he and lus-
cious Miss Swoonsudden are isolated on a pinnacle during the
Merry Loafers' picnic—but he must be rescued by the kids. Later
a rich woman is intrigued by the tiny jet which saved him. Donald
ruins this prospect of love-cum-wealth by burning off the poor
lady's hair. While the entire Disney studio is notorious for its moral
anatomy—no nipples or navals—the theme of foiled flirtation gives
young readers a peculiar joy when imputed to Donald. He presents
no rivalry to an audience whose growing sexuality is constantly
threatened in subtle ways by the father. His very name implies a
kind of androgynous creature: "Donald" is clearly male, but
"Duck" is technically female. A famous parody of Disney ideals

shocks us into admitting how relentlessly sex is withheld from all inhabitants of the Magic Kingdom: During an orgy of unlikely couples (such as Snow White and a lecherous set of Dwarfs), Huey, Dewey, and Louie gleefully lift Daisy's skirt to finally view her (as Yeats might say) feathered glory.[10] At any rate, the nephews and their human counterparts are not troubled by a virile Donald who might, even imaginatively, deprive them of females.

The three shortcomings which soothe a young reader's anxiety when confronted by an adult (albeit a duckish one) are thus lack of paternity, respect, and sexual success. They make credible the fourth and most important device: Almost every moral or practical triumph is won by the nephews. They or their pets repeatedly provide the disciplined energy which wins the day. Pointedly, they often save Donald from himself, thereby reversing the normal roles of parents and children. If one entertains the hypothesis that modern literature rejects the genres of tragedy and comedy since the first requires a stable ethical universe while the second requires a stable social world (neither of which is palatable to disillusioned readers), then the kids' victories are symptomatically modern. If one remembers Sancho trying to curb Don Quixote's flamboyant imagination, then the kids' rescues are reassuringly timeless. It is the young rather than their teachers who provide an efficacious moral center in many episodes. Their activities do more than illustrate literary theory. They satisfy two urges in young readers which are ordinarily mutually exclusive: The urge to win at adult-approved endeavors and the urge to rebel against conventional directions dictated by adults. Heroics that would be deemed improbable fiction if attempted in everyday life—like saving Donald's job as coast watcher by capturing smugglers whom he hadn't seen—have been staples of children's literature for almost a century. But the plucky lads in G. A. Henty's historical tales or the relentlessly healthy youths in Harry Castlemon's ''Roughing It'' series seldom put down adults. In Duckburg, the kids both rescue erring grown-ups and remind them of their silliness. They save Donald from an octopus, primitive natives, an icy waterfall, an unclimbable rock, a falling rocket, disgrace as a skier, an avalanche, bankruptcy, an angry moose, the game warden, and the wilds of Ecuador. Though this list is long, it is far from complete. Even the kids' pets, whom Donald has usually scorned, save him. Whether the previously rejected rescuer is a mongrel, racing pigeon, chipmunk, squirrel

("Sidney"), falcon, or mixture of strays, it ultimately displays the same loyalty, intelligence, and timing which distinguish the kids.

Despite the cleverness of these ego-saving formulas, only disturbed children can sustain for long the fiction of parents who aren't parents, who do not garner some respect, who never reap sexual rewards, and who must be salvaged by their offspring. The aspects of adult failure which Donald illustrates are only temporary; his world is turned upside-down for only a short while. Most children fear total metamorphosis and sense that tampering with normal roles will lead to guilt or anxiety. (Our neighbor's child, now a bold three, announced, "Today I'm going to be Daddy"—pause, panic—"until Daddy comes home.") Therefore most tales end with Donald in the same relation to his world as he had maintained in the beginning. For him, the universe is static. Several stories grow out of his chronic unemployability: "Four hours is about as long as he ever lasts on any job." One episode begins with his chagrin and resolution to change. He becomes an insurance saleman and talks Scrooge into buying a one-billion-dollar policy. The reformation is momentary, though. Cosmic toryism reasserts itself when the company demands that Donald protect Scrooge from harm and fires him anyway. The narrative allows our non-developing hero only two alternatives: A return to his original dreary condition or flight. The absurd means by which he almost inevitably returns to a former situation give readers of all ages a laugh. More important, the sameness of his connection to external circumstances offers young readers a welcome familiarity—a security in the face of apparent change, which no permanent realignments could effect. If Donald read T. S. Eliot he could aptly splutter, "In my beginning is my end." To cite only a few instances of his parodic hero journey from entanglement to apparent freedom and back to entanglement I would remember how a coin is lost, returned, and again lost; or how his temper is lost, reformed by a New Year's resolution, and then lost; or how Donald and Gladstone make rash vows, admit the impossibility of their boasts, and yet make still more foolish promises. Like an alchemist, Donald acts but does not finally alter the elements of his world.

Even the kids, who rack up their share of unqualified wins, often demonstrate that permanent change of relationships is impossible. Once they try to overlook Donald's unskilled job in the bucketworks since they wish to play hookey. Young Wordsworthians, they flee from school chanting, "We're smart already. . . . Old [people] think books more important than swimming and hunting." No matter what ruse they try, though, the system triumphs. Each escape route leads back to school or, at the end, to a convention of truant officers. For once, like Donald, they blame their lack of progress on "lowdown, flea-bitten luck." Blame it on Horatio Alger, capitalism (we need trained workers), conscience, our young fear of unlimited liberty—or luck. Their world is that of their elders, one in which excitements, schemes to reform, and avid resolutions are transient blips on a radar screen which always pictures the same landscape. In fact the settings of many adventures remind us that our endeavors are played against a static universe. Like the mediveal *plataea,* featureless stages such as oceans, beaches, and deserts throw into high relief the antics of Donald and company. Old and young must not hope to transform the universe but rather to live according to its constraints. This lesson, stoic in its tone, is finally optimistic. We are all, nephews and Donald, kids and parents, linked by invisible filaments. Whatever disagreements we have are negotiable, if not this month, then next. Despite antagonistic ambitions, both Donald and his nephews come to each other's aid in times of peril. The bullying, rebelling, and mutual invasions of privacy are aberrations, funny and sometimes moving, but only temporary.

That our interest in Donald springs from very deep curiosities about how far reorientations between adults and children may be enjoyed without regret does not, I think, exhaust the reasons for his enormous popularity during the 1940s and 1950s. Today *Walt Disney Comics Digest* sells around 215,000 copies monthly; then, the circulation of *Walt Disney's Comics* approached millions.[11] Several time-bound forces cooperated to keep him important to us. The Disney organization has always been brilliant at promoting its wares, of course. *WDC&S* was the successor to an already popular magazine, the *Mickey Mouse.* It is also true that the artwork was consistently excellent. (I recall how almost every mode of conveyance, from space ship to water ski, was clearly drawn.) In addition, the stories usually achieved a hypnotic balance between originality and familiarity. Whether or not a young reader recognized the plots, he was regaled with versions of perennial favorites like Jack and the Beanstalk, Snow White, Goldilocks, Rip Van Winkle, and so forth. It was easy to appreciate the Barks' twist given to proven entertainments such as jumping frog contests, the discovery of a floating island, or the search for the Loch Ness Monster. And the language, so important to us as a measure of belonging and understanding, included slang and puns as well as recondite words like "prevaricator" and "eons." Finally, the wartime paper shortage had curtailed alternate forms of children's literature, while postwar books often suffered from a dreary Dick-and-Jane prosiness.

If popular comic book heroes really do tell us much about communal assumptions, if the fey Asterix is somehow Every Frenchman, if the brutal Tarkan is *echt Deutsch,* then what else does Donald indicate about our shared American beliefs during his heyday? His licensed riot was important to children who had imbibed ideals spawned by the Depression and World War II. Without simplifying complex cultural issues, we may say that one lesson we all absorbed was that this world is a setting for perpetual conflict. Struggles against hunger and fascism were global restatements of the combat between parents and children. The previous antitheses between, say, Greek and barbarian, believer and infidel, or soul and flesh were never before so relentlessly propagandized. Everywhere, a highly literate population was met with posters, pictures, slogans, and pamphlets which told how "we" were fighting "them." The air was electrified (literally) with a crudely simplistic ethic of good characters who were resisting attacks by bad men. The Three Little Pigs pluckily confronted a wolf for some two decades. Although the aim of the duel was to annihilate poverty and the Axis, children knew that, somehow, their parents were neither totally obnoxious nor candidates for extinction. Thus Donald's world offered a moderate solution to conflict which the outside world denied. He was usually defeated—We win over Them—but preserved in the same state: We won't be abandoned. Certainly the typical development of a Duck adventure reinforced the bivalent knowledge that the 1930s offered our parents: If you do what you're supposed to do, you may prosper. But then again, you may not prosper. Barks wisely mediated between stories that had a logical set of consequences which grew inevitably from his premises—analogues, perhaps, of a secure Ben Franklin plan—and stories in which luck rules, the same inscrutable force that allowed hard-working men to become destitute and peaceful nations to be blitzed. Perhaps Donald's picture on so many unit emblems and war machines indicates the longing felt by American soldiers for the more bearable combat situations in Disney comics. To many G.I.'s, there had not been much time separating *WDC&S* from field manuals.

Whatever personal and cultural factors elevated Donald in the past seem to have diminished. I suppose that the variety, quality, and availability of pre-teen books helps to explain our reduced dependence. As a duck, he was an amphibian who waddled in two worlds, the land and the water. As a comic character, he also participated in two worlds, one of fantasy and the other (more important) realm of parenthood. Today the decline, in official terms, of the necessity for children to obey parents has eliminated some of the need to rebel. Indeed, covert statements in which adults are satirized are largely unnecessary since we have apparently enthroned the adolescent, the revolutionary, and the outsider as roles that literature should explore. Whatever symbolic figure may be chosen by future historians of American culture to represent the past decade or so, I think it fair to suggest that, for a brief time in the 1940s and 1950s, our most satisfying center of personal and public fascination was, not the patriotic eagle or the indigenous turkey, but Donald Duck.

NOTES

1. Sigmund Freud, *Totem and Taboo,* trans. James Strachey (New York, 1950), pp. 126–127.

2. Footnotes usually help scholars, but their presence here may be more bane than boon. As an academic, my natural inclination is to document each of these incidents. The full list of references numbers over 500 and, as Hedda Gabler's pedantic spouse says, "One can never have too many of them." But such Dunciad-like documentation would be fruitless in our case. The sad fact is that there are almost no collections of Disney comics open to a general public. Thus I hope readers will trust the accuracy of my citations and, more important, realize that one example often stands for many more. Themes and situations persisted throughout the entire period under study. The evidence is drawn from *Walt Disney's Comics and Stories,* Numbers 31–243, (Apr. 1943–Dec. 1960), with a few references to later issues. I exclude three classes of Duck tales: Numbers 1–30, since these were reprints of short newspaper episodes; Numbers 37, 113, 115, 116, 118–123, since these were not drawn by Carl Barks; stories which may include Donald but which feature Daisy, the Nephews, Scrooge, Gyro Gearloose, or Grandma Duck.

3. *The Disney Version* was published in New York, 1968. Ariel Dorfman and Armand Mattelart originally published *Para Leer al Pato Donald* in Valparaîso, Chile, 1971. The English translation by David Kunzle appeared as *How to Read Donald Duck: Imperialist Ideology in the Disney Comic* (New York, 1975). There are virtually no other studies of Donald's significance in American life. A preliminary index of *Walt Disney's Comics,* Numbers 31–60, may be found in *Comicollector Rocket's Blast,* 123 (Nov. 1975), [unpaginated, p. 18–19].

4. *Comic Art,* 7 (1968), 19. The interview took place in 1962.

5. Fredric Wertham, *Seduction of the Innocent* (New York, 1953, rept. 1972), p. 114.

6. The theory that modern literature generates its own moral systems is explored by William Van O'Connor in *The Grotesque: An American Genre* (Carbondale, Ill., 1962). Other analyses which help to define aspects of Donald's modernism are: Ernst Kris, *Psychoanalytic Explorations in Art* (New York, 1952); Wolfgang Kayser, *The Grotesque in Art and Literature* (New York, 1963); Frances K. Barasch, *The Grotesque: A Study in Meanings* (The Hague, 1971); Philip Thomson, *The Grotesque* (London, 1972).

7. Penrod and his friends decide to put on a circus: "News of the big show and museum of curiosities had at last penetrated the far, cold spaces of interstellar niceness, for this new patron consisted of no less than Roderick Magsworth Bitts, Junior, escaped in a white 'sailor suit' from the manor during a period of severe maternal and tutorial preoccupation" (*Penrod* [New York, 1914], 140). A current memoir of an upper-class childhood in fascist Italy by Susanna Agnelli is titled *We Always Wore Sailor Suits* (New York, 1975).

8. There is a conveniently annotated index of Scrooge's adventures by Kim Weston in Jack L. Chalker, *An Informal Biography of Scrooge McDuck* (Baltimore, 1974).

9. This episode appeared in *WDC&S* Number 104 (May 1949). In 1966 a Danish inventor was denied a patent for his method of raising sunken ships. He suggested injecting bouyant foam into them but the court ruled that Donald's scheme anticipated him. See *Chemistry* for Sept. 1966.

10. *The Realist,* 74 (May 1967), 12–13.

11. This circulation figure for August 1975 was kindly supplied by Mr. Thomas McTaggart, Western Publishing Company. Carl Barks wrote me a warm letter dated November 30, 1975 in which he speculates about the declining sales of comics in the late 1950s: "Most comic book publishers, editors, and others in the business feel that several factors brought on the demise. The first was the growth of TV entertainment in the homes of the kids who had previously *paid* for such entertainment. The second was the price of paper and labor which brought on raises in newsstand prices to twelve cents, then fifteen cents. Third and most important was thievery. Merchants simply stopped handling comic books because their profits went out the door under the shirts of countless kids."

The Sea-Dream: Peter Pan *and* Treasure Island

Kathleen Blake

According to Robert Louis Stevenson's "A Gossip on Romance," romances "may be nourished with the realities of life, but their true mark is to satisfy the nameless longings of the reader, and to obey the ideal laws of the daydream. The right kind of thing should fall out in the right kind of place; the right kind of thing should follow; and not only the characters talk aptly and think naturally, but all the circumstances in the tale answer one to another like notes in music."[1]

Treasure Island (1883) is the fulfillment of the "sea-dreams" of its boy hero, Jim Hawkins, who broods over the treasure map before he even leaves England (*TI*, p. 49),[2] and of the sea-dreams of generations of boys like him, who knew what was the right thing to go with what, what should follow, what answered. There was a shape to the ideal, or a limited number of shapes. Stevenson says, "For my part, I like a story to begin with an old wayside inn where, 'toward the close of the year 17____,' several gentlemen in three-cocked hats were playing bowls. A friend of mine preferred the Malabar coast in a storm, with a ship beating to windward, and a scowling fellow of Herculean proportions striding along the beach."[3] In the verse addressed "To the Hesitating Purchaser" of *Treasure Island,* Stevenson names his models—Cooper, Ballantyne, and Kingston—promising the reader "the old romance, retold / Exactly in the ancient way." He had his followers too. The romance received another inspired casting. But whereas *Treasure Island* is the dream, *Peter Pan* (1911) is about dreaming, and waking.[4]

The dream, the music, the game, as Stevenson also calls it, had been available to boys since *Crusoe,* whose classic outlines define a tradition of juvenile literature, the Robinsonnade. *Robinson Crusoe* was published in 1719 and has never been out of print. It entered early into a career of adaptation, channeling towards the specifically juvenile in Johann Wyss's *Swiss Family Robinson* (English translation, 1814), which then itself prolifically spawned. Frederick Marryat's *Masterman Ready* (1841), James Fenimore Cooper's *The Crater* (1847), R. M. Ballantyne's *The Coral Island* (1853), Jules Verne's *Their Island Home or The Later Adventures of the Swiss Family Robinson* (1900) are only the most famous among many, which also include *The Island Home* (1851), *Canadian Crusoes* (1852), *Arctic Crusoe* (1854), *The Desert Home or English Family Robinson* (1858), two separate *Rival Crusoes* (1826, 1878), and many another account, as in W. H. G. Kingston's book *Shipwrecks and Disasters at Sea* (1873).[5] The hunger for stories of the South Seas and their lonely islands extended, yet insatiate, into the last third of the nineteenth century. It was shared by Robert Louis Stevenson, who at fifteen stopped Ballantyne in the street to express his admiration, and by J. M. Barrie, who wrote an introduction to *The Coral Island* in 1913 which began: "To be born is to be wrecked on an island" and for whom "R.L.S." were the sweetest initials in contemporary literature.[6]

The appetite was stimulated by novelties such as Ballantyne's *The Dog Crusoe* (1861), where the formula expands to render Crusoe a dog and to accommodate "redskins" and the prairies of the Far West. The prize of novelty must rest with W. Clark Russell's *The Frozen Pirate* (1887). Though an admixture of pirates is nothing new—Crusoe himself fought with mutineers—it is unusual for the island to be an iceberg. The castaway finds upon it a frozen pirate ship and frozen pirates. One of the pirates thaws to tell the tale of the pirate treasure, which opens the way to many a chilling adventure.

Stevenson has kind words for Russell's *A Sailor's Sweetheart* (1880): Russell excels in setting and incident and stops there. His books presumably belong to the category of the "amoral" in literature, of which Stevenson approves and which had been steadily gaining ground in the sea-adventure school. If Crusoe's shrewd practicality lay deeper than his religion, and the edifying passages in the *Swiss Family Robinson* served as overlay for a good adventure story, the trend toward the morally superficial is headlong in, for example, Marryat's *The Privateersman* (1846). Reflecting on his part in a bloody pirate attack off the coast of Hispaniola, the privateersman's mind misgives him—for a moment: "But employment prevented my thinking; the decks had to be cleaned, the bodies thrown overboard, the blood washed from the white planks." As Stevenson says, interest in such romances turns "not on the passionate slips and hesitations of the conscience, but on the problems of the body and of the practical intelligence, in clean, open-air adventure."[7]

Losing no time on edification, writers of penny dreadfuls made fast-moving medleys of the standard repertoire, as did Samuel Bracebridge Hemyng, creator of Jack Harkaway's countless and variegated adventures. One page of *Among the Pirates and On the Island of Palms* (c. 1890) moves the hero from the defeat of the pirates to the storm to the shipwreck to the island. Jack is a formidable boy. When the pirate chief lays eyes on him, he exclaims, " 'Harkaway!' . . . turning ghastly pale and recoiling a step." Jack and his man Monday confront every danger there is in their quest to save Jack's father from the pirates. In this world, sons save fathers and boys triumph over seasoned and ruthless men for the favors of contested heroines. When the piratical black flag appears and the ship's captain is killed in the fray, Jack takes over: "It's the fortunes of war, men. I'll be your leader; don't despair."[8]

In Jack Harkaway we see the superboy of whom Stevenson's Jim Hawkins is a somewhat subtler example (he is responsible for every success on the island, benefiting from the lucky folly of a Crusoe) and to whom Peter Pan also owes his cockiness (on his island it is boy over man). By contrast, S. R. Crockett's *Sir Toady Crusoe* (1905) represents the type of the precious, small-boy, make-believe adventurer in the pirate and castaway mode—which had become by this time—less than a year after Barrie's play of *Peter Pan* appeared—just that, a mode. It is a short step from the let's-play-at-shipwrecks-and-islands sort of book to Neverland, and after a century of *Boy Voyagers* (1859) to every romantic fragment of land within the reach of the imagination, there was almost no interesting place left to send them to except the land of imagination itself.[9]

Treasure Island is the dream come true in the full-bodied glory of verisimilitude, which had belonged to tradition since Crusoe experienced the romance of his island in terms of common sense, a providential tally sheet, and the sound use of capital, and which allows Jim Hawkins to dream his island and to go there, returning with real pieces of eight. "*Robinson Crusoe* is as realistic as it is romantic," says Stevenson, and that is the model for his own boys' book. It is not that Stevenson believes in art as illusion or as hallucination. We do not forget, he says, that we are reading. Our minds waver between consciousness that we are watching a performance and the fancy's active participation with the characters. In *Treasure Island* the pleasure of aesthetic distance—isn't this just the way things should have happened—is never quite lost in the gripping appeal of the verisimilar—what really happened is before your eyes. But for Stevenson, the latter is the triumph of the romance writer.[10]

Abandon realism, tip the mind toward consciousness of the story as a story, and you have the sea-dream as the Neverland. Stevenson says that the words of a good book "should run thenceforward in our ears like the noise of breakers."[11] *Treasure Island* is a good book. So is *Peter Pan*—but of a different sort utterly, for Barrie is concerned with showing how the palpable absolute conjured by such as Stevenson is both forever and never, and in particular, never again. "On these magic shores children at play are forever beaching their coracles. We too, have been there; we can still hear the sound of the surf, though we shall land no more" (*PP*, p. 44).

Robinson Crusoe built a canoe and set out to sea. He found himself caught in a current and his island of despair, as it receded, looking more and more desirable. Jim Hawkins sets out in the coracle built by the resident Crusoe of Treasure Island, the marooned wild man Ben Gunn.[12] An unexpected current turns his cruise into a fearful drift toward the open sea. Rocks and surf cut him off from the land, except that the currents of this island, like Crusoe's, run north, allowing the clever navigator to ride it out with the added aid of sail to a beachable northern inlet. Peter does not have this adventure; that is Barrie does not relate it, though perhaps he might had his narrative coin toss not come up for the lagoon. All that remains of this part of the dream are those children always beaching their coracles—of course they are coracles—on a shore familiarly surf-pounded. The surf and the coracles define Neverland. It isn't that what happens in Neverland never happened before, never would, and never could. Just about everything that happens there has happened before—in books.

In Neverland life falls into ideal shapes, "like in a book." Who is James Hook? He is the pirate captain, part history and part literary creation. Stevenson, writing *Treasure Island,* read up on pirates in one of the great source-books on the subject, the 1724 *Pyrates* by "Charles Johnson" (actually Defoe).[13] He uses Defoe's Blackbeard to define his own Flint: "Blackbeard was a child to Flint" (*TI*, p. 41). Barrie extends the system of piratical relations. James Hook was Blackbeard's bo'sun, and if Long John Silver (alias Barbeque, the Sea-Cook) is the only man who did not fear

Flint or even the ghost of Flint, Hook is the only man "of whom Barbeque was afraid" and whom "the Sea-Cook feared" (*PP*, pp. 90, 99).

Captain Hook is also the Byronic hero in his boys' book manifestation. Like Byron's Corsair he is a "man of loneliness and mystery" (I, VIII).[14] "Where his frown of hatred darkly fell / Hope withering fled—and Mercy sigh'd farewell!" (I, IX). Hook's eyes express their balefulness in two glowing red spots. He suffers the "blighted bosom" of a Corsair (I, X), a self-torment as ineffable as Manfred's. Hardened by his thousand crimes, he yet harbors in his soul an unlooked-for reservoir of exquisite sensibility: "No little children love me!" (*PP*, p. 202). But no such inklings of humanity soften his relations with the general rout. Like the Corsair among his band on the pirate isle, "With these he mingles not but to command" (I, II). Hook is a "grand seigneur" (*PP*, p. 99).

Boys' book pirates are typically high-born like the Corsair and tend to be bigger than their men, better dressed, well-educated, and European. The pirate antagonist of Jack Harkaway is a "man of gigantic size . . . wielding a large broad scimitar. . . . But he was no Malay . . . for he had a white, thoroughly European face." Ralph Rover of *The Coral Island* beholds "a man of immense stature and fierce aspect regarding me with a smile of contempt [later a "Sardonic smile"]. He was a white man—that is to say, he was a man of European blood." Marryat's *The Pirate and the Three Cutters* (1836) offers a clear progenitor of Hook: "Superior in talent, in knowledge of his profession, in courage, and moreover in physical strength—which in him was almost Herculean. Unfortunately, he was also superior in all villainy, in cruelty, and contempt of all injunctions, moral and Divine." Scion of a great border family (recall that to reveal Hook's identity would have set the country in a blaze) and well-educated (Hook never forgets that he has been at a famous public school), this pirate, known as Cain, would have been handsome (like Hook) were it not for his scars. And "strange to say, his eye was mild, and of a soft blue" (the same color we find in the forget-me-not eyes of Hook, which are blue with a profound melancholy when they are not lit up red with murder).[15]

The pirate chief always exacts a shuddering respect, for his is a "not wholly unheroic figure" (*PP*, p. 222). Above all he has class. Often born an aristocrat, he possesses, even more importantly, the inner stuff of the gentleman. Failing noble birth, the resource of the superior man is to become the self-made "gentleman o' fortune," like Silver, who looks forward to retirement from the sea with money in the bank and a carriage to ride in. Silver is always as spruce as possible in his fine broadcloth suit, in contrast to his slovenly cohorts, while Hook cringes to oberve Wendy's eyes upon his soiled ruff. Silver despises his unruly, rum-sodden crew as unworthy of the sea, a pack of low tailors, while Captain Hook is "frightfully *distingué*," so superior to the rest that he "never felt more alone than when surrounded by his dogs. They were socially so inferior to him" (*PP*, pp. 186, 200). To be genteel is to inspire fear, according to the code of Long John Silver. Hook too has the breeding to be most sinister when he is most polite. The line of literary inheritance connects Hook to the attractively wicked Silver; to Ballantyne's pirate, whose straightforward ferocity of expression "rendered him less repulsive than his low-browed associates";[16] to the Byronic hero, whose "name could sadden and his acts surprise, / But they that feared him dared not to despise (I, XI)." Captain James Hook draws his crew from Flint's *Walrus* (drawn by Stevenson from the pages of Defoe), and his life's blood from printer's ink.

While life on any desert island goes by formulas, Neverland *is* formulas, and on it form is a way of life. The island is the land of dreams (it is the landscape of a child's mind) and its presiding spirit, Peter, is good form, a kind of embodiment of the play spirit, playing at islands.

There are moments when Jim Hawkins strides the thin line between living his adventures and playing them, as for instance, when he enjoys the confrontation between Captain Smollett and Silver— "It was as good as the play to see them"—realizing at the same time that the issue is deadly earnest—"them that die'll be the lucky ones" (*TI*, pp. 141, 143). The "air of adventure" (*TI*, p. 170) and elán in the doing take precedence over prudence or even utility. Why else would Jim sneak off the *Hispaniola* to go to the island, where he can expect nothing at all but trouble? The treasure map offers "the sport of the search" (*TI*, p. 42). As Squire Trelawney says, "Hang the treasure! It's the glory of the sea that has turned my head" (*TI*, p. 52). On this island a fusillade is no more to be minded than a game of cricket. The final treasure hunt seems "child's play" to Silver (*TI*, p. 232). Jim compares his desperate dodge and feint before the knife of Israel Hands to a game, a kind of sinister fulfillment of a boy's sport back home.

But if there is a hint of the game player in Jim, it is outright in Peter. Make-believe and real are the same thing to him. He does nothing to simply get something done. He never just lives; he has adventures. And he organizes his life in order to have them. Even *not* having adventures, doing the sorts of things John and Michael have done all their lives, is something he plays at, "a new game that fascinated him enormously" (*PP*, p. 130). After saving Tiger Lily, Peter engages the forbidding Hook when he doesn't have to because he "could never resist a game" (*PP*, p. 145). The sport of the combat is the point, and the lines of opposition are arbitrary. For example, having once led his boys nearly to victory in battle with the redskins, he suddenly switches the sides; the encounter continues with boys as redskins, redskins as boys.

In Neverland the ideal displaces mere contingency:

By all the unwritten laws of savage warfare it is always the red-skin who attacks. . . . Through the long black night the savage scouts wriggle, snake-like, among the grass without stirring a blade. . . . Not a sound is to be heard, save when they give vent to a wonderful imitation of the lonely call of the coyote. The cry is answered by other braves; and some of them do it even better than the coyotes, who are not very good at it. . . . Every foot of ground between the spot where Hook had landed his forces and the home under the trees was stealthily examined by braves wearing their moccasins with the heels in front. . . . That this was the usual procedure was so well known to Hook that in disregarding it he cannot be excused on the plea of ignorance [*PP*, pp. 179-180].

Of course, the "unwritten laws," the "usual procedure" are formulas well established in literature. Cooper leaps to mind, or Twain on Cooper:

In his little box of stage-properties he kept six or eight cunning devices, tricks, artifices. . . . A favorite one was to make a moc-casined person tread in the tracks of the moccasined enemy, and thus hide his own trail. Cooper wore out barrels and barrels of moccasins in working that trick. Another stage-property that he pulled out of his box pretty frequently was his broken twig. . . . Every time a Cooper person is in peril, and absolute silence is worth four dollars a minute, he is sure to step on a dry twig. There may be a hundred handier things to step on, but that wouldn't satisfy Cooper. Cooper requires him to turn out and find a dry twig; and if he can't do it, go and borrow one.[17]

The formula adventures that make up *Peter Pan* are presented in a style insistently "like in a book." It is as if the narrator (I call him Barrie for convenience) were saying: I tell it this way because this is what is needed for the sort of story I am telling. In Stevenson's words: "The right kind of thing should fall out in the right kind of place; the right kind of thing should follow." But it is a kind of cheating to reveal this principle of order within the story itself. Barrie's content is the content of romance, but his style subverts romantic illusion. He wants to establish the character of the terrible pirate captain; he proceeds as follows: "Let us now kill a pirate, to show Hook's method. Skylights will do" (*PP,* p. 100). He wants us to know that the pirate chief is not beyond all admiration; he stills the ticking of the crocodile as it waits below to receive Hook: "We purposely stopped the clock that this knowledge might be spared him: a little mark of respect from us at the end" (*PP*, p. 222). Things happen because the story requires them: "Will they [the children] reach the nursery in time? If so, how delightful for them, and we shall all breathe a sigh of relief, but there will be no story. On the other hand, if they are not on time . . ." (*PP*, p. 81).

Barrie assumes certain conventional narrative stances that appear particularly artificial because they are contradictory. He elaborately insists that he is bound, if reluctantly, to stick only to the truth. He wishes he could report that Peter talked to the Never bird, "but truth is best, and I want to tell only what really happened" (*PP*, p. 153). At the same time, Barrie is constantly intervening. He controls what happens much more than it controls him. For instance, he says that he might interfere with the denouement by breaking the news of the children's return to Mrs. Darling in advance so that she could give them the cold shoulder they deserve.

He has the power to lead his readers astray, as for example when he slips and writes the wrong ending. Two things are suggested here. One is that the narrator doesn't know everything and that something new has happened to change the plot since he heard the children's plans upon leaving Neverland; this implies the primacy of the story over its teller. Yet a second effect is just the reverse, for we have just read an ending as straightforwardly reported as any in the rest of the book, which then turns out to be a pure fiction, something that never "happened" at all. We are reminded of the narrative presence and power—not to mention caprice.

He asks us to time the events of the great battle between boys and pirates by our watches. Again the suggestion is double. Barrie invites us to the illusion—you are there, your time is the characters' time. Yet he strains the illusion by addressing us as readers. How can readers time the events themselves? We can only time the telling (or the reading) of those events.

Barrie hovers in the background in the form of addresses to the reader, rhetorical questions, asides on mothers. He speaks to his characters and they talk back.

The narrative presence suggested by a line like "We now return to the nursery" (*PP*, p. 78) is conventional and unobtrusive in itself, but Barrie makes a point of obtruding conventions: "In the meantime, what of the boys? We have seen them at the first clang of weapons, turned as it were into stone figures, open-mouthed, all appealing with outstretched hands to Peter; and we return to them as their mouths close, and their arms fall to their sides" (*PP*, p. 184). The forward action of the characters and the plot comes to a dead stop when the narrator is not there to supervise it.

Such action is not the most important thing. Some passages have nothing to do with forwarding it. Barrie writes a conversation between himself and Mrs. Darling. He says he could spare her ten days of pain by announcing the children's return in advance. She replies that the cost would be too great in the children's loss of ten minutes of the happiness of surprising her. This interchange is curious because it takes place on some secondary (or is it primary?) plane, outside of "the story" and without effect on it. Mrs. Darling *is* surprised on the night of the children's return. Her foreknowledge is entirely hypothetical. In fact, the hypothetical is the presiding narrative attitude, which the reader is obliged to share: "Let us pretend to lie here among the sugar-cane and watch them [the boys] as they steal by in single file" (*PP*, p. 96).

Peter Pan never allows us to enter for long into the sea-dream because the story repeatedly reminds us that it is pure dream, or game—arbitrary, conventional, made-up, literary. "Let us pretend." Art so overtakes nature in these woods that the coyotes come out second best at coyote calls. The Indians traverse every inch of ground between the lines of the boys and the pirates wearing their moccasins backwards because that is what they are supposed to do.

These "confiding savages" confide in the rules (*PP*, p. 181). Hook breaks them by failing to wait for the traditional dawn attack. The daring originality of this breach stands testimony to his "subtle mind," his "gigantic brain" (*PP*, pp. 181, 208). But in a realm where the game properly played is what counts, he suffers the bad conscience of the ulterior-minded cheat. Hook knows that the highest value is good form, but he violates it here as elsewhere—in an unfair fight with Peter on the rock, and in fretting about good form itself: "was it not bad form to think about good form?" (*PP*, p. 201). The true game player plays it straight, like the Indians, like Peter, like Stevenson. He may know that it is a game and enjoy its formal dimension, but he stays inside the frame so that its artificial limits do not impinge. In Barrie's work they impinge. He constantly reminds us of the frame. One might say that the narrator of *Peter Pan* is a dramatization of bad form. To rough out an equation: Hook is to Peter as Barrie is to Stevenson as adult is to child.

Peter remains a perpetual child because he does not remember things. In particular, he does not remember when he has been treated unfairly. He is fighting fair on the rock in the lagoon, and Hook bites him. This would undermine the faith of any other confiding boy by revealing the instability of the whole of idea of fair fight, precisely because it is just an idea. "No one gets over the first unfairness; no one except Peter. . . . I suppose that was the real difference between him and all the rest" (*PP*, p. 148). When Mr. Darling slips the medicine behind his back instead of taking it on the count of three as Michael does, Michael presumably begins to grow up. Adults cheat. They do not cut clean of the game. Mr. Darling wants to be admired by his children just as if he had taken the medicine, except that he happened to miss his mouth. And Hook has a passion for good form. The cheat upsets the system because he is both in it and out of it. One doesn't know where one is with him, and the game is demoralized.

Peter Pan, that "terrible masterpiece" as Peter Davies calls it, is a *tour de force* of literary demoralization.[18] Barrie presents himself as an adult forever banished from Neverland, a disgruntled onlooker cut off from his characters and doing maximum damage to their romantic world. His subversion is occasionally deliberate: "Nobody really wants us. So let us watch and say jaggy things, in the hope that some of them will hurt" (*PP*, p. 228). More often it comes of trying too hard to do the right thing. He goes through all the forms of the island narrative—in fact he hates to let any of them go and has to toss a coin to choose between them—but he is a fallen man because he perpetually shows that he knows they are forms. A narrator who writes, "Hook did not blanch, even at the gills" (*PP*, p. 144), is a fallen narrator. Good form is not to know one has it, like the childish Smee. Consciousness of form is bad form—a truth which is torture to Hook and, for Barrie, theme, style, and a last great desert-island book. (Let me not claim too much; it is just that to read *Peter Pan* is to feel that it *should* have been the last, as *Don Quixote* should have been the last knights-in-armor romance.)[19]

Barrie was a great admirer of Stevenson although he never met him. He thought of him as an inspired and lifelong boy, as "the spirit of boyhood tugging at the skirts of this old world of ours and compelling it to come back and play." Modern reclaimers of Stevenson's deteriorated fame are at pains to refute the much-worn biographical / critical judgment of his boyishness. It cannot be denied that Stevenson sometimes invites such a judgment, for example, when he draws a parallel between the writer of romance and the playful child. And it is worth noticing that even those who now argue his artistic maturation date it after *Treasure Island*. But whatever Stevenson's actual boyishness, the point is Barrie's opinion, for which he had his reasons. For example, in a letter of April 1893 from Vailima in Samoa, Stevenson gives Barrie a self-portrait: "general appearance of a blasted boy—or blighted youth—or '. . . Child that has been in hell.' " So according to Barrie, Stevenson was Jim Hawkins in the apple barrel. On one occasion he cites a letter from Stevenson giving directions for Vailima; he makes them parallel the phrasing of Peter Pan's directions for Neverland. Apparently for Barrie, Stevenson was a kind of Peter Pan.[20]

He was immensely attracted by the boy in Stevenson and he loved his works. "Over *Treasure Island* I let my fire die in winter without knowing that I was freezing." Many would of course say that he was attracted to what he saw in Stevenson because he was himself the ultimate Peter Pan, an identification made for instance by Max Beerbohm and John Skinner in articles with the definitive titles, "The Child Barrie" and "James M. Barrie, or The Boy Who Wouldn't Grow Up." Yet Barrie did not altogether approve of the boyish insouciance of Stevenson. In a humorous sketch of how it might have been had the two ever met, Barrie describes his original inclination to suspect this man in a velvet suit and with a manner "doggedly debonair," though resistance eventually capitulated to his smile. Barrie wasn't happy with Stevenson's philosophy of life, which is, he says, "that we are but as the lighthearted birds. This is our moment of being; let us play the intoxicating game of life beautifully, artistically, before we fall dead from the tree." The philosopher could be Peter, who is youth and joy and "a little bird that has broken out of the egg" (*PP*, p. 221). Barrie says that the keynote of Stevenson's writing is an indifference to matters of life and death. He says he looks forward to a great book from Stevenson after all the wonderful "little" books, but "He will have to take existence a little more seriously."[21]

The curious thing is that *Peter Pan* is a more serious book than *Treasure Island*. Whereas, essentially, as Richard Aldington says, "an adult can get nothing more from *Treasure Island* than a boy does," *Peter Pan* is a boys' book not only for boys. Though Stevenson's book is "serious like a game properly and strenuously played," it is not a serious statement about "existence."[22] Neverland adventures are only pretend; yet Barrie's book is very much about matters of life and death because it is about the loss of the island and the loss of childhood. To grow up is to hear the clock ticking for you, like Hook; to be "dead and forgotten," like Mrs. Darling (*PP*, p. 246); to be replaced by your daughter in Peter's affection, like Wendy, and she by her daughter after her. Good form means absorption in the shape of the moment, taking it absolutely for granted as when playing or dreaming. Peter lives eternally because for him each moment is all there is. But Barrie calls him "heartless," and he calls him "tragic" (*PP*, p. 251) for the same reason. In notes for a never-written play (c. 1922) Barrie recalls the desperation that is part of Peter Pan's situation: "It is as if, long after writing P. Pan, its true meaning came back to me, desperate attempt to grow up but can't." Peter sneers at the "laws of nature" as figured by mothers (*PP*, p. 234), who represent the cycle of life that transforms a child into someone who has children into someone finished off altogether. Comparing the essays of Lamb and Stevenson, Barrie places Lamb higher because "he did not play at pretending that there is no cemetery around the corner." One cannot quite get away with being an eternal boy, it seems, for even Peter has mysterious bad dreams and cries in his sleep, and Stevenson writes books that are marvelous good form but "to those who want more than art for art's sake, never satisfying."[23]

In *Sir James Barrie* Harry M. Geduld sums up the prevailing modern reaction to Barrie's works: "serious critical interest in his novels and plays has recently been hostile, when it has not been negligible or non-existent." Since the waning of the tremendous popularity that he enjoyed in his lifetime, Barrie has been of interest, if at all, mainly biographically, for his pathology. His personal oddities were made for Freudian critics: his love for his mother; his short stature; his take-over of somebody else's children and the extravagance of his immersion in the games he created for them; his idealization of women, which kept him at safe arm's length from them; his probable impotence; his divorce. Because he himself was preoccupied with childhood (in some ways doubtless even arrested in childhood), a misleading simplification has been practiced on his most famous work: *Peter Pan* is taken as representing the charming fulfillment of the desire for perpetual childhood, being as such sentimental and even neurotic. Only very recently, with Alison Lurie's essay in *The New York Review of Books,* has a voice been raised contrary to the general chorus. Lurie attributes to Barrie a more self-conscious and even self-critical treatment of the theme of childhood than he has been given credit for before. She bases her analysis on *Tommy and Grizel* and *Mary Rose.* Her reading of *Peter Pan* is more conventional however since it stresses the attraction of eternal youth, whereas I think that here too the attraction (and surely it is attractive—we shouldn't be so bent on psychological well adjustment as to deny that) is explored in large part as a *dilemma.* It is worth dipping into the play version to illustrate Barrie's undercutting of a position like Peter's. Peter has no weight, he doesn't eat, and he can't be touched. There is pathos, even tragedy, in his isolation from the life force. When she leaves him, Wendy says she would like to give him a hug. He half understands, as the author tells us between the lines of dialogue: "If he could get the hang of the thing, his cry might become 'To live would be an awfully big adventure!' but he can never quite get the hang of it." There has been considerable distaste of Peter's line in both play and novel: "To die will be an awfully big adventure." It should be realized that no matter what his life—or maybe because of his life—Barrie was aware of and more than hints at the sterility, and even morbidity, of the ideal of perpetual youth.[24]

An index of the ambivalence, far from naive, of his attitude toward childishness as a way of life is the sophisticated self-reflexiveness—more possible in the novel than the play and thus giving the novel the fuller resonance—in his handling of boys'-book formulas as a way of literature.[25] *Treasure Island* is the sea-dream pure and fine, its apotheosis. *Peter Pan* is the dream's deathblow, elegy, and obsessive half-life, artfully rendered in the medium of bad form. Just about everything that happens in Neverland has happened before in books. But these things can never happen again in the same way for the grown-up narrator and the grown-up reader. Barrie makes it all the harder for us to play the dream straight, to beach our coracles one more time.

NOTES

1. Robert Louis Stevenson, "A Gossip on Romance" (1882), *The Works of Robert Louis Stevenson,* South Seas ed. (New York: Scribner's, 1925), XIII, p. 136.

2. *Stevenson's Works,* VI; this is the book version of 1883, slightly modified from the serial version appearing in *Young Folks,* 1881–1882. Page references appear in parentheses in the text, identified as *TI.*

3. "Gossip," *Stevenson's Works,* XIII, p. 132.

4. I use the novel version published in 1911 as *Peter Pan and Wendy* (*The Works of J. M. Barrie,* Peter Pan ed. [New York: Scribner's, 1930], IX (page references appear in the text identified as *PP*), more commonly known since as *Peter Pan.* The play first appeared in 1904, though it was not published until 1928, after a good deal of modification. In the novel version, there is the very substantial addition of a narrative voice, which would not figure on stage, and which complicates the story's character and especially its implied audience. As Roger Lancelyn Green says in *Fifty Years of Peter Pan* (London: Peter Davies, 1954), p. 115, there are passages in the novel more understandable to adults than to children, who might be put off by Barrie's elusive prose style. The theme of bad form is absent from the play as are the demise of Mrs. Darling and other elements of the mortality theme that conclude the novel. Barrie did write an additional act showing Wendy grown up and beyond flying, but it was only performed once in 1908. I find the novel more interesting and complex in style and theme. It is also the version sold in children's bookstores as *Peter Pan,* although once having read it one is a little surprised to have found it there.

5. Authors of the additional titles listed are, in order: James F. Bowman, Catherine Traill, Percy St. John, Mayne Reid (with this title in 1858, but first published in 1852), Agnes Strickland, and W. H. G. Kingston. Interesting histories of the Robinsonnade appear in J. Harvey Darton, *Children's Books in England, Five Centuries of Social Life,* 2nd ed. (Cambridge: Cambridge University Press, 1958), pp. 114–120; in Eric Quayle, *The Collector's Book of Boys' Stories* (London: Cassell & Collier Macmil-

lan, 1973); in Harold Francis Watson, *Coasts of Treasure Island, A Study of the Backgrounds and Sources for Robert Louis Stevenson's Romance of the Sea* (San Antonio, Texas: Naylor, 1969). Stevenson lists some specific sources for *Treasure Island* in "My First Book" (1894), *Stevenson's Works*, VI, pp. xxv–xxxiv: the parrot comes from *Robinson Crusoe* (1719); the pirates from Defoe's *Pyrates* (1724, under the pseudonym of Charles Johnson); Billy Bones and the first chapters from Washington Irving's *Tales of a Traveller* (1824); the stockade from Marryat's *Masterman Ready* (1841–1842); the skeleton pointer from Poe (probably the *Gold Bug* [1843]); the Dead Man's Chest from Kingsley's *At Last, A Christmas in the West Indies* (1871).

6. Quayle, p. 62; Darton, p. 318; "R.L.S.," in *Margaret Ogilvy* (1896), *Barrie's Works*, VIII, p. 85.

7. "Gossip," *Stevenson's Works*, XIII, pp. 141, 134; Marryat (London: Dent, 1896), pp. 5–6.

8. Samuel Bracebridge Hemyn, *Among the Pirates and on the Island of Palms*, Harkaway Series, V (London: Hogarth House, n.d.), pp. 120, 119.

9. Ann Bowman, *Boy Voyagers* (1859).

10. "Gossip," *Stevenson's Works*, XIII, pp. 140–142.

11. "Gossip," *Stevenson's Works*, XIII, p. 132.

12. The parallel between Ben Gunn and Robinson Crusoe has often been noticed. Gunn seems to caricature Crusoe, with his piety and filial devotion dating from his residence on the island. This passage almost suggests the tongue in the cheek, though as most critics agree, *Treasure Island* is straightforward and without irony in its overall impact. Robert Kiely says it has the ingenuousness of Blake's "Songs of Innocence" or Wordsworth's "We Are Seven," in (*Robert Louis Stevenson and the Fiction of Adventure* (Cambridge, Mass.: Harvard Univ. Press, 1964), p. 80. Richard Aldington makes a similar observation; [see n. 22]. Also [see n. 22] on the minimal moral depth of *Treasure Island*.

13. On the pirate tradition as it influenced Stevenson see Watson, also John Robert Moore, "Defoe, Stevenson, and the Pirates," *ELH*, 10 (1943), 35–60.

14. Byron, "The Corsair," *Complete Poetical Works of Lord Byron*, Students Cambridge ed. (Boston: Houghton Mifflin, 1933), pp. 337–366; canto and stanza references appear in parentheses in the text.

15. Hemyng, pp. 119–120; Ballantyne, *The Coral Island, A Tale of the Pacific Ocean*, illus. Daziel (London: T. Nelson, 1874), p. 255; Marryat, *The Pirate and the Three Cutters* (London: Seeley, n.d.), p. 51. Watson notes that Stevenson hated Marryat's *Pirate* but counts it as an influence since it made so strong an impression (p. 172).

16. Ballantyne, p. 260.

17. "Fenimore Cooper's Literary Offences," *The Complete Humorous Sketches and Tales of Mark Twain*, ed. Charles Neider, illus. Mark Twain (Garden City, New York: Hanover House, 1961), pp. 633–634.

18. Janet Dunbar, *J. M. Barrie, The Man Behind the Image* (Boston: Houghton Mifflin, 1970), p. 165. Peter Davies was the youngest of the three Davies brothers with whom Barrie played out many of the adven-

tures that go into *Peter Pan* at Black Lake near his Surrey home in the summer of 1901. These adventures were photographed by Barrie, who then made them up into a manuscript book, virtually without text, called "The Boy Castaways of Black Lake Island" and attributed to the editorship of the small Peter. After their parents' death, Barrie took all five Davies boys under his wing.

19. Of course a hardy literary tradition often shows itself impervious to its *coup de grace*, as notably, in Arthur Ransome's *Swallows and Amazons* (1931) and Scott O'Dell's *Island of the Blue Dolphins* (1960). In my view William Golding's *Lord of the Flies* (1954) is more original than these, a continuation that is also a new departure.

20. "R.L.S.," in *Margaret Ogilvy, Barrie's Works*, VIII, pp. 94–95 (Stevenson as "spirit of boyhood" and as Jim Hawkins). Refuters of the Stevenson-as-boy theory are: David Daiches, *Robert Louis Stevenson* (Norwalk, Conn.: New Directions, 1947); Kiely, *Stevenson and the Fiction of Adventure;* and Edwin Eigner, *Robert Louis Stevenson and Romantic Tradition* (Princeton, N. J.: Princeton University Press, 1965). Eigner hardly talks about *Treasure Island,* which is odd in a book treating the romance tradition in prose fiction. He seems to lend Stevenson respectability by ignoring the boys' book romance, which is largely what Stevenson understands and praises as romance in his "Gossip," even though he had been more critical of pure adventure stories without moral resonance eight years earlier in "Victor Hugo's Romances" (1874 *Works of Robert Louis Stevenson* [New York: Bigelow and Smith, 1906], X, pp. 13–35). *R.L.S. To J.M. Barrie, A Vailima Portrait,* introd. Bradford Booth (San Francisco: Book Club of California, 1962), p. 3.

21. "Robert Louis Stevenson," in *An Edinburgh Eleven* (1889), *Barrie's Works,* VIII, p. 249. Lady Cynthia Asquith, his secretary and close friend, is one of the few to deny a boyish streak in Barrie (she says she doubts he ever was a boy [Dunbar, p. 307]). There was a time when he was congratulated for keeping his child's heart, as in a 1905 review in *Outlook,* where he is named the successor of Stevenson in this respect (Dunbar, pp. 176–177). But Beerbohm (1905 review, rprt. in *Around Theaters* [New York: Simon and Schuster, 1959], pp. 357–361), and Skinner (*American Imago,* 14 [1957], 111–142) represent the trend toward devaluing his presumed childishness. Martin Grotjahn, in "Defenses Against Creative Anxiety in the Life and Work of James Barrie"—a commentary on Skinner's article (*American Imago,* 14 [1957], 143–148), carries Skinner's psychoanalysis to its damaging conclusion—that Barrie's immaturity led to bad writing. Harry M. Geduld says much the same in *Sir James Barrie* (New York: Twayne, 1971). Barrie's letter to Miss Masson, December 1922, *Letters of J. M. Barrie,* ed. Viola Meynell (New York: Scribners, 1947), p. 251; "Robert Louis Stevenson," *Barrie's Works,* VIII, 254, 257.

22. Aldington, *Portrait of a Rebel, The Life and Work of Robert Louis Stevenson* (London: Evans Brothers, 1957), p. 143; G. S. Fraser, "Afterword," *Treasure Island* (New York: Signet, 1965), p. 213. There is some disagreement as to the moral depth of *Treasure Island.* In *Stevenson and the Art of Fiction* (New York: privately printed, 1951), pp. 9–10, Daiches

finds interesting moral ambiguity in Long John Silver; Kiely, pp. 42–80, discounts such profundities and talks about the classicism, formalism, abstraction of Stevenson's early work, which approaches pure ritual or design, he says. Daiches (*Robert Louis Stevenson,* p. 34) and Kiely (p. 71) agree, however, that *Treasure Island* shows no serious concern with the issue of mortality.

23. Dunbar, p. 362; "Robert Louis Stevenson," *Barrie's Works,* VIII, 256, 254.

24. Geduld, "Preface, *Barrie's Works,* X, 145; Lurie, "The Boy Who Couldn't Grow Up," *New York Review of Books,* XXII (February 6, 1975), 11–15.

25. See n. 4.

Gorky and Soviet Children's Literature

Ron Walter

High-flying birds and burning hearts are typical images in the works of Maxim Gorky (1868–1936). His *Song of the Falcon* and *Song of the Stormy Petrel* were paeans to the forthcoming Revolution, and the image of Danko saving his people from the dark forest by holding his own ripped-out heart, burning like the sun, above his head is well-known to Gorky readers.

Gorky himself was all fire and flight. His brilliant humanitarian spirit soared above the world of narrow-minded politicking and for this reason he is regarded with a combination of respect, reverence, and awe in the Soviet Union by liberal and dissident thinkers as well as by orthodox communists—a rare accomplishment in a country where heroism is often determined by the ideological camp one belongs to. Though he is the acknowledged father of Socialist Realism, it is not so much Gorky's greatness as a writer, which is questionable, that Russians admire so deeply in him. Rather, it is his unique role in preserving life and culture in Bolshevik Russia. In the years directly following the Revolution, Gorky edited the only oppositionist newspaper in the country; singlehandedly preserved art works and architectural monuments from wanton destruction; saved countless lives (Lenin never refused a Gorky request for help or intervention); founded a large-scale literary translating house to save starving writers; and was a moral center around which gathered the best minds of Russia. Even in exile during NEP Gorky's influence was immense: a *Who's Who* of the writers of the twenties would show that virtually every writer of note regarded Gorky as something of a literary spiritual father. He maintained voluminous correspondence, reading all important literature of the day and giving valued advice to the authors. From the time of his permanent return to the Soviet Union till his death in 1936 Gorky worked indefatigably on establishing a firm basis for his brainchild—the literature of Socialist Realism.

Gorky's writing and his humanitarian pursuits are well-known in the West. Almost unknown, however, is the great role he played in fostering children's literature in the Soviet Union. In fact, if any one figure can be said to be the "father" of Soviet children's literature, it certainly has to be Gorky (an appellation which may, to some degree, exculpate him from being the undeniable father of a rather hapless brainchild—Socialist Realism). Such parentage is not to be scoffed at, for Soviet children's literature is certainly one of the richest in the world, partially because Gorky incessantly encouraged the best Soviet writers to write children's literature, partially because the best writers have naturally moved toward children's literature to avoid writing obligatory tendentious literature, and partially because it appears that a collective society shows more concern for its children (albeit sometimes for the wrong reasons) than a free-enterprise society.

Gorky's concern for the well-being of children dates back, as it naturally should, to his own childhood. In one of his acknowledged best pieces of fiction, Part One of his well-known autobiographical trilogy, appropriately entitled *Childhood,* we see Gorky as a sensitive child exposed to arbitrary brutality (his grandfather, for example, was given to counting the daily sins of the children and ritualistically whipping them every Saturday for the accumulated transgressions of the week) and resolved to right the wrongs of the older generation when he himself grows up. (Among his later methods, incidentally, was often to recommend to children that they read his own *Childhood.*)

From early in his literary career Gorky showed concern for children by organizing holiday programs for poor children in his hometown of Nizhny Novgorod (since renamed Gorky), directing children's plays, helping to select books for children's libraries, not to mention writing children's stories himself. By 1910 his role in children's lives was sufficiently respected that he was invited to speak at the Third International Conference on Family Education in Brussels. He couldn't attend, but the letter he wrote the Conference represents the first in a long series of theoretical formulations of his views on children's literature. Gorky was a tireless propagandizer and in this letter, as in many others, he wrote with great feeling about the urgent need to have children read about the accomplishments of mankind, about the great role of reading in the raising of children and the formation of their world view. When he was the head of a publishing house during World War I he decided to put into effect the thoughts expressed in his letter by publishing a series of books for children on outstanding people written by recognized authorities. He wrote letters asking people to write biographies—H. G. Wells on Edison, Romain Rolland on Beethoven, Nadson on Columbus, Temiryazov on Darwin, and he himself would write on Garibaldi. These were to be books written for children, not adult literature usable by children. Though in the Soviet Union they are by now used to having children's literature written by top-rank writers, at the time the idea was revolutionary and indicative of Gorky's fervor and breadth of vision in promoting children's literature. When all his correspondents showed their willingness, Gorky went on to compose a long list of the world's best children's books, which he proposed to have translated and published in Russia. But all this was during a time of war and revolution—and severe paper shortages—so that Gorky's ambitious plan had to wait for more stable times. It eventually formed the basis of a similar project taken on by the world's first Government Children's Publishing House (Detgiz, then called Detizdat), which Gorky helped found in 1933. At the time he had to content himself with a more modest project, the founding of the new country's first children's journal, *Northern Lights,* published between 1919 and 1920, through which Gorky hoped to realize his dream of founding a solid new children's literature based on "respect for the power of reason, for the searches of science, for the great task of art—to make a person strong and beautiful," as he wrote in the editorial of the first issue. Once again, however, his vision far exceeded its realization as governmental pressures (Gorky readily employed ideological enemies of the revolution as children's writers) eventually caused the journal to fold.

With *Northern Lights* began Gorky's history of resistance to narrow political pressures in the area of children's literature. As the free development of Soviet literature was halted in the late twenties when Stalin and his minions came into firm control of the country, children's literature came under siege. The Russian Association of Proletarian Writers, an organ of the Party that had gained virtual hegemony over literary output, came out against, among other things, fantasy in children's literature. It was argued that the "new man" of the socialist world should develop from childhood a purely "realistic" view of the world. Having animals talk, for example, only encouraged a retreat into an individualistic fantasy life characteristic of the old bourgeois world. The literary slogans of the day were "removal of the veils" and "for the living man"—both calls for a highly realistic literature accurately reflecting the evolving socialist world as it was. In children's literature the attitude was to regard a child as a small man and to appeal purely to his rational faculty, to write informational literature for him, to propagandize him from the dawn of his consciousness to become a sturdy builder of communism. The polemic excited by these views was intense and Gorky, ever the defender of culture, was in the thick of the battle, publishing a series of seminal articles in *Pravda* on his theory of children's literature. In these articles, from 1928–1930, we see Gorky as no less a propagandizer than his adversaries, no less interested in cultivating a socialist mentality in children and extirpating capitalistic values, but his views are incomparably better informed, based on long experience with children's mentalities. Gorky convincingly argues that a child naturally absorbs the external world through the medium of play, and it is through words as play that a child learns the subtleties and spirit of his native language. Furthermore, the fantasy and play elements in children's literature develop the sense of intuition, so that later in life the adult raised on a strong fantasy literature will be more likely to pass beyond the merely practical in his solutions to scientific, artistic, and life problems.

Gorky's theory of children's literature, as evolved during this polemic on the "right" way to cultivate young socialist minds as well as in later speeches and articles, could form a substantial study in itself. Here it is enough to observe that Gorky always maintained an extremely broad-based stance and was never narrowly didactic in his approach. True, in the spirit of the theory of Socialist Realism which he developed his attitude toward children's literature was always tinged with romanticism, with the distinct tendency to see people as larger than life. So deep was his faith in the power of a book and so urgent his desire to extract from children their noblest instincts, their highest flights of imagination, their deepest respect for the accomplishments of their forebears, not to mention their most antiacquisitive impulses, that he felt perfectly justified in fostering the creation of a literature molded on the Dostoevskian formula of "realism in a higher sense." But within this general romantic bias Gorky consistently remained both the practical and theoretical enemy of the politicos, hacks, and Party hard-liners who were out to use children's literature to turn young people into pragmatic, obedient, orthodox communist thinkers.

Gorky's theoretical formulations were not based simply on his own literary ideas adapted for children. He constantly checked his ideas with children themselves. During the 1920s, for example, he maintained a lively correspondence with members of the so-called "Gorky Colony"—a group of three-hundred or so boys being raised at a former reform school near Kiev, and with Anton Makarenko, their headmaster and disciplinarian. It was at Gorky's insistence, incidentally, that Makarenko, a household name in the Soviet Union in the area of children's education, wrote his magnum opus on his experience at the Gorky Colony, the *Pedagogical Poem* (translated recently into English under the title *The Road to Life*). And when Gorky embarked on another of his many grandiose projects, the founding of the government publishing house for children in 1933, he had letters sent all over the Soviet Union to children and children's organizations, asking them what kind of reading they wanted. The over two-thousand replies he received were carefully analyzed and formed the basis for the many book contracts offered by the newly established enterprise.

It was Gorky's dream to establish children's literature in the Soviet Union as a pursuit equal in value to adult literature and to draw upon the best talent in the country to write it. When in 1934 Gorky presided over the first congress of Soviet writers he had the introductory general lecture on Soviet literature followed immediately by a report on the state of and possibilities for children's literature. It was certainly in large measure due to Gorky's influence that many of the Soviet Union's best writers, who normally wrote for adult audiences—Olesha, Zoshchenko, Kaverin, Kataev, Paustovsky, Prishvin, Aseev, Tikhonov, A. Tolstoy—also wrote for children. And Gorky himself set an example by writing a variety of tales for children filled with fanciful situations and imaginative language.

There can be no doubt that had it not been for Gorky, Soviet children's literature, which comparativists will someday discover to be one of the world's richest and most sophisticated bodies of contemporary children's literature, would not have developed so broadly or so freely. Gorky was the patron saint of Soviet children, constantly looking out for their interests, constantly inspiring writers to give their best to them, constantly withstanding political pressures to use children's literature as an instrument of narrow indoctrination. To this day his influence is strongly felt. Almost every Soviet book devoted to children's literature, a subject of considerable scholarship in the USSR, contains reminiscences of Gorky or articles about him or numerous references to his role in establishing Soviet children's literature on a firm foundation. In a country where pressures toward doctrinaire literature are constant, Soviet children are fortunate that Gorky's spirit is an enduring part of their heritage.

REFERENCES

The sources of the material contained in this article are from numerous texts. The principal ones are given below:

Ya.A. Chernyavskaya, *Sovetskaya detskaya literatura,* Minsk, 1971

Detskaya literatura 1967 (Moscow, 1968).

Detskaya literatura 1970 (Moscow, 1970).

Alexandr Ivich, *Vospitanie detej* (Moscow, 1969).

L. Kon, *Sovetskaya detskaya literatura 1917–1929* (Moscow, 1960).

Dan Levin, *Stormy Petrel: The Life and Work of Maxim Gorky* (New York, 1965).

Anton Makarenko, *The Road to Life* (New York, 1973).

N. B. Medvedeva, *M. Gorkij o detskoj literature* (Moscow, 1968).

Miriam Morton, *A Harvest of Russian Children's Literature* (Berkeley, 1968).

Vera Smirnova, *O detjax i dlja detej* (Moscow, 1967).

Irwin Weil, *Gorky, His Literary Development and Influence on Soviet Intellectual Life* (New York, 1966).

Reviews

Recent Trends in Children's Literature

The Newbery and Caldecott Award Books 1975–1976

David L. Greene

Arrow to the Sun, a Pueblo Indian Tale adapted and illustrated by Gerald McDermott. New York: Viking, $6.95. Caldecott Medal 1975.

The Grey King, by Susan Cooper. Illustrated by Michael Heslop. New York: Atheneum, $6.95. Newbery Medal 1976.

M. C. Higgins, the Great, by Virginia Hamilton. New York: Macmillan, $6.95. Newbery Medal 1975.

Why Mosquitoes Buzz in People's Ears, a West African tale retold by Verna Aardema. Illustrated by Leo and Diane Dillon. New York: Dial, $6.95. Caldecott Medal 1976.

Recent children's literature has developed in two directions: realism/naturalism and fantasy. The three fantasies and one realistic novel which were awarded the 1975 and 1976 Newbery and Caldecott Medals are excellent examples of what can be achieved in each area and of the pitfalls that await even the best authors.

Virginia Hamilton's 1975 Newbery book, *M. C. Higgins, the Great,* is one of the most impressive recent realistic novels for children or adults. Hamilton avoids the extreme naturalism of many recent children's books (have publishers just discovered Emile Zola and Frank Norris?). The title character is a thirteen-year-old black boy who lives with his family on Sarah's Mountain near the Ohio River. The Higginses have lived on the mountain since M.C.'s great- (or great-great) grandmother, Sarah McHigan, fled from slavery in 1854. Sarah's descendants are part of Sarah's land, and leaving it seems impossible to all of them except M.C. The mountain, however, has been violated by strip mining, and M.C. decides that they must leave before a great spoil heap slides down upon them.

M.C.'s mother, Banina, is a natural singer. And he believes that when the "dude" comes to tape her voice, she will get a recording contract and the family will have to leave with her. But the dude finally tells M.C. that he is only a collector—that he is driven to preserve music, just as Banina has to sing and M.C.'s father, Jones Higgins, cannot think of leaving Sarah's Mountain. Even if the dude were able to obtain a contract for Banina, it would change her; "it'd never be the voice, the woman, singing like this evening, walking home from far."

The dude is an outside force coming onto the mountain; he recognizes the danger of the spoil heap, but he is unable to do anything about it. The other outsider in the novel is Lurhetta Outlaw, a black girl driven to wander. M.C. feels a strong sexual attraction toward her, which he recognizes only partially. Lurhetta realizes instinctively that the separation between the Higginses and the Kilburns, "witchy" folk with six fingers on each hand, is unnatural. She sees the contradiction between the fact that M.C.'s best friend is Ben Kilburn and the fact that M.C. and his family have not seen the Kilburn's land since Banina was frightened long ago by Viola Kilburn's healing powers.

M. C. Higgins, the Great is a marvelously rich, but flawed, work. Hamilton is at her best when she shows the unity of the mountain people with their land, the tension and love between M.C. and his father, the glory of Banina's singing. She is not so successful with her symbols: the forty-foot pole on top of which M.C. spends much of his time; the giant web of vine and rope which links all the Kilburn buildings; and, at the end of the book, the wall the Higginses begin to build from dirt, automobile parts, and Sarah's gravestone to protect their home from the spoil heap. M. C. 's pole stands in the middle of the family graveyard; the stone markers have been replaced by portions of automobiles. Therefore the pole not only symbolizes M.C.'s isolation and dominance, but also, as Banina says, serves as "the marker for all of the dead." All this somehow manages to be contrived, obvious, and muddy at the same time.

The 1976 Newbery Medal book, Susan Cooper's *The Grey King*, is part of the modern heroic fantasy movement dominated by J. R. R. Tolkien, C. S. Lewis, Lloyd Alexander, and Ursula K. Le Guin. It is, I think, more flawed than other recent fantasies and certainly more flawed than *M. C. Higgins, the Great*. Yet it is a work of great power. *The Grey King* is fourth in Cooper's The Dark Is Rising sequence. The first three are *Over Sea, Under Stone; The Dark Is Rising*; and *Greenwitch*; the fifth and concluding book will be *Silver on the Tree*.[1]

Cooper's fantasy sequence involves the eternal struggle between the powers of Light and Dark, a struggle which suggests the influence of Manichaeism (though many of the incidents come from Welsh mythology and the Matter of Britain). The Light is represented by immortals known as the Old Ones; the central figure in *The Dark Is Rising* and *The Grey King* is Will Stanton, who is both a young boy and the last of the Old Ones to be born. Cooper's chief problems are especially obvious in the second book: Will Stanton is not fully developed, and the role of the Old Ones is not clear. I am especially disturbed that even though they live out of time (or at least are able to go back and forth in time), the implied foreknowledge is never of the slightest use. In addition, how the Old Ones can be both all-powerful and limited is never clearly worked out. In *The Grey King,* I am glad to say, Will has more individuality than he does in earlier books and succeeds in his quest to gain the harp and waken the sleepers, without much interference from the other representatives of the Light.

Much more interesting than Will and the figures of both Dark and Light are the Welshmen and their land. Cooper, like Hamilton, emphasizes the unity of man and his surroundings. Owen Davies, the Rowlands, Caradog Prichard, and the other Welshmen in *The Grey King* are completely realized. Will Stanton and the other Old Ones are much easier to accept when we see what they are trying to preserve. The most fascinating character in the book, and indeed in the sequence thus far, is the albino boy, Bran. The boy was left by his mother, Gwen, with Owen Davies, a man who turned to rigid Calvinism when Gwen disappeared. Bran is complex, moody, not especially likeable, and both proud and ashamed of his difference from others. His grief at the loss of his dog, Cafall, is the most moving moment in the novel. Although we see the action through Will's eyes, we are most concerned with Bran, whose story *The Grey King* really is. Bran's true identity, which is not especially well-disguised and probably not meant to be, brings together Welsh legend, the influence of the past on the present, and the timelessness of the struggle of good against evil.

The two Caldecott books, *Arrow to the Sun* and *Why Mosquitoes Buzz in People's Ears,* are very different fantasies from *The Grey King.* Gerald McDermott's *Arrow to the Sun,* which received the Caldecott medal in 1975, was described by Leo Schneiderman in Volume 4 of this journal as "a graphic production of exceptional power and beauty." Of all recent books for children, *Arrow to the*

Sun is probably the most successful combination of text and illustration. The story itself is impressive. It tells of the coming of a "spark of life" from the sun to an Indian maiden and of the search by the boy who comes from the spark for his father. Finally the boy becomes an arrow and is shot by the Arrow Maker to the sun. There he is made to prove himself by passing through "the four chambers of ceremony—the Kiva of Lions, the Kiva of Serpents, the Kiva of Bees, and the Kiva of Lightning." Each trial is depicted by a full-page illustration without text. The boy then returns to earth to bring the spirit of the sun to men, and "The People celebrated his return in the Dance of Life."

This evocative tale, with mythic elements found in many different cultures, is completely captured in the illustrations. McDermott bases his drawings upon Pueblo designs. The figures are reduced to stylized masses in bright, almost garish, colors. The pictures are filled with action, yet the action is so stylized that the scenes seem almost static. Like the young Indian boy's achievement, *Arrow to the Sun* is a timeless and universal book.

Why Mosquitoes Buzz in People's Ears, the 1976 Caldecott medalist, is beautifully illustrated in muted colors by Leo and Diane Dillon. Like McDermott, the Dillons reduce form to stylized masses. The pictures, not surprisingly, dominate the text. More surprising and very effective is the way in which the Dillons emphasize each animal mentioned in the text by reducing the relative sizes of the other animals in the corresponding illustration, thus making visual the shifting focus of the tale. The story itself is slight and charming. It tells how a simple statement by a mosquito ("I saw a farmer digging yams that were almost as big as I am. ") has ramifications that result in the owl's refusing to wake the sun. This is the old "for the sake of a nail the kingdom was lost" fallacy, which is delightful so long as it is not taken seriously.

There is surprising unity of vision in the 1975–76 Newbery and Caldecott books. All four show that actions have significance even when they are harmful. It is good that much of modern literature, in this post-Eliot age, celebrates life.

NOTES

1. I am indebted to Margaret Esmonde's excellent series of articles on Cooper's Dark Is Rising sequence: *Fantasiae,* Nov. 1974, pp. 6–7; Jan. 1975, pp. 7–9; Feb. 1975, pp. 5–6; Feb. 1976, pp. 7–8. Professor Es-

monde's incisive comments have greatly influenced my own thinking on Cooper's work. (*Fantasiae* is published by the Fantasy Association, P.O. Box 24560, Los Angeles, California 90024.)

Trends in Poetry for Children

Alethea K. Helbig

Ego-Tripping & Other Poems for Young Readers, by Nikki Giovanni. Illustrated by George Ford. New York: Lawrence Hill and Co., 1973. $4.95.

Figgie Hobbin, by Charles Causley. Illustrated by Trina Schart Hyman. New York: Walter and Co., 1975. $4.95.

I Became Alone, compiled by Judith Thurman. Illustrated by James and Ruth McCrea. New York: Atheneum, 1976. $6.25.

Let's Marry Said the Cherry! And Other Nonsense Poems, by N. M. Bodecker. Illustrated by author. New York: Atheneum, 1974. $4.95.

Modern Poetry, selected by John Rowe Townsend. Photographs by Barbara Pfeffer. Philadelphia: J. B. Lippincott Co., 1974. $5.95.

My Black Me, The Ethnic Expression of Fourteen Contemporary Poets, edited by Arnold Adoff. New York: E. P. Dutton and Co., Inc., 1974. $6.95.

New Coasts and Strange Harbors, selected by Helen Hill and Agnes Perkins. Illustrated by Clare Romano and John Ross. New York: Thomas Y. Crowell Co., 1976. $5.95.

One Winter Night in August & Other Nonsense Jingles, by X. J. Kennedy. Illustrated by David McPhail. New York: Atheneum, 1975. $5.95.

Opposites, by Richard Wilbur. Illustrated by author. New York: Harcourt Brace Jovanovich, Inc., 1973. $3.75.

The Oxford Book of Children's Verse, chosen and edited by Iona and Peter Opie. Oxford: Oxford University Press, 1973. $10.00 ,

Room for Me and a Mountain Lion: Poetry of Open Space, selected by Nancy Larrick. Illustrated with photographs. New York: M. Evans and Co., Inc., 1974. $5.95.

Settling America. Edited by David Kherdian. New York: Macmillan Publishing Co., Inc., 1974. $6.95

The Skin Spinners: Poems, by Joan Aiken. Illustrated by Ken Rinciari. New York: The Viking Press, 1976. $6.95.

The Star in the Pail, by David McCord. Illustrated by Marc Simont. Boston: Little, Brown and Co., 1975. $6.95.

To See the World Afresh, compiled by Lilian Moore and Judith Thurman. New York: Atheneum, 1974. $4.95.

The poet and critic William Jay Smith commented not long ago that "most recent collections of poetry for the young appear to concentrate on the realistic poem that offers little dimension to the imagination and no rhythmic assurance or consolation."[1] In addition to lamenting the banality and lack of imagination of the poetry currently being offered to children, Smith presented the criteria by which he judges poems for young people. Poems for children must, he said, be graphic, lilting, precise, concrete, and above all, well-written. He asserted, "And the basic requirement [of a writer for children], so often forgotten, is consummate skill; only the most accomplished poetic technician should be allowed to write for children."[2] An examination of books of poetry published for young people during the last three years lends support to Smith's criticism. A good deal of what has been published recently is indeed uninspired and unimaginative in concept and trite and prosy in language. It is also sadly lacking in music, that quality of poetry to which children are probably first attracted and by which perhaps they are longest held. Fortunately, however, in the last few years there have been some books which give us encouragement that good poetry is still being written for children by "accomplished poetic technicians" and that poems which meet Smith's criteria are being collected and put together in interesting and challenging arrangements by imaginative and competent anthologists.

While books of ethnic poetry are often marred by the inclusion of pedestrian and poorly constructed material, they also contain some of the most expressive poems we have for children. In *Ego-Tripping,* Nikki Giovanni, one of the best of today's writers of the Black experience, has put together twenty-two poems, some new and some previously published, which she felt young readers would like. Although the poems vary in quality, this collection appeals to the intellect as well as to the emotions with pieces about childhood memories and feelings, Martin Luther King, music, H. Rap Brown, and a lost, one-eyed kitten. Sometimes she jokes, sometimes she is serious, at other times she is angry or sad. She talks pensively about Flora who went to Sunday School and learned about the Queen of Sheba who "was Black and comely / and she would think / I want to be / like that." She chides boys who play Indians: "You should play run-away-slave / or Mau Mau / These are more in line with your history." Some poems are rich in music and are highly sensory: "everytime it rains if its summer / the sky turns pink and the earth smelling / very sweaty calls my feet to play." The sometimes realistic, sometimes dreamy black-and-white illustrations which accompany nearly every poem make *Ego-Tripping* a particularly attractive volume.

Some of Nikki Giovanni's poems appear in Arnold Adoff's anthology *My Black Me*. Other poets included in this small, only fifty poems, but rich harvest are such twentieth-century writers as Lucille Clifton, Don Lee, Langston Hughes, Barbara Mahone, and Imamu Amiri Baraka. *My Black Me* is intended as a *"beginning book of Black"* for "young brothers and sisters of every race" to enjoy reading now and to arouse the urge to read more. Adoff has wisely avoided the sensational and the topical to put together an anthology which is predominately hopeful in tone and which demonstrates that, while only Blacks could have written most of these poems, one need not be Black to identify with them. A broader selection of ethnic voices appears in *Settling America*. Fourteen young poets from various cultural backgrounds, among them Japanese-American Lawson Fusao Inada, American-Indian Joy Harjo, Lebanese-Muslim Sam Hamod, and Puerto Rican Victor Cruz, write about their families, their neighborhoods, their loves, their memories, their disappointments, hopes, angers, and celebrations. Although some of these poems are weak in diction, bland in imagery, or peter out at the end, most of them give a good sense of the coming together of two cultures in the life and thought of the various poets, as in Armenian David Kherdian's:

> Years later, reading the solemn and bittersweet
> stories of our Armenian writer in California,
> who visited as a paperboy coffee houses in
> Fresno, I came to understand that in these
> cafes were contained the suffering and
> shattered hopes of my orphaned people.

The best feature of this book is that it combines one hundred poems reflecting different ethnic experiences in sufficient number from each culture so that the uniqueness of each way of life can be caught and savored and compared with the others.

It is very difficult to write good nonsense verse. Humorous or funny poetry which is poorly conceived simply does not hold up, and many a verse has given one good laugh and soon been forgotten. It takes a writer of indeed "consummate skill" to produce a book of nonsense with staying power. Each of the last three years has fortunately seen the publication of nonsense made to last. In *Opposites,* Pulitzer-prize-winner Richard Wilbur invites the reader to look at things backwards and upside down as in thirty-nine short, concise, delightfully witty pieces, he has fun with the meanings and sounds of words. He lets his whimsy roam as he talks about the opposites of mostly ordinary things or actions, investing them by his inventiveness with new life and interesting appearances.

> The opposite of *doughnut*? Wait
> A minute while I meditate.
> This isn't easy. Ah, I've found it!
> *A cookie with a hole around it.*

A greater variety of nonsense appears in the books of Bodecker and Kennedy. In the thirty-three short verses in *Let's Marry Said the Cherry,* Bodecker defies logic to create absurdly illogical worlds that seem perfectly normal within the context of the poems. Here are pieces about an alligator who runs an elevator, about a snail who goes to "Yale / likes mutton / and ale," and about timid Harry Docer the Grocer who locks up all his merchandise. Gentle, genial absurdity is evident with Johnson Prior's "mixed but earnest choir" of seven pigs, a mule, fourteen parrots, a monkey, sixteen cats, and Mrs. Ford on the harpsichord and with Violet Amanda Bitter, who quite literally discharges her babysitting responsibility by sitting on the baby. Most of the poems make use of word play, often in tight, deft fashion, as in "Mr. Slatter," a hatter who "made his hats / of brittle-batter." While these poems are well done, still more finely crafted and more lasting are the poems in *One Winter Night in August.* Among the wacky characters appear a wicked witch, Medusa, a boa who eats bowling balls, a dinosaur, a walking skeleton, and great-great-grandma who sleeps in a treehouse. Here are domestic situations gone awry, with exploding gravy and a monstrous mouse who grabs the birthday cake. Some verses are close to real life, like the one about "baby [who] eats our rugs so clean / He beats a carpet sweeper." These happy, rollicking verses demand to be shared orally. They show a delightful sense of the absurd, love of verbal play, and above all a good awareness of the necessity for restraint in producing nonsense that will wear well and give pleasure for many readings.

It is hard to classify the books of Joan Aiken, Charles Causley, and David McCord since they offer examples of both humorous and serious poetry. *The Star in the Pail* contains twenty-six poems selected by McCord from his previously published poems, some originally published as long ago as fifty years. Here are old friends, like "Our Mr. Toad," as well as poems not so well-known, like "Gone" and "The Star in the Pail," pieces with sharp and clear images, gentle rhythms, and McCord's genius for seeing and feeling from the child's point of view in an uncomplicated, uncluttered, and ungimmicky way. Marc Simont's full-color paintings make this book a visual as well as a literary treat. In English Poet-of-the-Year Causley's thoroughly delightful *Figgie Hobbin,* moods range from the utterly nonsensical, " 'Quack!' said the billy goat, / 'Oink!' said the hen" to the rollicking "Colonel Fazackerley" who scares away a ghost to the poignant "My Mother Saw a Dancing Bear," a commentary on people's insensitivity to the plight of wild creatures held in captivity. Some poems rely on word play for their comic effect, like "King Foo Foo sat upon his throne / Dressed in his royal closes, / While all around his courtiers stood / With clothes-pegs on their noses." The mystery and melody of "At Nine of Night I Opened My Door" to see a creature like Father Christmas crossing the new-fallen snow recalls De la Mare, as does the haunting "Riley": "What strange secret had old Riley? / Where did he come from? Where did he go? / Why was his heart as light as summer? / *'Never know now,' said the jay. 'Never know.' "* Imaginative and well-constructed, the poems in *Figgie Hobbin* should bring years of reading enjoyment to poetry lovers of all ages.

The most outstanding recent work by an individual poet is *The Skin Spinners* by English novelist Joan Aiken. Aiken can be gentle, playful, provocative, or terrifying in poems of varying lengths and differing forms about bad dreams, alligators in New York sewers, ghosts of children in an old house, and the boy with the wolf's foot who goes howling through the street. She asks us to pity the girl whose hair was turned to crystal because she mocked a wizard and to be sure not to step on the train platform by "that door" because we might never come back again. Touching is the poem about the grandmother who converses with her long dead husband: [She] "Keeps a smile in her bedside cupboard / Soft in the morning you hear her say / 'Tom? Do I feel like smiling today?' " The poem about how Miss Pallant's shadow got tacked to the map of Spain on the schoolroom wall is funny, and there is a tidy four-liner about Old Mog, the "Old fat sociable cat / [who] Thinks when we stroke him he's doing us a favour." Some poems are highly musical, such as the ballad about the sirens on the rocks who sit "A-nodding and a-gossiping and knitting winter socks." Although varied in quality, this collection shows that Aiken is able to "make of air and dust and flesh / a subtle or a silver mesh" ("The Skin Spinners") of ingenious, unpretentious, and highly appealing poems.

While the works of individual poets can bring hours of reading and listening pleasure, anthologies probably offer the widest range of opportunity for personal enjoyment. The last three years have seen the publication of many collections which vary greatly in approach, in size, and in the quality of the poetry they contain. The Opies' *The Oxford Book of Children's Verse* is a comprehensive gathering of over three-hundred poems by mostly British poets arranged chronologically from Chaucer to Ogden Nash and supplemented by copious notes. The compilers' objective was " to make available in one place the classics of children's poetry," poems written for children or with children in mind. These pieces are not only interesting for their own sakes, but the arrangement of the poems makes it possible to detect poetic trends and changing social values and attitudes toward children.

More innovative collections have been done by Thurman and Larrick. *I Became Alone* discusses the work of five women poets from different cultures and times, Sappho, Louise Labé of France, Ann Bradstreet, Juanna Ines de la Cruz of Mexico, and Emily Dickinson, in brief biographies and in their poetry. These poems deserve to be widely known, for as Thurman says in her preface, "Quality has no gender: there are no 'poetesses.' These five poets wrote, and are, for everyone." *Room for Me and a Mountain Lion* is the latest in a series of tasteful anthologies done by the noted authority on children's literature, Nancy Larrick. An imaginatively arranged collection, this book contains over one hundred mostly modern American poems in varying moods about mountains, woods, fields, prairies, the sea and dunes, the animals who live in these open spaces, and the humans who share the openness with them. Here are such choice pieces as Francis' "Skier," Jerome's "Deer Hunt," Smith's "Morels," Swenson's sea poems, and Jarrell's bird and bat poems. Electric with movement and sharp with imagery, these poems project a keen sense of the vastness, the lure, and the mystery of wild nature.

Increasingly anthologists are making their selections from modern poets because the twentieth-century cadences and ways of seeing and speaking of recent writers seem particularly suitable for today's young people. No good general anthologies of modern poetry have come out for younger children; anthologists seem to be concentrating on the junior- and senior-high-age groups. Among the best of the latest of these is *To See the World Afresh,* which is intended to move readers to see in a new way what they have looked at but not really experienced before. Although included are such keen observers and fine spokesmen as John Updike, Adrien Stoutenburg, Denise Levertov, Robert Bly, and Slyvia Plath, as a whole the book is thin, static, and bland. Much more exciting because of its diversity of content is English critic and novelist John Townsend's *Modern Poetry,* a collection of over one hundred-thirty poems done by British and American poets starting with those who were young in the 1930s because "this seems to be the point at which poetry begins to speak in our own tones of voice." Among the poems, about half of which were published during the last five years, are some by such well-known writers as Auden, Spender, and Hughes, while less well-known poets include Edwin Morgan, Ann Beresford, and Douglas Livingstone. In varying moods of happiness, cynicism, despair, anger, celebration, and optimism, this is a choice collection which gives a good sense of the variety of the concerns and feelings of poets of the mid-twentieth century.

In *New Coasts and Strange Harbors,* Hill and Perkins have demonstrated well that they have the qualities which critic Lillian Smith says a good anthologist must possess: understanding of and respect for children, courage to avoid the used and the ordinary, knowledge of and love for poetry, and an artist's sensitivity for effective arrangement.[3] In putting together their over two-hundred short lyrics, most written in the last twenty years, the compilers set out to find good poems that would give pleasure, "poems that catch the ear" and "speak about the feelings we all share as we are growing up and even after we are grown." By eighty-four British and American poets, arranged in fifteen sections, these pieces speak of such subjects as family activities and relationships; play, love, the passing of the seasons; singing and dancing; death; and the weather. Some are angry ("Traveller's Curse"), some joyful ("buy me an ounce"), some reflective ("Daedalus"), or frightening ("beware: do not read this poem"), but all are highly melodious and sharp with imagery so that the words fall happily on the ear, have appeal for the eye, and taste good on the tongue. A handsomely designed and illustrated book, *New Coasts and Strange Harbors* should be enjoyed for a long time to come. It stands as one of the best collections for young people of the past few years. Like the works of these other poets and anthologists, it too shows that much fine poetry is being made available for children these days.

NOTES

1. William Jay Smith, "Sounds of Wind, Sea and Rain," *The New York Times Book Review,* May 2, 1976, p. 42, cols. 1–2.

2. William Jay Smith, p. 23, col. 4.

3. Lillian H. Smith, *The Unreluctant Years* (New York: The Viking Press, 1967), p. 101.

Juvenile Science Fiction, 1975—1976

Francis J. Molson

Conversations, by Barry Malzberg. Indianapolis: The Bobbs-Merrill Company, Inc., 1975. $4.95.

Dragonfall 5 and the Royal Beast, by Brian Earnshaw. Illustrated by Simon Stern. New York: Lothrop, Lee & Shepard Company, 1975. $4.50.

Dragonfall 5 and the Space Cowboys, by Brian Earnshaw. Illustrated by Simon Stern. New York: Lothrop, Lee & Shepard Company, 1975. $4.50.

Dragonsong, by Anne McCaffrey. New York: Atheneum, 1976. $7.95.

End of Exile, by Ben Bova. New York: E. P. Dutton & Company, 1975. $7.95.

The Heavenly Host, by Isaac Asimov. Illustrated by Bernard Colonna. New York: Walker and Company, 1975. $5.95.

No Night Without Stars by Andre Norton. New York: Atheneum, 1975. $6.95.

The Pale Invaders, by G. R. Kestevan. New York: Atheneum, 1976. $6.95.

Star Ka'at, by Andre Norton and Dorothy Madlee. Illustrated by Bernard Colonna. New York: Walker and Company, 1976. $6.85.

Star Prince Charlie, by Poul Anderson and Gordon R. Dickson. New York: G. P. Putnam's Sons, 1975. $6.95.

Science fiction for readers aged 7 to 10 continues to be difficult to find. Consider, for example, the two *Dragonfall 5* books by Brian Earnshaw, a British author. Presumed to be science fiction because of references to space ships, rocket engines, and stunners, the books are really adventure stories in which futuristic technology is a prop but is in fact nonessential to the plot. In *Dragonfall 5 and the Royal Beast* the starship *Dragonfall 5,* with its crew of Old Elias, Big Mother, and their two sons, Tim and Sanchez, is forced down upon the Forest Planet. Looking for their missing cargo, the Royal Beast, the boys are surrounded by the Shanchi and persuaded to side with them in their rivalry with the evil, meat-eating, giant bears, the Molok'ki. In a dog fight between Shanchi balloons and Molok'ki dirigibles, the Molok'ki are beaten back but manage to capture *Dragonfall 5* along with Old Elias and Big Mother. Before any serious damage can be inflicted upon any of the participants, Sanchez discovers that the Molok'ki are in fact vegetarian and peace loving. Hostilities cease, the crew is reunited, and harmony is restored.

The resemblance between *Dragonfall 5 and the Space Cowboys* and science fiction is even more tenuous, for the book is in reality a camouflaged western. The starship and its crew land on the Kench ranch and into an old-fashioned feud between the Kenches and their cousins, the Maxwells. Before their Uncle Richard disappeared, he left behind riddling clues as to who is to inherit his ranch and cattle. His nephews, however, have been too obtuse to decipher the first clues, which Tim and Sanchez do in a very short while. Ma Maxwell steals the first clues and to find a second set heads out for the great cave of the Condavees; the Kenches follow. Both parties are captured by musical monkeys, who require the quarreling families to pass a test originally set up by Uncle Richard. The Maxwells fail and the Kenches obtain title. Learning that the Great War had been fought over cattle and land, the Kenches decide to share their legacy with the Maxwells.

If a category must be assigned to these books, space fantasy may be more appropriate, especially in view of the ample exaggeration in the stories. The books are not particularly exciting or suspenseful, but they are easy to read and fun. Earnshaw employs exaggeration to good effect, especially in his selection of names for his characters. The simple black-and-white illustrations are humorous and add to the fun. Contributing also to the books' humor is the absence of any moralizing or insistence upon any contemporary relevance, except entertaining young readers.

Juvenile science fiction has not been spared the currently widespread theory that children's literature should teach a belief, which has flawed, weakened, and dulled so many children's books. Witness, for instance, the new offerings in the Walker Science Fiction for Young Readers series. In spite of their endeavor to engage readers with intelligent presentations of several compelling topics, both books suffer from their authors' desire to offend none of today's more vocal pressure groups.

Star Ka'at seems to have much going for it. One of its authors is Andre Norton, a well-known science fiction writer with a fine reputation for successful juveniles. Its subject matter is standard science fiction fare: imminent catastrophe facing earth and earth's visitation by agents of a morally superior, other-world civilization, the Ka'ats. Several contemporary problems are dramatized—the loneliness experienced by parentless children, the effects of poverty on minorities, and the abuse animals have suffered from humans. But these themes are not enough to render the book satisfactory. Also, constant explanation and commentary on the part of the invaders reflect not the logic of inscrutable beings, but of stuffy and boring pedants.

The second of the Walker series offerings, *The Heavenly Host,* is by Isaac Asimov, but it is unlikely that this novel, a science fiction Christmas story, will further enhance his reputation. Shortly before Christmas Jonathan Derodin arrives with his mother on Planet Anderson Two. It is Mrs. Derodin's task to certify that the planet is uninhabited by any intelligent life and, hence, open to human colonization. Jonathan accidentally meets a small Wheel, one of the planet's native inhabitants who, he has been warned, are unintelligent and dangerous. The two become friends and Jonathan learns that Wheels are intelligent and able to communicate through teleflashing, the flickering of color and spatial patterns. When Jonathan is unsuccessful in convincing his mother of Wheel intelligence, Yellger, his small friend, and some of the other young Wheels fly over the human colony on Christmas day. The Wheels' display of flying and teleflashing is so dazzling that the colonists are not only convinced of Wheel intelligence but also imagine that the angels at Bethlehem must have looked like Wheels in flight.

Asimov's novel is a strangely anachronistic book. Although set in a future when tremendous scientific advances have made feasible interplanetary travel and colonization and have, presumably, affected many other aspects of human life, the book's illustrations depict human beings clothed and coiffured in today's fashion. The colonists live, think, and form value judgments as if they are unaffected by the tremendous technological innovations which have occurred. Perhaps Asimov is intimating that in spite of all the changes humanity will experience in the future, the species will still be inclined to xenophobia and the urge to manipulate or exterminate whatever stands in the way of its progress. In any case, the import of the novel is unclear. The religious message seems intrusive as the two elements do not meld.

In *No Night Without Stars,* Andre Norton returns to her metier: the fast-paced novel that stresses adventure and eschews any explicit social or political relevance. Sander, a smith, and Fanji, a shaman, are among those who must reassemble the pieces after natural disasters have destroyed civilization. Accompanied by several dog-like animals, the two set out for a Before place where each hopes to find something important: Sander, skill in his craft so that he can impress his uncle; and Fanji, knowledge, especially of weapons, so that she can avenge the death of her people. After reaching their destination, the pair is shocked to discover the existence of Big Brain, a series of artificial brains. This gigantic computer is controlled by Maxim, the final survivor of the Chosen Ones who had prepared for the demise of civilization by consolidating all available technology under one roof. Grown insane from loneliness and a lust for power, Maxim seeks to dominate the earth. Sander and Fanji, against all odds, kill Maxim and destroy Big Brain, but not before Sander realizes the worth of doing well what one is best suited for and Fanji resists collaboration with Maxim.

No Night Without Stars begins slowly. Then, like all good adventure stories, it builds to an exciting climax as Sander and Fanji struggle to overcome the array of electronic weaponry deployed against them. Depth is added to the traditional quest format: the protagonists must first overcome their own internal hang-ups before they can conquer the external dangers. Thus Sander learns to control his jealousy and anger, and Fanji tempers her pride in her special abilities. Both cease looking to the past for all their answers. Consoled by the realization that every night has some stars and trusting in themselves, they set their eyes to the future. Also enhancing the novel's effectiveness is Norton's style, a distinctive blend of economy and directness with a pinch of formality and archaic diction.

Ever since Robert Heinlein published his first juvenile, *Rocket Ship Galileo,* many science fiction authors have written for both adults and children. The motives of these authors may not always have been the best interests of children and their books, but one consequence is that of all genres of contemporary children's literature only juvenile science fiction can boast of so many of its authors having stature in the adult market also. The new releases of the past twelve months reveal that this boast is still valid. In addition to Norton, Ben Bova, Poul Anderson, Gordon Dickson, and even Barry Malzberg have entered the field.

Bova's new juvenile, *End of Exile,* concludes his loosely interrelated Exiled trilogy begun by *Exiled from Earth* and continued in *Flight of Exiles.* Born and raised on board a space ship, a small group of young people have lived according to rules promulgated by Jerlet, the great scientist who had designed complex machinery which would satisfy the small community's needs until it reached a new home. After Jerlet left, the machines began to break down and the rules became transformed into sacred laws that could be interpreted only by Magda, the priestess. Growing anxiety and superstition permit the power-hungry Morel to gain ascendancy. Linc, who wants to know how the machines work, decides to seek out Jerlet's help. The finding of Jerlet, Linc's return to the group with new instructions and hope, his struggle to overcome Morel and convince Magda to help him, and guiding the space ship to its new home constitute the remaining, and major, part of the plot.

End of Exile is recommended for any young reader already fond of or curious about "hard" science fiction. The novel describes in detail the rocketry, computers, and life-support systems required to run a gigantic space ship. The novel also lays out a plausible scenario of the way in which a small community (in spite of the most sophisticated social and psychological planning) deteriorates when left to itself too long and becomes an increasingly ossified society, flirting with superstition and violence. The novel contains exciting incidents, suspense, a surprise ending, and conflict aplenty. There is even a hint of romance between Linc and Magda. Besides being a writer Bova is also an editor and as such appreciates the importance of a clear, fast-moving style that is "with it" for today's readers. The style of his novel easily meets this criteria.

Poul Anderson and Gordon Dickson, coauthors of *Star Prince Charlie,* are at home in either science fiction or fantasy, so it is no surprise that their new juvenile contains both elements. The events of the novel take place on Talyina, a planet technologically and politically behind earth, and involve Charlie Stuart, who is mistaken for a hero whose coming will bring down the usurper, King Olaghi, and restore peace and unity. Except for Charlie and his tutor, Bertram, a teddy bear, Hoka, the characters are the typical tyrants, knights, soldiers, and peasants found in any heroic romance. Rather than plot and characterization, what gives the novel its distinctiveness is its blend of humor and mocking tone: a big teddy bear affecting Scottish ways and using "British Broadcasting Company English"; the yachina, a wagon that resembles a gigantic baby's push toy; the faked or twisted-into-heroic-looking deeds that are made to fulfill the five prophecies pointing to Charlie as the long-sought hero; the tongue-in-cheek correspondences between British history and events on Talyina. Whatever serious side the novel has is quite muted. Charlie does acquire some wisdom as he realizes that ruling demands not only a knowledge of the difference between right and wrong but skill in public relations. Essentially, *Star Prince Charlie* is fun. Its tone is so light and its events so happily teetering on the ridiculous that one wonders whether its authors put the book together over a case or two of beer.

Barry Malzberg never wrote for young people before *Conversations,* and this inexperience may be responsible for the book's failure. Like *Star Ka'at,* Malzberg's novel has a lot going for it. Its author is prominent. It is about the right topics for young people: the individual resisting his peers, romance, a future in which a Council of Elders controls the young, adult fear of change, and youth's curiosity. The protagonists are young. The plot seems uncomplicated. "Crazy" Lothar encourages twelve-year-old Dal to look at the former's scrapbooks that record the past. Since such books are forbidden, Nan, Dal's close friend and future marriage partner, turns Lothar in to the authorities, but he escapes. Before doing so he gives the scrapbooks to Dal so that knowledge of the past will not be lost. Dal studies the books and, inexplicably fascinated, becomes their unofficial custodian. Ten years later the Council of Elders is overthrown, and Dal lives like any other of his peers.

Malzberg chose to narrate the story in the first person through Dal. The upshot is that the only character the reader has a chance to know is Dal; all other characters are mere name-pegs upon which snatches of conversation are hung. Malzberg uses, moreover, a somewhat dense, allusive style and, in general, eschews explanations. Thus, what impels Dal to accept the books and become their custodian is not clear. Also unclear are the reasons for the overthrow of the Elders, the part played by Lothar in the revolt, and Dal's final conformity. It is possible that the author deliberately intended not to provide explanations, suggesting in this way the subjectivity and ambiguity of life. Such an intention with its consequent obscurity may whet the sophisticated reader, but it guarantees that very few young readers are going to read *Conversations*, let alone enjoy it.

In *The Pale Invaders* G. R. Kestevan, a British author, investigates the moral ambiguity of contemporary technology. One group of survivors of the Upheavals inhabit a small, secluded valley and believe that life as they live it has never changed. One day strangers intrude into the valley and ask to dig what they call coal. The valley faces a difficult decision. What the decision is and what happens to the valley and its way of life are narrated by young Gerald. An intelligent, perceptive child, he has always been curious, especially about the stories told by Old Carz concerning life before the Upheavals, stories the rest of the elders insist are make-believe. Gerald persists in asking questions and begins to explore. Gradually he, and the reader, learn the truth—that exhausted land, shortages, and riots led to the Upheavals. Gerald also begins to appreciate the difficult decision confronting the elders—whether to cooperate and risk possible moral contamination from a reliance on technology or to reject the strangers and preserve the relatively primitive life of the valley. An air of mystery, a sensitive rendering of a young teen's deepening awareness, and an analysis of the morality of technology make *The Pale Invaders* a superior work.

Anne McCaffrey's *Dragonsong* is also superior science fiction. Surprisingly, the novel's plot is slight and unexciting. Menolly, a very musically talented girl, gains her dream of becoming a harper despite parental disapproval and an injury to her hand. More impressive is the novel's portrait of the girl's growth in self-confidence, and most impressive is its setting. McCaffrey has created an original and credible world, Pern, complete with a geography and ecology, and settled by people whose social organizations reflect the physical environment.

Pern is a planet that has been colonized by humans who soon find themselves under attack by Thread, a hostile, carnivorous spore life drifting down from the sky. To defend themselves, the colonists selectively breed a life form indigenous to Pern into creatures that can destroy Thread. These the people call dragons because they spit fire and can teleport through space and time. A select few of the colonists who manifest ESP are recruited to "partner" the dragons, a process called impressing. Because of the necessity to have dragons and their human riders prepared at all times and in all places for defense, the people of Pern develop very specialized social and economic organizations, the Holds. Descriptions of the life and routine of two of the Holds make up a large part of *Dragonsong*. Although a brief preface records the past history of Pern and provides necessary background—a history derived, presumably, from McCaffrey's other adult novels about Pern—enough of the physical texture and culture of Pern exists in *Dragonsong* so that the reader can believe in it. So convincing and attractive is Pern that it seems safe to predict that it will be remembered when many other secondary worlds have disappeared into oblivion.

From the moment the Carstairs family enters the large house which aged Mrs. Aylwood sells to them, fifteen-year-old Jan senses someone or something in the woods watching her, her parents, and her younger sister, Ellie. Jan's foreboding is reinforced by the broken mirrors that begin to appear around the house. A family outing in the woods convinces her that there is something powerful and potentially dangerous there. Such an ominous beginning marks what is perhaps the best science fiction juvenile of the past year, Florence Engel Randall's *A Watcher in the Woods*. To effect her outstanding achievement Randall has expertly combined elements

from several genres—mystery, the family story, and the adolescent
novel—and has expressed them in a style that is, as the occasion
requires, colloquial, evocative, formally cadenced, sensitive.

The identity of the force in the woods and its relationship with Mrs.
Aylwood constitutes the mystery. The science fiction has to do with
the nature and origin of the force and the means it used (part of which
resembles the electronic disturbances that enhance the ominous atmosphere of Alan Garner's *Elidor*) to communicate with Jan and the
others. The qualities that characterize the Carstairs—intelligence,
affection, forbearance, and willingness to sacrifice—will remind
readers of the Murry family in *A Wrinkle in Time*. There is nothing
original about a shy fifteen-year-old, given to day dreaming and
wonder, blossoming into a poised sixteen-year-old. But Randall has
managed to instill freshness in her portrayal of Jan. Particularly good
is Jan's poignant realization that Mrs. Carstairs is, even before she is
mother and wife, an individual who needs understanding and support
like any other person. All the strengths of the novel, however, could
simply amount to a competent novel at the hands of a competent
writer. Fortunately, Randall is no neophyte, having already published five novels and many short stories. One passage should suffice
to demonstrate both the quality of Randall's style and her ability to
isolate those moments when the small universes people wall themselves inside begin to break apart under pressure from the much
larger universes—actual and potential—existing all around.

> All she had wanted was her family and this house. She had
> looked at it and had had a vision of candlelight and crackling flames
> and snow softly falling, and now she couldn't hold onto her dream,
> finding even on a hot July evening, no warmth anywhere.
> She didn't want to explore the mysteries of the universe. She
> didn't want to hear the pulsing song of quasars; but a strange,
> unknown door had opened, and long ago a girl had been lost, and
> my mother, standing in her kitchen, leaning against an old,
> cracked, porcelain sink, was crying. (p. 123)

These novels by no means represent all the juvenile science
fiction published during the past twelve months. They do suggest
the quality of books currently being written and the directions the
genre has been taking. In general, attempting to write science
fiction for the young has yet to be proven feasible. Yoking socially
relevant material to science fiction has been only partially successful. The phenomenon of science fiction authors writing for

both adult and juvenile markets persists. Established writers continue to publish but, as might be expected, with mixed results. New talent does appear, occasionally producing outstanding entertainment. Taken as a whole, the output of the past year bodes well for the future of juvenile science fiction and attests to its slowly growing stature.

After Armageddon

The Post Cataclysmic Novel for Young Readers

Margaret P. Esmonde

And All Between, by Zilpha K. Snyder. New York: Atheneum, 1976. $6.95.

Below the Root, by Zilpha K. Snyder. New York: Atheneum, 1975. $7.50

Children of Morrow, by H. M. Hoover. New York: Four Winds Press, 1973. $5.95.

City of Darkness, by Ben Bova. New York: Charles Scribner's Sons, 1976. $6.95.

House of Stairs, by William Sleator. New York: Dutton, 1974. $6.95.

No Man's Land, by Simon Watson. New York: Greenwillow Books, 1976. $6.95.

No Night Without Stars, by Andre Norton. New York: A Margaret McElderry Book. Atheneum, 1975. $6.95.

Noah's Castle, by John Rowe Townsend. Philadelphia: Lippincott, 1976. $6.95.

The Pale Invaders, by G. R. Kestevan. New York: Atheneum, 1976. $6.95.

The People of the Ax, by Jay Williams. New York: Henry Z. Walck, 1974. $6.95.

Ransome Revisited, by Elisabeth Mace. London: Andre Deutsch, 1975. £ 2.25.

Treasures of Morrow, by H. M. Hoover. New York: Four Winds Press, 1976. $6.95.

The Turning Place: Stories of a Future Past, by Jean E. Karl. New
York: Dutton, 1976. $7.95.
Wild Jack, by John Christopher. New York: Macmillan, 1974.
$5.95.
Z is for Zachariah, by Robert C. O'Brien. New York: Atheneum,
1975. $6.95.

Whether we trace its origin to Plato's *Critias,* More's *Utopia,* or
Wells' *The Time Machine,* the best science fiction has always
provided an excellent medium for social criticism and speculation
about man's possible future. Though contemporary science fiction
writers generally avoid the mantle of prophet, their works are often
quite consciously didactic and reflect the anxieties of the society in
which they live, especially the growing disbelief that technology
will save the world and the growing acceptance of the fact that, one
way or another, the destruction of our society, and perhaps our
world, is inevitable. These repressed fears have given rise to a
special type of science fiction—the postcataclysmic novel—an unusual number of which are being published in the United States and
Great Britain.

Though atomic warfare and alien invasion were once the most
popular way to accomplish the end of the world, the majority of
disaster novels for young readers produced between 1973 and 1976
predict the overthrow of our way of life through socioeconomic
breakdown—often coupled with ecological disaster. Included in
this first category are John Rowe Townsend's *Noah's Castle,*
Simon Watson's *No Man's Land,* G. R. Kestevan's *The Pale
Invaders,* Elizabeth Mace's *Ransome Revisited,* William Sleator's
House Of Stairs, Ben Bova's *City Of Darkness,* and John
Christopher's *Wild Jack.*

Most realistic of these dystopian novels is Townsend's *Noah's
Castle,* which is set in England "two or three years after the time
you are reading it." The novel's protagonist tells the story of his
father, Norman, the manager of a shoe store, who purchases an old
Victorian mansion which he fortifies and provisions to carry his
family through the period of chaos he sees looming as the pound
sterling becomes worthless and England experiences economic
collapse. Using the unsympathetic viewpoint of the teenage son,
Townsend characterizes the father with psychological acuity. Lower
class in background because *his* father drank away the family's
money, forced to leave school without a diploma at the

age of fourteen, Mr. Mortimer nonetheless rose through the ranks to become an officer in World War II, only to find himself relegated shortly thereafter to the status of a shopkeeper by the British class system. A martinet, he runs his family like an Army regiment, demanding unquestioning obedience from all. His obsession with providing for his family alienates all of them in the end, as they choose to endure the hardships of the famine rather than the guilt of hoarding while others starve. Though one might observe that his description of the suffering lacks full impact because the central characters do not experience physical privation, the great strengths of the book—the characterization of the father and the presentation of the moral dilemma of hoarding—overshadow this weakness.

On the dedication page of *No Man's Land*, another British author, Simon Watson, writes: "This story takes place in a possible future." In this future, not much further away than Townsend's, his dystopian vision sees man regimented, depersonalized, separated from nature, encased in concrete "campuses," which are described as gigantic units "housing over three-thousand people, containing all the shops and services that anyone could require. . . ." The countryside has been "rationalized," carefully cleared of all living things, by the science-fiction device of the novel "Giant," the ultimate machine—"Man's first invention to have a mind of its own." Pitted against this technological Frankenstein are thirteen-year-old Alan, his friend Jay, an adamant nonconformist, the sixty-five year-old "General," who hides to avoid the compulsory welfare home, and his female counterpart, an escapee from such a home, where she was "waited on night and day, never allowed out, no chores to do . . . built-in television and scented bedlinen, breakfast in bed—a gilded cage indeed." Watson's real monster—the ultimate, depersonalized welfare state—the gilded cage—is more insidious in some ways than Orwell's Big Brother, for the government sincerely believes itself to be the benefactor of its citizens. Watson keeps the reader off-balance by presenting the government as logical, efficient, progressive, and well-intentioned—opposed only by the ignorant youths and the eccentric old people. He hurls some challenging ideas at his readers, subtly underscoring the choice men have to make in governing themselves—the Hobson's choice of the ennui of total security versus the risks of individual freedom. Watson's England has chosen security and material comfort, and the government discourages all variety in people and in nature. The defeat of the science fiction *bete noire,* the supermachine, by the boy, Alan, is merely camouflage for this larger issue which remains unresolved. Though Watson pays lip service to qualified conformity, he does allow Jay to reach an island refuge where he can find a new life, "not comfortable" but "interesting." The reader is left to consider for himself which life is preferable.

A third British novel, *The Pale Invaders* by G. R. Kestevan, takes place in England eighty years after "the Upheaval," a time of social and economic breakdown. A small group of people takes refuge in a mountain valley on the Welsh border and remains totally isolated, living in virtually a Stone-Age culture. Two of the more imaginative young people begin to suspect that the wild stories told by Old Carz, one of the original settlers, are based in truth. At this point, the village is discovered by pale-faced men who want to open the old coal mines in the region to provide energy for the slowly recovering society. The confrontation between this isolated community and a more sophisticated society is realistically treated and makes a very effective, low-key statement about today's situation, as our oil-hungry world probes remote areas for new energy supplies. Perhaps more pointedly, it observes that man is not as far from his Stone-Age ancestors as he may think.

One of the bleakest of these postcatastrophe novels is Elizabeth Mace's existential nightmare, *Ransome Revisited.* A "Great War," followed by pestilence and natural catastrophes, reduces Britain's population to a few-thousand people. The children, "pale, thin, and sadly dressed," have numbers instead of names, and they look forward to going "Out There" to earn their names and, perhaps, help to regain the "secret of flight to the glorious stars." Instead of the stars, the young protagonist and several others are assigned to work in a quarry, doing pointless labor under the direction of a brutal supervisor who drives them to escape by his cruelty. A pathetic group of misfits—the boy, his retarded brother, a little orphan girl, and enigmatic Susannah, whose one treasure from before the "Terrible Disaster" is an old copy of Arthur Ransome's *Swallowdale*—travels north in search of a legendary place where people are free. After an arduous trek, trailed by Will, a ruthless, amoral young man who has killed the supervisor and caused the death of the retarded brother, they reach Scotland only to discover that "the Colony" is an island which lies some three-days journey across the sea. Too tired to continue, Susannah remains in Scotland; Will goes on to seek "the place in the far North where clever men work to find the way back to the stars." The boy and the orphan girl undertake the last journey and reach their goal. Mace paints a surrealistic nightmare filled with pointless cruelty and characters too exhausted to experience emotion, even grief for the dead. What the author intends by her story is hard to say for certain. The amoral Will (perhaps a symbolic name) pursues the stars, representing technological knowledge, while Susannah longs for the past of Ransome's novel. Neither crosses into the Promised Land. Only the two innocents achieve the vision: "Swallowdale sheep waiting like white stars . . . on the green universe, the mountain."

Perhaps because economic problems are not as threatening, American writers examine a variety of tensions. In the *House Of Stairs*, William Sleator creates a nightmare of behavioral psychology. Five sixteen-year-old orphans—Lola, the nonconformist; Peter, the dreamer; Abigail, who just wants to be liked; Oliver, the self-centered; and fat, vicious Blossom—find themselves imprisoned in a strange building that consists of a maze of intersecting staircases. Unaware that they are human guinea pigs in a psychological experiment in conditioned human response, the five teenagers quickly become dependent on a machine as their only food supply. As time passes, they determine that cruelty and physical abuse are the keys to the operation of the machine. Lola and Peter are appalled by this knowledge and refuse to take part, resisting to the point of starvation. In a chilling concluding chapter, the doctor in charge of the experiment reveals the full purpose and the extent of the conditioning. Sleator's novel sustains the feelings of suspense and horror which are only increased as explanations of the house of stairs are made. Set in what might possibly be our near future, the *House Of Stairs* is a chilling glimpse of man's inhumanity as well as a vision of man's indomitable will to resist the darker side of his nature.

Well-known science fiction writer Ben Bova chooses as his theme racial prejudice, coupled with ecological disaster, to present a grim look at the future of our large cities. A domed New York City, supposedly evacuated because of killing pollution, is opened up each summer as a vacation resort to prosperous tourists from the Tracts, the endless suburbia of conformity and upper-middle-class white ambition. The young protagonist, Ron Morgan, is trapped inside when the city closes on Labor Day because his ID pass has been stolen. During his enforced stay, Ron discovers that, when the city was originally evacuated, some people were left behind. Trapped, they survived by forming ethnic gangs which wage incessant warfare. The black gangs, under the leadership of the Black Muslims, have united and are planning to break out and seize a decent life, by force if necessary. By the book's end, Ron has recovered his ID card; and in a confrontation with the Black Muslim leader, he learns to his horror that the government had forcibly prevented the Blacks and Puerto Ricans from leaving New York City, sentencing them "to starve, to freeze, to be rat bait." Ron is permitted to exit and returns to the Tracts vowing "to change things." Though no one can quarrel with Bova's message, the thinly disguised social criticism remains just that. His characters are one-dimensional and his science fiction device, a domed, doomed New York, where people come for a summer holiday, seems as implausible as does Ron's enforced detainment in that city. The grim warning to complacent suburban whites is so obtrusive that the book scarcely deserves the label "fiction."

A similar plot serves British author John Christopher in *Wild Jack*, though the conflict is one of class prejudice rather than racial prejudice. No stranger to this particular type of science fiction, Christopher is off and running in this novel, reversing the theme of his previous work, *The Guardians*. *Wild Jack* takes place in twenty-third-century England, after "the Breakdown"; the population of London and other English cities is limited to a few-thousand people each, living in luxury thanks to their "energy towers." Outside the walled cities in the Outlands live the Savages, descendants of the people who had been expelled generations before. The protagonist, Clive Anderson, son of a London councillor, is an over-privileged young man who accepts without question the status quo until a political maneuver against his father results in the son's deportation to a prison island for social deviants. His escape in the company of an American and a Japanese boy seems rather contrived, but never mind that. The trio find their way back to the English Outlands and live among the Savages whose leader is a Robin Hood figure called "Wild Jack." In the Outlands Clive learns to appreciate the more demanding life outside the walls. This is quite obviously the first book of a series and is Christopher's usual fast-paced adventure story about courageous and resourceful boys who regain long-lost freedom for England. But Christopher's standard plot, reworked again and again, is getting a bit threadbare; his latest story seems rather perfunctory.

A second major pattern in the postcataclysmic novel can be found in the six books which focus on man's longing for peace and his struggle to free himself from the curse of violence. In each book in this group, the survivors of earth's ruin develop psychic powers which help them cope. This group includes Andre Norton's *No Night Without Stars,* H. M. Hoover's *Children Of Morrow* and *Treasures Of Morrow,* Jay Williams' *The People of the Ax,* and Zilpha K. Snyder's *Below The Root* and *And All Between.*

In her usual capable fashion Andre Norton, who might well be considered the originator of this type of science fiction novel, offers *No Night Without Stars.* In a North America largely destroyed by volcanic eruption, tidal waves, and pollution, Sander, a young metalsmith of Jak's Mob, a clan of nomadic herdsmen, sets forth to discover the lost metallurgic knowledge of the Before Time in order to regain his rightful place in the tribe. In his wanderings, he encounters Fanyi, a young shaman whose people have been slaughtered during her absence. She too seeks the secret stronghold of the Before People to gain knowledge which will enlarge her psychic powers so that she may revenge her people. After encountering a number of standard mutated horrors, the pair confront an evil master computer which seeks, in its endless hatred of its creators, to eliminate all life from earth. When Fanyi's mental powers fail in the contest, Sander succeeds in badly crippling the malevolent machine. At the conclusion, Fanyi voices Norton's understated message: "There is no night without a star, so the blackness of our night can be lighted by our own efforts. We are ourselves, not the Before Ones. Therefore, we must learn for ourselves, not try to revive what was known by those we might not even want to call kin were we to meet them. . . ."

H. M. Hoover's novels, *Children Of Morrow* and its sequel *Treasures Of Morrow,* deal with the adventures of Tia and Rabbit, young misfits in a harsh, primitive society comprised of descendants of survivors of an army-missile-base shelter. Hoover's world has been destroyed by "The Death of the Seas" which diminished the world's oxygen supply and ultimately resulted in the death of 93 percent of all living creatures by simple suffocation. The children's unusual appearance and telepathic power draw down upon them the wrath of the chief, and they flee toward the Pacific Ocean, encouraged and advised by the highly intelligent members of another survival community named Morrow, with whom the children have inadvertently established telepathic contact. Hoover maintains the suspense of the chase nicely with a last-minute rescue which will satisfy young readers.

In the sequel, the children learn that their grandfather was a Morrowan scientist who, on a field trip to the San Francisco area, had artificially inseminated one of the women of the Base. The Morrowans, who have developed telephathic abilities through genetic mutation, return to the Base taking the children with them— though the reasons for the return seem contrived. It appears that Hoover is leading up to a choice for the children: to return to the idyllic existence of Morrow Hall or to stay at the Base and try to raise the people from savagery. But, no. Tia is glad to see how savage the people are because if they "were anything more, then I couldn't leave again." Interesting enough as escape tales, Ms. Hoover's books fail to offer insight into the human condition. The enlightened Morrowans display a surprisingly inhuman attitude toward their debased fellow men. Smug in their own superiority, the Morrowans' solution is to leave them to their misery and ignorance. One finishes the second book wondering: was this trip really necessary?

Similar in general theme but superior to Hoover's books is Jay Williams' *The People Of The Ax*. In an Iron Age culture, Arne and Frey, young initiates into the People of the Ax, are sent by the village council to Osan, the wise woman of the mountains, to learn how the hairy, apelike Crom have suddenly acquired iron clubs. Arne's discovery of mysterious writing in the caverns beneath Osan's mountains gives the reader the first intimation that this novel is science fiction not fantasy. Arne learns from Osan that he possesses "tendo," the psychic power to manipulate matter and, as he comes into his full power, he proposes that the Crom are not bestial but "unfinished people" to whom souls may be given. In the course of a council, Osan tells of atomic holocaust coupled with volcanic action which destroyed the materialistic civilization of the forefathers of the Crom, who are now systematically eradicated so they cannot regain control. Repelled by this heartlessness, Arne risks his life to prove that the hapless Crom are people like themselves who can be rehabilitated. Though reminiscent of LeGuin and Boule, Williams' simple but powerful style and deft handling of plot enhance the thought-provoking examination of man's inhumanity to man.

In her books, *Below The Root* and *And All Between,* Zilpha K. Snyder chooses to examine man's inhumanity to fellow man arising out of the abuse of power. She sets her story on a planet called Green-sky to which, long ago, the people came after "a desperate flight from a far distant planet, which had been totally destroyed by the terrible curse of war." The Kindar, as they called themselves, built their cities in the giant trees of the planet and, through rituals of joy and peace, developed remarkable mental powers of psychokinesis and telepathy. The only shadow in this utopia is the Pash-shan, vicious monsters who dwell below the impenetrable roots of the forest floor waiting to kill Kindar unwise enough to descend from the trees. After rescuing a little Pash-shan girl, three young initiates into the priestly ruling class discover that the Pash-shan are not monsters but only imprisoned Kindar who had disagreed with the Ol-zhaan, the ruling caste. *Below The Root* ends with the promise to "rekindle the light of the dream for all Green-sky." In her sequel *And All Between,* Snyder attempts an interesting literary experiment. The same story told in the first book is now told from the point of view of Teera, the rescued girl. Snyder repeats the identical dialogue expanding only Teera's part of the story. The first reaction to the technique is "what an easy way to write a second novel," but a fairer assessment of Snyder's attempt to provide a dual point of view must be made. The dual narration is an interesting innovation, but it would have been more effective if the two points of view could have been integrated into one novel to avoid the repetition of so much of the dialogue. In this second book, the plot is carried beyond the conclusion of the first book to a confrontation between the power factions of Green-sky. Snyder poses the age-old question: should one submit to evil, or use evil methods to oppose it? Her thought-provoking portrait of a society seeking to escape the curse of violence and her experiment in narrative technique make these books stimulating reading.

In this abundance of postcataclysmic novels, even the old standard catastrophes—the atomic war and the alien invasion—are given new vitality by contemporary authors. Utilizing the atomic holocaust popular in the 1950s, Newbery medalist Robert C. O'Brien presents his novel as the diary of teenage Ann Burden, who escapes death from atomic cataclysm because atmospheric inversion protects the small valley in which she dwells. Having lost her family to radiation, she lives alone with her dog and a few farm animals until the arrival of a chemist from Cornell, who escaped by wearing a radiation "safe suit." She nurses him through a bout of radiation sickness and even dreams that together they will be a new Adam and Eve. This daydream of a new Eden is ruthlessly shattered by the chemist when he recovers and demands that Ann serve him with unquestioning obedience. The new Eve chooses to go out into the unknown world without Adam, having refused to repeat the old mistakes. O'Brien does not soften the edges of his apocalyptic vision by providing a happy ending for Ann. As in real life, he gives her only hope and faith that someone might be out there to give life purpose and meaning.

Last, and perhaps the most creative of all the postcataclysmic novels, is Atheneum editor Jean Karl's *The Turning Point*. In a dazzling display of imagination, Ms. Karl takes as her starting point that old chestnut, the alien death ray. In the first episode, Ms. Karl eradicates most of the world's population by means of the "Clordian Sweep," and in the eight subsequent sections, she spans thousands of years of the development of a new mankind, taking us eventually out into the vast reaches of space. Never consciously didactic, the taut stories read like abstracts from some future history, giving a tantalizing view of the millenia. Like poetry, her compressed narratives run the risk of obscurity, which she seeks to alleviate by means of "Some Notes on Sources." These "notes" not only provide additional information but also lend an air of historical authenticity to her work. The reader finishes the book hoping that Ms. Karl will expand each of her stories into a novel.

The Turning Point sums up the mood of the 1970s. We are at a turning point; the good old days are gone, and we must find a new course. As her space traveler says at the novel's close: "There are always problems. They change. Patterns change. And sometimes things get worse, sometimes better. But no matter what happens, problems remain." A large part of the appeal of contemporary science fiction for the young reader is its ability to delineate these eternal problems and to suggest that their answers lie within each man's grasp—love of fellow man.

Folktales and Fantasy

P. L. Travers in Fantasy Land

Michael Patrick Hearn

About the Sleeping Beauty, by P. L. Travers. Illustrated by Charles
Keeping. 111 pp. New York: McGraw-Hill Book Company, 1975.
$7.95; $7.71 library edition.

The *volksmärchen* (traditional fairy tales), unlike the *kunst-
märchen* (literary fairy tales), exist in a constant state of flux. As
they pass from culture to culture, from storyteller to storyteller,
they are reshaped retaining, however, the basic mythic truth.
There is no definitive version of any tale; it has many authors and
many versions. Perhaps the most durable story in this tradition is
"The Sleeping Beauty" with its archetypical image of dormant
sexuality. Elements of the popular version date from the fourteenth
century in the lengthy romance *Perceforest*. In the "Histoire de
Troylus et de Zelladine," the princess Zelladine under the curse of
a slighted goddess falls into a deep sleep while spinning and is
found by Prince Troylus. This recording is only the germ of the
folk tale. The earliest collected version of the complete story is the
Neapolitan "Sole, Luna e Talia" ("Sun, Moon and Talia") in
Giambattista Basile's *Lo Cunto de li Cuenti* ("The Tale of Tales,"
popularly called *Pentamerone,* 1634–1636). In this version the
princess, under a spell induced by a splinter in her finger, is ravished
by a young king, a fate similar to one endured by Zelladine at the
hands of Troylus. When the princess awakes, she has become a
mother. Her illegitimate children are discovered by the king's wife
who orders them made into a meal for her husband. Talia, too, is
condemned to death. Through the kindness of the cook, the children
are saved. Talia is recognized by her lover, and the jealous queen is
burned at the stake. The classic retelling of this tale is "La Belle au

bois dormant" ("The Beauty in the Sleeping Wood) included by Charles Perrault in *Histoires ou contes du temps passé* ("Stories or tales of past time," 1697). Perrault did not merely collect old stories; he was a man of letters who argued the superiority of the moderns over the ancients, and like the other authors of fairy tales at the French court, he believed in refining and elevating the old nurse's stories. His fairy tales, dedicated to the young niece of Louis XIV, are free of Basile's earthy humor; Perrault changed the theme of the earlier sleeping princess from that of rape and infidelity to one of patient virginity. Perrault's heroine, blessed by the fairies with beauty, wit and grace, must sleep for a hundred years, like Brynhild, until the proper prince be found. Perrault retained the rest of Talia's tale, though he discreetly introduced a priest who legitimized the two children, and he transformed the jealous wife into an ogress mother-in-law. In the next collected version, "Dornroschen" ("Briar Rose"), of the Grimms' *Kinderund Haus-märchen* ("Children and Household Tales," 1812–1822) Perrault omitted this episode entirely and concluded the tale with the marriage of the prince and princess. The story has since gone through many transformations, primarily in the popular theater, but the power of those versions by Perrault and that perceptive longforgotten storyteller known to the Grimm brothers has not diminished. The only significant addition to the tale has been the tender conceit of the prince awakening his beloved with a kiss.

Now P. L. Travers, the celebrated creator of Mary Poppins, has published her version of the popular story. *About the Sleeping Beauty* is a deceptive title. The book is not an analytical study; it is an anthology, containing the new story with an afterword that acts as a defense for presuming to improve on the folk tale and a selection of five stories using the "sleeping beauty" image. No explanation is given for the choice of these particular translations. Why was Margaret Hunt's "Dornroschen" preferred to Edgar Taylor's? Why was Geoffrey Berenton's "LaBelle au bois dormant" chosen rather than Roger Samber's? And why was Perrault's moral in verse dropped from the story? Although the inclusion of these tales (which Ms. Travers feels are over-wordy, graceless, full of sophistries) provides an opportunity for comparison between the traditional and her literary version, they seem to be included merely to flesh out a rather slim volume.

Novalis argued that the fairy tale was a form of poetry, and the writing of a fairy tale requires the same care as a sonnet. Every word must be precisely chosen, each phrase delicately balanced to fit the whole; no choice may be arbitrary. Ms. Travers explains that she does not wish to retell the old story (she follows the structure of the Grimm version), but rather she wants to present a few reflections on the old theme. Although generally well-written and occasionally perceptive, these passages are in the nature of digressions. Without much justification, she has placed the story somewhere in Arabia—a device similar to performing Shakespeare in modern dress or Bizet in blackface. It is a theatrical trick allowing all the elaborate trappings of an exotic locale, but Ms. Travers' Arabia has as little to do with the Near East as Shakespeare's Athens of *A Mid-summer Night's Dream* has to do with ancient Greece. Her story remains rooted in the European tradition. The new version is full of stage machinery. The characters talk in dreary platitudes ("When you are given a lily, do not protest that it should have been a tulip"), and the Wise Women, like caricature fairies, bless the princess in doggerel. Each of the thirteen women must speak, and they go on at length about each gift. As in poetry, brevity in a fairy tale is a blessing. Elaboration is not necessarily improvement; this excess is reminiscent of the pirates of Dickens' *A Christmas Carol,* who argued that by adding an original song of sixty lines to represent the carol sung by Tiny Tim they were improving the story. The only new character is the slave Buraba who plays Uncle Tom to Rose's Little Eva. He is abused by a regular buffoon of a sultan, who speaks in cliches and is totally lacking in imagination. This sultan is the cause of the court's troubles; he recognizes that one of the thirteen wise women will be slighted by not receiving a gold plate, but he persists in inviting only twelve. Ms. Travers makes him conscious of his sin and so contradicts the moral of the folk tale: that a ritual can be debased by an innocent mistake. This stolid potentate laments that the fairies do not bless the child with gold and silver; he (or Ms. Travers) seems not to realize that the daughter will inherit his domains—all the silk and damask, gold and jewels, she so elaborately describes at the opening. He even argues at the conclusion of the story that all the marvelous events were impossible, that his daughter has only dreamed them. The scene is anticlimatic and does not increase our understanding of the tale. Ms. Travers is most original in her depiction of the princess; there is a magic power, a psychological depth, developed in her character as she approaches the hidden tower. But these moments are rare in this new "Sleeping Beauty," which through its high intentions and dismal excesses could easily put a princess to sleep without aid of a spindle. Sadly she cannot awaken with a copy of *Mary Poppins* by her bedside to prove how exceptional a writer Ms. Travers can be.

The same excess found in the story is evident in the book's design, a genuine candy box of a binding whose endpapers and gaudy jacket have no relation to one another. The drawings by Charles Keeping are unremarkable; they have the stiff polish of a greeting card. And the use of color increases nothing but the price of the book. The design, like Ms. Travers' retelling, lacks balance; although ambitious, it fails to illuminate or amaze.

Six Beauties Sleeping

Joseph Cary

About the Sleeping Beauty, by P. L. Travers. Illustrated by Charles Keeping. 111 pp. McGraw-Hill Book Co, 1975. $7.95.

"The proper METHOD of studying poetry and good letters is the method of contemporary biologists, that is careful first-hand examination of the matter, and continual COMPARISON of one 'slide' or specimen with another." This sentence, from the first chapter of Ezra Pound's *ABC of Reading*, gives a good description of the procedure of P. L. Travers in the book at hand.[1] Drawing upon various tongues and times and cultures she has assembled six versions of a matter distinguishable as being "about the Sleeping Beauty." Part One (a little over half the book) presents Miss Travers' own reworking of the materials, plus a sixteen-page afterword composed of her reflections—from the double view of devoted reader and thoughtful storyteller—on the fairy tale in general and the tale of Sleeping Beauty in particular. Part Two gathers, in translation, five earlier metamorphoses of the same tale: the "Dornroschen" "Briar-Rose" set down by the Brothers Grimm in the early 19th century; Perrault's "La Belle au bois dormant" of 1697; Basile's

"Sole, Luna e Talia" of 1636; and two anonymous tellings, from Ireland ("The Queen of Tubber Tintye") and Bengal ("The Petrified Mansion"), published at the close of the last century.

Such are the slides proffered. They are not intended to be exhaustive; in the course of a single paragraph of her afterword the author lists fifteen alternative instances of the figure of the hidden sleeper "waiting until the time shall ripen." Nor is there here any question of a lost, inferred, or recovered "one story only" or original. " 'The Authors,' " Miss Travers quotes, " 'are in Eternity,' and we must be content to leave them there." Like any good teller she trusts the tales.

I think that *About the Sleeping Beauty* is an absorbing experiment in definition on Pound's model and that it sheds lights on both subject and genre. But the author has chosen to go further and to join herself—on the line—in the telling and for this reason I am touched and call her venture gallant. "To be in jeopardy is a proper fairy-tale situation," she says, and I shall leave it at that. What follows is no "review" but notes in response to the stimulus provided. I begin with Part Two.

Plus ca change plus c'est la même chose . . . but is it so? Metamorphosis—my term, after all, not the author's—means not *change* but *conversion,* or change-into-equivalence (in Hugh Kenner's phrase: "[an] identity persisting through change,")[2] What are the persistent items threading these exhibits?

1. There is a sleeper, female, unmarried, of royal blood and beautiful, whose sleep—like the torpor of the Fisher King—infects the realm (i.e., either extends over the entire court and palace or—as in Basile—causes the palace to be abandoned by a grieving king who believes his daughter dead). The sleep is abnormally long and measured in years not hours; Perrault and the Grimms call it an even century. The effect is to approximate Basilean abandonment and to create in time an oblivion; the remote island of Tubber Tintye and Perrault's thorny *bois dormant,* absent from the earlier versions, provide spatial images for this perfectly natural (under the circumstances) general neglect. In these several senses the sleeper is "hidden."[3]

2. There is a male, of royal blood and—except in the case of Basile, where he has a monstrously jealous wife—unmarried, who is variously, but crucially, associated with her wakening. In "The Petrified Mansion" and "Sole, Luna e Talia" the prince has no

prior inkling of the princess but "happens" upon her and is instru-
mental in returning her to waking life: in the first case by luckily
touching her with the life-giving stick of gold he has found by her
pillow, in the second by seeding her in her sleep with twins—one of
whom, confusing the princesses' finger with her breast, sucks forth
the sleep-inducing splinter. (Fortuity and happenstance *may* be
read as destiny of course; my point is that these wakeners have no
conscious awareness of their possibly fated roles). In the Irish version the prince does have a quest in mind, but the sleeper—the
Queen of Tubber Tintye in this instance—seems incidental to it.
His task is to procure three bottles of life-giving water for the
Queen of Erin and in the course of doing so, he cohabits with a
sleeping beauty who then wakens after seven years (the term of
sleep) to find a child (their child of course but a mystery to her)
playing on the floor. Only in the versions of Perrault and the Grimms
does the prince *set out* to find the princess; "all he has to do," as Miss
Travers points out, "is to come at the right time." In both cases she is
awakened not with a kiss but by the turn of a century—though the kiss
follows quickly after.

3. Whether in the long run ("Sole, Luna e Talia," "LaBelle au bois
dormant," "The Queen of Tubber Tintye") or the short ("The Petrified Mansion," "Dornroschen") they marry and live happily ever
after.

A beautiful sleeper, an awakening which involves a fortunate
meeting, a marriage: the short run in general and the Grimms'
"Dornroschen" in particular satisfy best. Miss Travers judges that
this version (on which her own is squarely based) has been
"purged of dross" and become "all essence," a "clarification." I
couldn't agree more, but not everybody does. The Opies, for
example, unaccountably find oral-based renderings, such as they
suppose "Dornroschen" to be, "flat and foolish" in comparison
with the literary "quality" of Perrault: Bruno Bettleheim compares
the Grimms' tale with those by Basile and Perrault and finds it morally
deficient since "the evil fairy is not punished."[4] It is worth examining
the long run to see whether—exquisite image!—a baby has been
thrown out with the bathwater.

"The Queen of Tubber Tintye," "Sole, Luna e Talia," and "La
Belle au bois dormant" all contain a fourth element: the figure of
the Other Woman. In the Irish tale she is the Queen of Erin, the
prince's (unknowing) stepmother who concocts murderous tasks

for him which lead in the end to her own undoing. But the focus here is primarily upon the prince and his exploits his prodigious week-long "rest" with and later marriage to the sleeping beauty seem merely "perks" attaching to the heroic mode. In Basile it is the sleeper Talia who, strictly speaking, should be nominated Other Woman since her lover the King is already married. But since Talia's amorous role has been wholly passive and unconscious, we judge the sleeper innocent. On the other hand the Queen-wife has "the heart of a Medea" and no one's sympathy. Rather than injured party, she seems the vile intruder and in the end is consumed by her own destructive fire. This pattern holds true for Perrault except that he, doubtless in the interests of clearing the affair of any overtly sexual naughtiness (he also suppresses what the Opies call *the rape*), makes his Other Woman the prince's ogress-mother, who is also finally hoist with her own petard (a vat of vipers).

So in the long run the tale involves an Other Woman, older than the sleeper, who savagely persecutes the sleeper and, although the "rightful" (i.e., legal) queen, will inevitably be replaced by her.[5] She is, however, a trial for the wakened beauty and for this reason I believe she falls beyond the waking-sleeping-reawakening movement which the Grimms saw was right: the best movement because it is the simplest pattern for the naturally cohering tale-to-be-told. An added fact is that the wakened beauty is never a bride, but a mother (of twins, or a single child depending on the tale), and she is persecuted by the Other Woman chiefly through her offspring. For me, as for Miss Travers, this is another story, legitimate perhaps, but another. So it turns out that in their short run the Brothers Grimm threw out at least one—probably two—babies with the bathwater. Quite properly so.

The sleeper wakes, the virgin becomes the bride, a threshold is crossed, a curtain lowers even as another rises, and the story is over.

And now, let us look more closely at "the curse." Why does the sleeper sleep? No clues forthcoming from Bengal. There she lies in her petrified mansion: perhaps she misplaced the golden stick. But what does it mean? On Tubber Tintye it is a question of, "When they get drowsy, and sleep comes on them, they sleep for seven years without waking. . . . When the seven years are over, they all wake, and none of them sleep again for seven other years." I find this boring. In these (for me) less interesting tales such sleep is a mere *donnée*.

The same is true for Basile's Talia, though for her it is a matter of early death, not sleep (a death of course from which she will be roused).

> There was once a great king who, on the birth of his daughter . . . commanded all the wise men and seers in the kingdom to come and tell him what her future would be. These wise men, after many consultations, came to the conclusion that she would be exposed to great danger from a small splinter in some flax.

The king, as kings can and will, takes certain steps: "flax or hemp or any other similar material" is outlawed from the premises and with this the distaff and spindle. Infernal or not, the machine slips into gear: the attempt to circumvent destiny actually promotes it. The princess grown glimpses an old woman spinning; her curiosity is quickened; and the game is up. Hindsight shows the poor king to have been a foolish, fatuous, kicker against pricks. When the time comes for me to write my *Sleeping Beauty* he shall be my hero.

Who or what is the old woman? In Basile her horrified reaction to catastrophe is surely genuine: she flees from the room, "rushing precipitously down the stairs." Sardonic Perrault presents her as a "dear" old creature out of touch with the times: she "had not heard of the King's proclamation forbidding the use of spindles" and is "greatly upset" when the Princess pricks herself. She calls for help. The Grimms' old woman with a spindle discovered at the top of an abandoned tower on Briar-Rose's fifteenth birthday is far more reticent and mysterious. "I am spinning," she says in response to the question and having provided the link she disappears from the tale. (Miss Travers responds to the possibility, which is at most only suggested by the Grimms, by explicitly making *her* shrouded spinster the thirteenth wise woman). Supernatural or natural, in all four cases the old woman with the spindle discloses an inevitable but "forbidden" experience to innocent eyes and serves, like the tragicomic king who forbade, as the witting or unwitting servant of destiny.

To his everlasting credit it is Charles Perrault who seems to have first furnished a proper account of why the sleeper sleeps. She sleeps because . . . and the well-loved elements appear like a promise kept: (1) a childless king and queen at last have their prayers answered; (2) a potentially benevolent power (eighth fairy godmother in Perrault, thirteenth wise woman in the Grimms) is ceremonially neglected and offended; (3) the curse of early death by spindle-prick is uttered and then modified to sleep-with-a-term by a companion power who, in tandem with the other, shows that a curse may be mixed and even conceal a blessing. Perrault alone includes the prince in the revised sentence (". . . a hundred years, at the end of which the son of a king will come to wake her"). The Grimms and Miss Travers are silent on this issue, which of course predicts the nature of the blessing.

But to pursue the point: why *sleep* rather than, say, imprisonment or hard labor? The answer, as always, is in the story. And the Grimms, as always, say it best: the sister power cannot "undo the evil sentence but only *soften* it . . . 'It shall not be death, but a deep sleep of a hundred years, into which the Princess shall fall.' " Such sleep is death softened then—a painless period of quiescence filled with pleasant dreams of the future. ("Is it you, my Prince?" Perrault has her say upon waking. "You have been a long time coming.") It is the adequate expression of the curse, tempered with mercy.

In his *Hero with a Thousand Faces* Joseph Campbell ranges the sleeping beauty in company with Brynhild of the *Volsunga Saga* who "was protected in her virginity, arrested in her daughter state for years" until the coming of the proper hero.[6] But despite the fact that the princess, like Brynhild, is miraculously exempted from time's usual inroads for a protracted period, it is surely wrong to think of her as lying in a frozen purity or a state of arrest. She is after all the *sleeping* beauty, hidden not absent, neither dead nor translated nor in suspension.[7] Sleep may mean a deadness, a loss of touch with reality (cf. Rip van Winkle, the submarine dream-fugues of J. Alfred Prufrock, or the rebuke made to Peter in Mark 14:37: "Sleepest thou? couldest not thou watch one hour?"). But I think the right way to read its quality in stories of the sleeping beauty is as a state of latency, both biological and psychological, wherein a presence is concealed and awaiting, ripening towards its proper moment of manifestation. Her sleep is the sleep we would wish ourselves—a rest and a refreshing—a gathering of strengths moving towards a waking that at once fulfills and begins anew. Throughout she remains, as Valéry says in his lovely sonnet, "secretement sensible."[8]

Why then talk about a curse at all? The answer is simply that that is the way it looks to us. What happens is not told from a knowing or privileged viewpoint. When the offended power speaks, we hear—like our poor brother His Majesty the King—an "evil sentence" only dimly mitigated by the subsequent "softening" sentence it elicits. A hundred years is long and more than a lifetime! "The King, who would fain keep his dear child from the misfortune, gave orders. . . ."

The theme-refrain of the tale as told by Miss Travers is precisely this: *This is the way it looks to us. And how little we know.*

In the Afterword Miss Travers characterizes the intention underlying her version:

> The story in its present guise may be thought of as a series of reflections on the theme of the Sleeping Beauty, particularly as it appears in "Dornroschen." . . . It was not written at all to improve the story—how could one improve on the Brothers Grimm?—but to ventillate my own thoughts about it.

In keeping with this meditative design, she has invented a revolutionary new personage who is far more central and influential than any other character—princess included—in the story. This person is the storyteller himself, a poetical Mohammedan gentleman every bit as reflective as—hardly indeed to be distinguished from—his creator. His leisurely, largely lyrical commentary on the action constitutes the bulk of her text, almost four times the length of Perrault's and almost ten times the length of the Grimms'.

"Once upon a time," he begins, "a time that never was and is always, there lived in Arabia a sultan and his wife. They were, as sovereigns go, reasonably benevolent and as much loved by their subjects as is possible for fallible human beings." These lines set the prevailing tone pretty fairly—amused and gently ironic with its "as sovereigns go" and "reasonably benevolent" and its touching on the basic theme of human fallibility; the deeper and mellifluent strain is also sounded in the opening subordinate clause ("a time that never was and is always") which suggests a dimension of being wholly other than the one we think we inhabit. We are in shrewd, professional hands.

I have used the word *influential* above with a purpose. Not only does the storyteller comment generously on the implications of his narrative but his creatures do as well. The frog for example, who in the Grimms version simply tells the queen that "Your wish shall be fulfilled; before a year has gone by you shall have a daughter," in the Travers version not only suavely delivers its good news but adds a little homily on human vanity and a gloss on its own symbolic status as well:

> Ah, so I must be human to be wise—is that what you think? Well, the sun rises promptly every morning, rivers flow downhill rather than up, the seed breaks the pod when the time is ripe. Were these taught their changeless ways by man? . . . A man sees no further than his nose. So, for that matter, does a frog. On the other hand, a frog lives in water, down by the roots, and senses what is stirring.

The humble woodcutter who witnesses the bristling and corpse-strewn hedge give way at the advent of the proper seeker interprets the ontological sense of the spectacle: "He is himself his own weapon. The time must be ripe." Above all the Sultana, queen-mother in the "vaguely Middle-Eastern world" where the tale is set, provides what Henry James would call the perfect *ficelle* for the author-storyteller's ruminations:

> At the same time she could not help wondering about all that had happened. And from that day forward . . . she pondered and dreamed and questioned. And the more she thought about it, the more it seemed to her that her daughter had stepped into another dimension—into, in fact, a fairy tale. And if this were so, she told herself, she would have to look for the meaning. For she knew very well that fairy tales are not as simple as they appear; that the more innocent and candid they seem, the wilier one has to be in one's efforts to find out what they are up to.

"But Mary kept all these things, and pondered them in her heart" (Luke 2:19). And Alice's motherly older sister reviews and wonders about the meaning of Alice's adventures in Wonderland. In the afterword Miss Travers goes so far as to call her story "the Sultana's interpretation" of the Grimms.

About Part One of *About the Sleeping Beauty*, I believe that the afterword is one of Miss Travers' premier creations. It charts a thoughtful, resourceful, intelligent probing into the sense of a well-loved tale. Its companionpiece, her story itself, is flawed in its very conception. But the flaw, like a diamond's, is light-giving—by which I mean she has taught me a great deal about what I think a fairy tale should be.

She has said it best herself, and most succinctly, in her review of Randall Jarrell's beautiful *Animal Family*: "the good story never explains."[9] In the afterword she phrases this in a significantly different way: "We can but guess, for the fairy stories never explain." In the Travers "Sleeping Beauty" the guesses, reflections, and explanations—whether of the Sultana, the storyteller, or Miss Travers herself does not matter since all are one. All are deliberately allowed to enclose and overrun, like the *bois dormant* itself, the luminous clarity of a pattern of events expressed in its perfection—as she happily acknowledges—by the Brothers Grimm. In the Travers version as never in the Grimms and hardly ever in their predecessors (even the facetious "superiority" of Perrault to his materials is only occasional) we are made aware of the artful knowingness of the teller. The tale itself lacks breathing-space. One reader's listing of the fairy tale virtues would include:

1. swiftness, spareness, dryness.
2. an anonymity: a "transparency" of tone and diction such that the tale shines through and we are scarcely aware of its medium, its art.
3. extroversion, a deed-boundness, in that all feeling finds expression in look or gesture.
4. an epistemological and metaphysical dumbness: no guesses or explanations unless these are part of the life-line ("plot") of the tale.

By extension this would impugn some of the stories of Anderson; Alice's sister's dream and the poems at the beginning and ending of Carroll's two books; and chapters like "The Piper at the Gates of Dawn" in *The Wind in the Willows*.

The Irish poet AE once told Miss Travers that Mary Poppins:
had she lived in another age, in the old times to which she certainly belongs, would undoubtedly have had long golden tresses, a wreath of flowers in one hand, and perhaps a spear in the other. Her eyes would have been like the sea, her nose comely, and on her feet winged sandals. But, this being Kali Yuga, as the Hindus call it—in our terms, the Iron Age—she comes in the habiliments most suited to it.[10]

But how lucky for us that Miss Travers had committed her Poppins before the wise and well-meaning AE could get at it and interpret it and even, as Miss Travers says, teach her how to read what she had written! Plain and prim and sharp, with no nonsense, Mary Poppins is her own person—a myth for the Iron Age. Someone in Miss Travers knew and knows that we are always born too late, that every age is iron and that the gold will have to be alembicated from the humble materials at our daily disposal.

Yet if we take Miss Travers at her own modest word, that is if we read her "Sleeping Beauty" as a series of reflections on a theme, as an essay reviewing the matter of a beloved story and culminating in the superb personal essay-meditation of the afterword—what a stimulating book she has produced! The length of and excitement, I hope, animating these notes should be the proof of it. She is to be read, reread, and pondered for her thoughts about the curse and the "wicked" fairy. ("The necessary antagonist," she calls her, "placed there to show that whatever is 'other,' opposite and fearful, is as indispensable an instrument of creation as any force for good.") She reminds us of a tradition where Judas might be thought of as a "saint," where the Lord of the Flies, Beelzebub himself, might be our helper.

NOTES

1. *Caveat:* the author has been poorly served by her publishers. The physical presence of the book is tawdry, the illustrations emanate from the plastic world of Barbie and Ken, who seem indeed to have modeled for the principals. The vulgarity of the "package" belies the spirit of the text.

And one textual amendment for the next edition: the translator of Giambattista Basile's "Sole, Luna e Talia" from the Neapolitan into "literary" Italian is Benedetto Croce, not *G*roce.

2. Hugh Kenner, *The Pound Era* (Berkeley and Los Angeles: University of California Press, 1971), p. 290.

3. But Frau Viehmann of Zwehren, one of the Grimms' most notable sources, was not only a master *raconteuse* but knew her Perrault well; also, "The Grimms often tightened, motivated, and clarified the plot and narrative in order to obtain a more closely knit story"—see Murry B. Peppard, *Paths Through the Forest: A Biography of the Brothers Grimm* (New York, Chicago, San Francisco, 1971), pp. 61, 65, 69-71.)

4. Iona and Peter Opie, *The Classic Fairy Stories* (London and New York: Oxford University Press, 1974), p. 81; Bruno Bettelheim, *The Uses of Enchantment: The Meaning and Importance of Fairy Tales* (New York: Alfred A. Knopf, 1976), p. 230.

5. There is a small generational lag in "The Queen of Tubber Tintye": the prince's *mother* replaces the Other Woman as Queen of Erin while the former sleeping beauty assumes her mother-in-law's role as Queen of Lonesome Island. But the general effect of beneficent upward-mobility (youth replacing age, good replacing evil) remains the same.

6. Joseph Campbell, *The Hero with a Thousand Faces* (New York: Pantheon Books, 1949), p. 62. The Opies view the story of Brynhild as "the tale of the Sleeping Beauty in embryo . . . [with] perhaps even a hint of its significance" (op. cit., p. 83).

7. Not like, that is, Randall Jarrell's "La Belle au bois dormant":

What wish, what keen pain, has enchanted her

To this cold period, the end of pain,
Wishes, enchantment: this suspending sleep?

—who is in fact a corpse concealed in a trunk; nor like Keat's
Madeline in "The Eve of St. Agnes," whose sleep seems to bracket her from natural process:

Blinded alike from sunshine and from rain,
As though a rose should shut and be a bud again.

8. Paul Valéry, *Poésies*: the poem is titled "Au Bois dormant." Cf.
Campbell, who cites the *Mandukya Upanishad* to the effect that "In deep
sleep . . . the self is unified and blissful; therefore deep sleep is called the
cognitional state" (op. cit., p. 220). And even Bettelheim, who in general
strikes me as frequently reductive so far as fairy tales are concerned (for
him "the curse" is menstrual), writes sensibly that "what may seem like a
period of deathlike passivity at the end of childhood is nothing but a time
of quiet growth and preparation, from which the person will awaken mature, ready for sexual union. *It must be stressed that in fairy tales this
union is as much one of the minds and souls of two partners as it is one of
sexual fulfillment.*" (Op. cit., p. 232, italics mine.)

9. *Randall Jarrell 1914–1965,* ed. Robert Lowell, Peter Taylor, Robert
Penn Warren (New York: Farrer, Straus & Giroux, 1967), p. 254.

10. *Only Connect: Readings on Children's Literature,* ed. Sheila Egoff,
G. T. Stubbs, L. F. Ashley (Toronto: Oxford University Press, 1969), p.
194.

Participating in Enchantment

Betty Jo McGrade

The Uses of Enchantment, by Bruno Bettelheim. New York: Alfred
A. Knopf, 1976. $12.50.

Bettelheim's new book is not addressed primarily to students of
children's literature who appreciate the enchantment, the complexity, and subtlety of fairy tales. The adults he hopes to reach are
those who advocate "realistic" stories for children, stories with
positive messages about handling everyday crises, recognizing ambivalent feelings, and working toward attainable goals. He argues

persuasively that "realism" is foreign to children's own ways of thinking and therefore fails to recognize, much less help resolve, their central problems. He goes beyond the enumeration of symbols in fairy tales to focus on the stories as a source of hope for the future which makes development toward maturity attractive and thus possible. Although Bettelheim clearly appreciates the literary qualities of fairy tales and identifies these as the source of our delight in hearing the stories, he disclaims any intention of analyzing their literary, historical, or religious characteristics. His focus is on these tales as the one art form fully comprehensible to children, one which speaks to them on unconscious as well as conscious levels, conveying an appreciation of their struggles and promising the happy ending which makes their struggles worthwhile.

The view outlined in the preceding paragraph clearly depends on a theory of child development—of how children think and feel at various ages and what enables them to mature. Bettelheim's orientation is psychoanalytic, and the familiar Freudian stages and symbols are referred to throughout the book. His handling of these topics is extraordinarily sensitive. Take, for example, the following quotation from his discussion of living "happily ever after" and the fact that fairy tales do not specify details of the hero's later life with the princess he has won:

> A child cannot and does not want to imagine what is actually involved in being a husband and father. . . . The little boy certainly doesn't want Mother to be busy with housekeeping or taking care of other children. He doesn't want to have sex with her either, because that is still an area full of conflict for him, if he has much awareness of it at all. As in most fairy tales, the little boy's ideal is just he and his princess (Mother), all their needs and wishes taken care of, living by themselves and for each other forever [*The Uses of Enchantment,* p. 112].

This is a description of Oedipal wishes and is identified as such, but it is both more accurate and more interesting than the stereotypes too often presented as "Freudian." Bettelheim's intimate knowledge of children and his feeling for them make this a very special book. He does not state his view of childhood and the human condition in any one part of the volume. Instead, he meshes fairy tale material and its interpretation with discussions of the human needs relevant to particular stories. This produces a loose structure which can be confusing and repetitive at times, but the book is rich enough to reward persistence. Indeed, this complexity of presentation may allow the reader, like the hearer of fairy tales, to accept what is helpful at the moment, returning to different aspects of the material later as different needs arise. I have summarized some of Bettelheim's central points below, but I encourage readers to work through *The Uses of Enchantment* themselves, making their own selections from its humane, literate, and curiously tough-minded contents.

Bettelheim's definition of fairy stories (which he differentiates from myths, fables, and cautionary tales) emphasizes their happy endings. As children hear many fairy tales and come to know that a satisfactory conclusion is guaranteed, they are increasingly able to enter into the events described. Children recognize intuitively that "once upon a time," is not "now" and that the stories are "unreal," although not "untrue." Their truth lies in the fact that they fit children's own preoccupations and ways of understanding the world. For example, the mortal terror, rage, despair, and triumph in fairy tales mirror the intensity of children's feelings. A belief in magic is not suggested to children by the stories but occurs spontaneously in their thinking, where animism, belief in the efficacy of wishes, and a conviction that death is reversible are characteristics well-established by contemporary research. Bettelheim feels that the punishments meted out to evil doers in fairy tales, which often seem cruel to adults, are reassuring to children, who feel more secure knowing that justice is done. Children are, he says, unable to identify their own intense and ambivalent emotions explicitly and need to organize their inner chaos by externalizing aspects of these feelings in different figures (wicked stepmother and fairy godmother, human child and his animal sibling, etc.). Fairy-tale characters, who are typically all good or all bad, gloriously beautiful or disgusting, facilitate this splitting and externalization, while the symbolic nature of the stories allows participation at whatever level of awareness the child is able to handle without too much anxiety or guilt. Bettleheim describes play and the fantasies children generate on their own as helpful in working out issues which are not too complex or anxiety provoking. The child by himself, however, tends to elaborate the developmental conflict he has actually reached. Fairy tales go further in suggesting types of solutions that may be effective and in promising a happy ending which the child himself cannot imagine. When Hansel and Gretel transcend their oral greed and act independently, they are able to live happily with their family; when Beauty gradually becomes accustomed to the Beast, she sees the appeal under his initially disgusting exterior and he turns into "Life's most delightful companion." The next developmental steps implied in fairy tales are psychologically accurate. The hope and fantasy satisfaction they consistently offer do not interfere with developing rationality, but give the child confidence enough to function in the world and develop realistic thinking. A rich fantasy life, as stimulated by the cultural heritage fairy tales transmit, does not interfere with mature functioning but provides additional resources for it. What makes fantasy unhealthy, on the other hand, is not effectiveness in providing pleasure but limited scope and compulsive repetition. To have heard about many kinds of monsters and ways of defeating them is to have hope and some sense of cultural support in one's efforts. To have met only one's interior monsters (through a conspiracy of silence about the darker side of others' lives) is to feel evil and alone. Unlike myths and cautionary tales, fairy stories "entice" children without telling them outright how they must choose. Fairy tales support the idea that individual striving against severe difficulties is essential, but the outcome pictured is independence, not obedience to instruction or custom. The reward is ruling one's kingdom (i.e., oneself) "as only those rule who have suffered many things."

Bettelheim prefers collections of fairy tales without illustrations, so the child's fantasy participation is maximized. He believes the stories are even more effective when told instead of read. The idea is to increase the interaction between adult and child, with parents' own motivations entering into the details emphasized or omitted, and the child's reactions modifying the story in turn. A fairy tale read only indicates that some adult, somewhere, understood the child's predicament. The same story told in the right spirit, with a parent responding to its pains and triumphs, makes a child feel understood in the deepest sense. "Understanding" here does not mean labeling what a child feels: "you enjoy Cinderella because you want to outdo your sisters," or "Little Red Riding Hood rather liked that wolf to begin with, didn't she?" The child's ability to respond to fairy tales without conscious awareness of the reason for his interest is crucial. To explain or label his involvement is to deprive him of an important way of working out feelings, to eliminate the very advantage which fairy tales have over "reasonable" discussion. Parents' conscious understanding of fairy-tales' themes may help guide their initial selection of stories to tell. But after this exposure a child's own preferences should be followed, while he is allowed to respond at his own level with time to mull over the story and freedom to ask for many repetitions if they're intriguing to him. The point is presenting delightful tales in which the child can gradually make discoveries for himself. Actually, although Bettelheim is discreet about making this point, fairy tales offer discoveries for adults too. We are reminded repeatedly of our blindness in undervaluing the "simpleton," the young child who understands in different but genuine ways; of the destructive force unleashed if we become jealous of a developing child; of children's need to go out into the world and win their own kingdoms; of the useful purposes served by periods of withdrawal and self-absorption, from which the "sleeping" child wakes to new maturity; of the importance of befriending our "animal" nature as a source of wisdom and pleasure. The focus on struggle and hope in fairy tales also speaks to adults and especially to parents. We must hope with our children— not by denying difficulties or presuming to specify outcomes but by affirming the value of effort, our own as well as theirs.

In comparison with other mental-health professionals, child psychologists, and educators, Bettelheim is distinguished by his emphasis on the ordeals children must face. These are not seen as unfortunate or unnecessary miseries to be prevented by good parents, good schools, and good children's literature. Bettelheim clearly views such struggles as essential to development, as the way we progress toward a more independent and satisfying life. His unflinching description of our fears and confusion is balanced by a lyric sense of the joy which can be found in relationships, in personal integration, and in achieving a sense of meaning. His book, like fairy tales themselves, presents the intensity and significance of life. That is a source of enchantment we should all seek to share.

Illustration

Collector's Items

Marian Parry

The Bear's Famous Invasion of Sicily, by Dino Buzzati. Illustrated by author. New York: Pantheon, 1947. Out of print.
Fletcher and Zenobia Save the Circus, by Edward Gorey. Illustrated by Victoria Chess. New York: Dodd, Mead & Co., 1971. $4.95.
Penny, by Beatrice Schenk de Regniers and Marvin Bileck. New York: Viking, 1966. Out of print.
What If?, by Joseph Low. Illustrated by author. New-York: Atheneum, 1976. $6.95.
Womenfolk and Fairy Tales. Edited by Rosemary Minard. Illustrated by Suzanna Klein. Boston: Houghton Mifflin, 1975. $5.95.

The application of Jung's ideas to children's literature has proved remarkably fruitful, particularly in articles which have appeared in this journal. Yet for some reason no mention has been made as yet of the Archetypal Collector of Illustrated Children's Books. In an art form where the basic assumptions are usually fantastic, it must follow that the Collector is no ordinary creature.

What is he like, this Imaginary Collector, the model for the widely varying real collectors?

I see him today as a lionlike creature, upright and often rampant. He has a powdered mane and 18th-century dress because of his devotion to elegance, form, charm, and the values of reason. The first assumptions in illustrated children's books may often be fantastic, but they are followed out in a reasonable and consistent manner.

The Collector's library is large, and the furniture in it is small; children come there to read in peaceful comfort. They must take off their shoes before they go in. Except for this detail, the reading room is exactly like the magic children's rooms in public libraries.

There are other rooms in the Palace of Illustrated Books, of course. The Imaginary Collector has genius, money, and space without limit. He has solved many seemingly insoluble problems which need not concern us here—such as how to display original book art in an unfolding consecutive sequence. It goes without saying that all his books have the best stories and/or the finest pictures. He buys many copies of each book; so he rarely has to think of touching the books in his innermost room, the Collector's Collection.

The Collector's Collection contains, in mint condition, one copy of every beautiful children's book which has ever been published. Very occasionally all other existing copies of a book are read "to pieces" by children. In ordinary libraries the vanishing of books is taken for granted: even the Archetypal Collector can't prevent it. And so it happens that at times museums and rare book libraries send emissaries to the library begging the Collector to allow them to display books from his inner collection. He always refuses, with a stance more rampant than usual: "You may display any of my other books, gentlemen," he says. "The choice is large. Isn't it a pity that you didn't collect children's books in the long period when illustration was out of fashion in New York art circles? I can remember when the word 'illustration' was an insult to a picture. Illustrated children's books were an economic miracle put together for a fraction of the cost of other illustrated books by laboring artists and devoted editors and art editors." A lecture, even by this remarkable creature, can become boring. The emissaries gnash their teeth and yawn at the same time: the Collector sees that it's time to end the conversation and get back to his books.

"My servant Ariel," he says, "will be delighted to show you the books which can be sent out for public display. I am sure you will not object to removing your shoes." And with gestures more courtly than his words, he bows them out of the palace office.

The Collector returns to the world of illustrated children's books, a world of imaginary worlds. Each fantasy book has its fantastic first assumptions:

> Sit still as mice on this occasion
> And listen to the Bear's Invasion
> Of Sicily, a long long while
> Ago when beasts were good, men vile.

The first assumption of the *Bear's Famous Invasion of Sicily* is a world inhabited in an organized way by bears. It is a world of precipices and mountains, castles and monsters, astrologers, magicians, and ghosts, drawn in ink and water color.

The actual drawing of each bear is just about identical. The story is full of crises and excitement. The reader is rushed from danger to danger, and as he goes along he searches eagerly in the pictures for clues so that he can be sure which bear is which.

There are clues, careful clues, altogether in character. And so while each eye is a dot and each shape is almost the same, the main bear-characters become important creatures, intimately known to the reader. Each character develops and grows in individuality. In the end it is surprising to realize how extremely simple and spare the drawing is. There is not an extra line or dot.

Some of the charm of this kind of drawing is like that of a stuffed animal or of a puppet skillfully handled. To a child his stuffed bear doesn't always have the same expression—quite the contrary. A good puppeteer can make us feel changes in physiognomy even of a tomato or a potato. There's an extra dimension to this kind of drawing when it works. The viewer, without realizing it, does a lot of the invention of the characters himself. In the *Invasion of Sicily* the viewer's imagination creates whole populations out of all the little, lively, identical bears.

Invasion is a small epic—a heroic tale. It contains both triumph and tragedy; shows us night, day, monsters, storms, and even a funeral; it explores the perils of success and worldly glory; and teaches about good and evil. All this is done with a world view which is even clearer in the pictures than in the story. We see the world in great panoramas. We see mountains, oceans, cities, a fortress, and a castle cut in half so that we can watch the ghosts dancing. And in all this we watch our bear-characters being heroes and villains. Monsters larger than a hundred bears attack them while the little figures fight bravely. But the greatest danger is the effect of luxury. Possibly the best of the pictures is the inner view of four stories of a gambling den, cut in half like a doll house. It repays lengthy perusal.

The illustrated books discussed here do not just present a fantastic world to a child. They also involve the child reader, who has only to accept the first assumptions in order to find himself in that world. Once there, he searches the illustrations and finds many things which are not in the story itself. The drawings are an invitation to continue imagining along the same line.

The story of *Penny* by Beatrice Schenck de Regniers, is a new version of *Thumbelina*. It is told with good pacing and a poetic style without adjectives or soppy embellishment. Old stories are often the best, but most retellings are not nearly as good as this one.

The illustrations are the best I've seen yet by Marvin Bileck. It is the world of a little girl "no bigger than a penny," a world of soft, mysterious, intricately detailed watercolor and pastel pencil colors. The main figures are colored just a little darker than the others. There are rushes by the water reminiscent of the "dream rushes" in Alice in Wonderland. One feels the presence of each leaf on the plants, each petal on the flowers, each scale on the turtle, each hair on the rabbit.

The viewer of course feels no bigger than a penny. Caught up in the story, the reader rides the enormous turtle past the giant columns of the lower rungs of a Victorian chair. The knobs have the dimensions of the temple of Karnak. The folds in the turtle's legs seem like the wrinkled legs of an old elephant or old socks falling about a giant's ankle.

This world is often seen in panorama—in far off views of whole worlds which are both fairy-tale and real at once. Villages, trees, rocks, wagons, and people are all parts of a perfectly meshed, pale puzzle. The pages are a kind of treasure hunt.

Some of the hunt takes place within the spaces of large capital letters—a new version of a medieval convention. A large letter *S*, for example, is above the paragraph: "So the old woman made a *big* wedding cake. And Penny made her own wedding dress." In the upper part of the *S* we see the old woman, working in her fairytale kitchen. There are crocks and a barrel, all in sepia pencil. The old woman's kind face, her bonnet, her smile, her skirt bulging out like the top of a pumpkin in distinct pleats, all are contained in a drawing no bigger than a penny. The eye searches eagerly in this little area, inventing crocks and churns and barrels, spoons and herrings, fairy-tale kitchen apparatus.

Miniaturization like Bileck's is psychically important to children. Children feel inferior to the world where they are always smaller. Miniaturization shows them objectively positive values in the very small and, more important, gives an objective distance to the place of various sizes in the scale of creation.

Three books discussed here are still in print and can be aquired by real as well as by imaginary collectors.

Womenfolk and Fairy Tales is a collection of fairy tales which "present their women as active, intelligent, capable, and courageous human beings." It contains many classic stories, among them "Mollie Whuppie," "Mr. Fox," "East of the Sun and West of the Moon." This is not the place to discuss the fantastic first assumptions of fairy tales, even if Bruno Bettelheim's *Uses of Enchantment* had not begun to explore their implications. These are stories of the highest literary and psychic merit.

The illustrations by Susanna Klein are curiously solid, unsentimental, original, and brilliant. They combine seeming opposites: the world of fairy tales and individual, even rather familiar, figures. A princess may look like your neighbor. There's no touch of Hollywood in this vision.

Susanna Klein works with pencil. Her pictures are full of shading and texture: walls and hills must represent many hours of work. Her patience and her original use of space and perspective combine to give a solid quality to her figures—a convincing feeling of reality in clearly invented fantasy. For example, the elephant on the cover has a round opening which shows people inside carrying on their lives with self-sufficient resourcefulness. The scene and the elephant are both two-dimensional and three-dimensional at once—both solid and flat—making the scene both fantastic and real simultaneously.

On p. 108 there is a particularly effective picture illustrating "the husband who was to mind the house." The husband stands in despair tearing his hair; he is a stalwart, mustached figure. You have seen his counterpart on the street, though not dressed in clothes of a peasant-past. In the foreground is the main figure, a pig standing in and drinking from a huge puddle of cream. He is a concrete abstract of all pigs: his white rump and body are like a sausage stuffed with lard. The pig's entire being is focused on the pleasure of swilling the cream; his snout is deep in the cream puddle. It is a drawing which ought to give the viewer some of the satisfaction the pig is feeling.

Susanna Klein's feeling for daily faces and her use of three-dimensionality can bring the child's vision back to the world around him. After looking at this book the child will be able to imagine his brother or sister or parents—even himself—in the world of the fairy tale and in a spirit far from Walt Disney flattery.

Collectors of children's books will surely want to acquire every book they can find by Joseph Low. *What If?* asks fantastic questions in riddle form. So, in a way, it is a quintessence of the fantastic assumptions of children's illustrated fantasy books: "What if a Martian wanted to marry you? Give him your bike and say, I'm sure you'd be much happier with my sister."

Joseph Low throws us into a wonderful imaginary world where little children with wit and presence deal happily and lightly with outrageous, impossible, and dangerous situations. We see them facing not only a creature from Mars but also a lion, Blackbeard, a shark, a dragon, a dinosaur, and other large and dangerous creatures.

The drama of turning the pages fits in with the riddle form. The question is on the right-hand page, and the child must turn the page to get the answer, which appears on the left side. And he finds a new danger waiting for him on the right.

This book is a *tour-de-force* as far as color is concerned. It is done in black line with grey and a yellow which shades from gamboge to a light orangey color: a feeling of lightness and great variety is achieved with only two colors.

Every line that Joseph Low has drawn in this book is alive. He draws and paints so that it seems that the ink and wash were put down only a moment before you looked. You feel the touch of Low's hand in each scratch of shading on a cloud, each whisker on the muzzle of a lion. There's not a clichéd dot or dash to be seen. Everything is fresh and immediately felt. Each creature and each child is a new invention—a new comic creation.

Fletcher and Zenobia Save the Circus is written by Edward Gorey, whose many illustrated books are collector's items. Victoria Chess is the right illustrator for his sophisticated text. What are the fantastic assumptions here? It's the world you would see if a cat named Fletcher could talk and was almost exactly the same size as an enterprising little girl named Zenobia. Paper maché heads that are used in an animal circus fit Fletcher exactly. Objects fly through the air and land with remarkable convenience where we all find ourselves, in a French café. The development which follows is logical and triumphant.

There are ten full-color pictures and a colored cover to emphasize the gaiety of this remarkable world. But it's the black-and-white pictures of Fletcher and Zenobia throughout the book that somehow weave the central thread of the story. The story unravels in highly sophisticated conversations and jokes which will amuse adults as well as children. Fletcher is like a loveable and not quite self-confident younger brother. Zenobia is fearless and brilliant and enterprising. Why are Fletcher and Zenobia so funny? Is it their zany smiles or Zenobia's girlish postures or Fletcher's bottom and tail? Luckily such charm cannot be put into any formula. "I know I'm fine figure of a cat," says Fletcher modestly, "but I wonder if I don't make a rather small rhinoceros?" Zenobia looks at him with a critical eye, and then shrugs. "After all, these *are* the provinces; they can't reasonably expect. . . " Fletcher looks downcast. "Besides," Zenobia adds quickly, "what you lack in quantity, as it were, you more than make up for—"

Criticism of Children's Literature

A Review of Children's Literature Anthologies and Core Texts

Claudia Lewis

Anthology of Children's Literature, by Edna Johnson, Evelyn R. Sickels, and Frances Clarke Sayers. Illustrated by Fritz Eichenberg. Fourth edition. Boston: Houghton Mifflin Co., 1970. $15.50.

The Arbuthnot Anthology of Children's Literature, by May Hill Arbuthnot. Fourth edition revised by Zena Sutherland. Chicago: Scott, Foresman, and Co., 1976. $15.95.

A Book of Children's Literature, by Lillian Hollowell. New York: Holt, Rinehart and Winston, 1966. $12.50.

Children and Books, by May Hill Arbuthnot and Zena Sutherland. Fourth edition. Chicago: Scott, Foresman and Co., 1972. $14.95.

Children Experience Literature, by Bernard J. Lonsdale and Helen K. Macintosh. New York: Random House, 1973. $11.95.

Children's Literature in the Elementary School, Charlotte S. Huck. Third edition. New York: Holt, Rinehart and Winston, 1976. $13.95.

Children and Their Literature, by Constantine Georgiou. New York: Prentice-Hall, 1969. $11.95.

A Critical Approach to Children's Literature, by James Steel Smith. New York: McGraw-Hill, 1967. $10.50.

An Introduction to Children's Literature, by Mary J. Lickteig. Columbus, Ohio: Charles E. Merrill Publishing Co., 1975. $11.95.

Literature for Children. Ed. by Pose Lamb. Dubuque, Iowa: Wm. C. Brown Co., Publishers:

Children's Literature in the Curriculum, by Mary Montebello. 1972. $3.50.

Enrichment Ideas, by Ruth Kearney Carlson. 1976. $3.50.

History and Trends, by Margaret Gillespie. 1970. $2.95.

Illustrations in Children's Books, by Patricia Cianciolo. 1976. $3.50.

Its Discipline and Content, by Bernice E. Cullinan. 1971. $2.95.

Poetry in the Elementary School, by Virginia Witucke. 1970. $2.95.

Storytelling and Creative Drama, by Dewey W. Chambers. 1970. $2.50.

Literature for Thursday's Child, by Sam Leaton Sebesta and William J. Iverson. Chicago: Science Research Associates, Inc., 1975. $10.95.

A New Look at Children's Literature, by William Anderson and Patrick Groff. Bibliography compiled by Ruth Robinson. Belmont, Cal.: Wadsworth Publishing Co., Inc., 1972. $12.95.

Now Upon A Time A Contemporary View of Children's Literature. Myra Pollack Sadker and David Miller Sadker. New York: Harper & Row, Publishers, 1977. $13.95.

Sharing Literature With Children, by Francelia Butler. Cover design by Maurice Sendak. New York: Longmans, Inc., 1977. $19.95. Paper, $9.95.

Word Music and Word Magic Children's Literature Methods, by James A. Smith and Dorothy M. Park. Boston: Allyn and Bacon, Inc., 1977. $13.95.

Children's Literature: An Issues Approach, by Masha Kabakow Rudman. Boston: D. C. Heath and Co., 1976. $11.95. Paper, $6.95.

A Critical Handbook of Children's Literature, by Rebecca J. Lukens. Chicago: Scott, Foresman and Co., 1976. $4.50.

A Parent's Guide to Children's Reading, by Nancy Larrick. With Illustrations from Fifty Favorite Children's Books. Fourth edition. New York: Doubleday and Co., Inc., 1975. $8.95. Paper, Bantam Books, 1975. $1.95.

Which anthology? Which text? Ten years ago this was not as difficult a question for college teachers of Children's Literature as it may be today. Anthologies were represented only by the two giants, Arbuthnot and Johnson, Sickels, and Sayers—plus Hollowell of slightly smaller scope and intent. And as for core texts—books about books and their use in the classroom—here again, two giants stood alone: Arbuthnot's *Children and Books* and the Huck and Kuhn *Children's Literature in the Elementary School.*

Today to my knowledge there is only one additional new anthology on the horizon, but the core texts have proliferated. Large and beautifully produced books—how does one make a choice among them? This review will attempt to pinpoint their purposes and appeals.

First a few comments about the anthologies. The two giants have both been brought up to date, Johnson, Sickels, and Sayers as of 1970 (1289 pp.) and Arbuthnot as of 1976 (1120 pp.), the latter a revision by Zena Sutherland. Both books use the genre approach; both take a broad look at the field and include more travel, fact, and science than in the earlier editions, as well as more literature from and about minorities in the United States.

It is the expectation of both editors that the books may be used as texts in the Children's Literature classes, and to this end there are expository introductions for each section and brief commentaries before each entry. Furthermore, both include important supplementary sections to round out the literary experience for the student. Johnson, Sickels, and Sayers offer appendices on storytelling, the history of children's literature, and illustrations and illustrators; while in Arbuthnot there are two full additional articles, one by Donnarae MacCann and Olga Richard on "Illustrations in Children's Books," including discussion of old and new trends, and a final full section by Sam Leaton Sebesta and Dianne L. Monson on "Guiding the Literary Experience." Abundant bibliographies and award lists are included in both books.

How to make a choice between them? It is up to the individual instructor. Some may be especially glad to find in Arbuthnot a great many of the poetry selections making up the popular Arbuthnot collection, *Time for Poetry,* or to find here a short section on Science Fiction. On the other hand, Johnson, Sickels, and Sayers offer "Sacred Writings and Legends of the Saints," including not only selections from the Bible but from Hindu, Taoist, and other Far Eastern scriptures.

This can be said of both books: the purpose is wide coverage, a skimming of the field to introduce students to the categories that exist and to some of the best in poetry, fiction, and fact, with the hope that in depth reading will follow. Criticism in depth has not been the aim, nor has there been an attempt to stir up the critical thinking of the reader relative to such questions as how a child finds meaning in what he reads. In relation to folk tales and myths, for instance, one looks in vain for thinking on the level of Bruno Bettelheim's in the book that has recently aroused the children's literature community, *The Uses of Enchantment: The Meaning and Importance of Fairy Tales.*[1] But one must say that the aims, limited though they may be, have been successfully realized. The two books are monumental achievements and surely no one would deny their overall usefulness.

The Hollowell anthology (580 pp.) is a well-produced, thoughtfully put-together introductory book for a one-semester course—as well as for librarians and parents. It also follows the genre approach, but its introductory sections and descriptive entries are extremely brief and often superficial, in view of the need to cover the field in about half the length of the two giants. Though it has not been revised since 1966, it is up-to-date in many ways, for instance in its stance on shunning stereotypes in books about Negroes and Indians, and in its bibliographies which aim to meet a variety of current interests. As in the other two anthologies, there are excellent appendices on the history of children's books and on illustrations. Brevity, however, seems the best word to characterize the overall result.

The new anthology, *Sharing Literature With Children,* offers an entirely different type of thematic approach, as the author, Francelia Butler, explains in her preface: "Besides being a collection of literature to be supplied to children, the book offers a theory about children's literature which grows out of something we have all experienced and sensed intuitively—that the most deeply moving literature seems to center in certain basic symbolic themes that keep recurring like the patterns in music." The genres emerge, but they are subsidiary in this approach, which uses as main topics "*Toys and Games,*" "*Fools,*" "*Sex Roles,*" "*Masks and Shadows,*" and "*Circles.*" The reader is caught up in a feeling of excitement over the book's grand design and is swept at once into large vistas where his thoughts are extended. The publication of this book, in the spring of 1977, is one of the major children's literature events of the year.

Now let us consider the core texts, those large, heavy, beautifully produced and illustrated books about books and children's use of them. As the two giants stand now, the Arbuthnot *Children and Books* is a 1972 expanded version (836 pp.) with Zena Sutherland coauthor. *Children's Literature in the Elementary School* is a new 1976 third edition, by Charlotte S. Huck (814 pp.). Both are indispensable and magnificent resource books providing up-to-date, broad coverage not only in their annotations but in what is offered to help the teacher in the classroom. Arbuthnot and Sutherland include new sections on television, series books, multi-media centers, comics, as well as articles by Anne Pellowski on "Internationalism in Children's Literature" and by John Donovan on "Book Promotion." A number of other articles by specialists round out this section.

Just as broad and up-to-date in its coverage and attitudes is the text by Charlotte Huck. Readers will find books representing all the contemporary issues in realistic fiction discussed and weighed here; poetry fully presented, with an eye on what pleases children today; a picture book section that aims to give the reader new perspectives; and a pervading attitude that shows a concern for making critical readers out of children. The final sections on literature programs in the schools are rich in suggestions for helping children get the most out of their reading.

Is anything lacking, then? Almost nothing. But just as in the case of the two large anthologies (where there is such a wide sweep), there is some loss in depth. In *Children and Books,* for instance, we are told that the psychological implications in Sendak's *Where the Wild Things Are* (Harper) are sound—but we are left to wonder just what these psychological implications are. And there is no hint of what Sendak's *Higglety Pigglety Pop* (Harper) may be all about. Likewise, the reader suspects that *Alice in Wonderland* really has more to offer than just "nonsense" and "wild logic." And in the Huck text one looks in vain for probing thinking regarding the enormous popularity of such picture books as Steig's *Sylvester and the Magic Pebble* (Simon and Schuster) and de Regniers' *May I Bring A Friend?* (Atheneum). Arranged thematically, *Now Upon a Time* is a book about children's literature, and *Word Music and Word Magic* has a methods approach. Both contain tips on how to teach.

Some of the smaller texts now appearing on the scene go into a little more depth, at least in certain areas. First let me mention briefly two that do not expand the picture at all in terms of critical thinking. Georgiou's *Children and Their Literature* (501 pp.) is short on in-depth discussion and long on enthusiasm. Its annotated bibliographies may be its most useful feature. Lickteig's *An Introduction to Children's Literature* (432 pp.) is strictly what its title indicates—an "introduction." Because the attempt is a brief coverage of the whole field, the result is a book crammed with titles and lists. Brief annotations may tell what happens in a book, but not what the book is really about. The bibliographies are unannotated and without grade-level indications.

A third new book, Lonsdale and Macintosh's *Children Experience Literature* (540 pp.) is not outstanding for what I have been calling "depth" yet has a fresh, original approach and a concern for practical application that should make it very useful for teachers. In the first place its plan of presentation is inviting. The authors use their own system of classification, eventually covering all the genres except information books. Teachers should welcome the chapters on "Teachers Study Children," "Meeting People Through Literature"—offering abundant listings of books about children in other countries—and "Literature and Personal Growth." It also offers very contemporary chapters on poetry and science fiction. Scattered throughout are pertinent bibliographies and suggestions for extending the experiences of both reader and children. The useful appendix lists numerous sources.

And now we come to three of the newer texts that do indeed expect of the reader some critical thinking in depth. James Steel Smith's *A Critical Approach to Children's Literature* (442 pp.) places emphasis all along the way on central critical questions such as the nature of literary value in children's literature. In Anderson and Groff's *A New Look at Children's Literature* (362 pp.) the attempt throughout is to encourage the reader's own critical, perceptive approach; while the stress in Sebesta and Iverson's *Literature for Thursday's Child* (565 pp.) is always on themes and values and the meaning of books to children. At the same time, all three texts aim to offer the student more than a brief coverage of the field.

More specifically, Smith's book, the work of a man who has been a college teacher of literature for both children and adults, gives the reader the feeling of moving along in a college course with a very stimulating instructor. The usual genre survey is avoided, but in the long run the major types of writings are covered. In addition there is a thought-provoking section on the cultural context today, including children's exposure to oral literature in the home, neighborhood, and school, as well as in advertising.

The Anderson and Groff book (362 pp.) does not attempt a broad coverage of every genre or of all today's controversial issues. However, it offers very full bibliographies and important highlights, often with a focus on helping the reader place pieces of children's literature in context. For instance, in the fantasy section several pages are devoted to a discussion of *Alice in Wonderland*

and its devices and similarities to fairy tale. (How refreshing to find more than just a brief annotation on *Alice*!) Throughout the text the suggestions for the teacher are provocative, specific, and helpful. The book is obviously addressed to the mature student who has some knowledge of child development and of Piaget and has the ability to read and appreciate well-written literary criticism.

In Sebesta and Iverson's *Literature for Thursday's Child* (565 pp.) a new format immediately strikes the eye. Booklists are set off in boxes at suitable points, and a number of complete stories and many additional single pages are reproduced from the original books. There is wide coverage of books, bibliographies, and activities here as in most of the other texts, but with some special emphases that give this book its own tone. Always in the forefront is the conviction that literature study should bring "high joy" to children. Again and again the authors stress that basic reading instruction and the teaching of literature should be treated as distinctive enterprises, and their major concern is with ways of enriching the reading experience—that is, of helping children find ways to relate *themselves* to a story. Some knowledge of "literary elements," they believe, enhances children's appreciation and enjoyment, and they offer many examples of how skilled writers have succeeded. Three and a half pages are devoted to *Charlotte's Web* (Harper) alone, to show how E. B. White has unified the elements of this story. In connection with this look at "Literature and the Creative Process," the importance of children's own writing is recognized, and an article by Helen Danforth on this topic is reproduced from *Elementary English* (April 1960). Throughout this fresh, innovative book, values and an exploratory, thinking approach are paramount.

This brings us to the end of the large core texts. However, there are the seven small books that form an entity under the overall title, *Literature for Children*, edited by Pose Lamb. A good deal of the content of the larger texts is covered in these separate, easily handled books, most of them only a little over 100 pages in length. Four are mainly utilitarian, with the teacher and his/her curriculum needs always in mind: *Children's Literature in the Curriculum* by Mary Montebello; *Storytelling and Creative Drama* by Dewey W. Chambers; *Enrichment Ideas* by Ruth Kearney Carlson; and *Poetry in the Elementary School* by Virginia Witucke. When we come to Margaret Gillespie's *History and Trends* we have a full coverage that brings the reader up to the present from beginnings in the 15th century, a more extensive treatment than can be found in the giant anthologies and texts. The same can be said of Patricia Cianciolo's *Illustrations in Children's Books,* a very thorough look that includes a sixty-page annotated "Bibliography of Illustrated Books." Finally, in Bernice E. Cullinan's *Literature for Children: Its Discipline and Content,* we have a scholarly yet very readable consideration of some of the literary elements of narrative fiction. The belief here is that "a sensitive recognition of what makes a piece of writing effective" can raise literary taste and increase pleasure in reading. (Sebesta and Iverson would no doubt agree.) Dr. Cullinan believes that arid analyses are inappropriate in the elementary school, but that children appreciate stimulating critical questions that elicit higher level thinking skills.

A small new book similar in intent though broader in its coverage is Rebecca J. Lukens' *A Critical Handbook of Children's Literature* (214 pp.). Not intended as a complete course in Children's Literature, it could be a useful supplement; and would-be writers for children might well study its careful examination of the elements of character, plot, setting, theme, point of view, style, and tone. The author considers not only fiction—with *Charlotte's Web* the touchstone—but also poetry, nonfiction, and biography. An extremely well-written book, it is a small work of art in itself.

Another new book that could be used as a supplement is Masha Kabakow Rudman's *Children's Literature: An Issues Approach* (433 pp.). The concern here is to help teachers—and children—examine books critically, actively reject all stereotyping, and search out basic values and attitudes when evaluating books. The issues covered here—very fully—are siblings, divorce, death and old age, war, sex, the Black, the native American, and the female. Reprinted (with adaptations) is the Council on Interracial Books for Children's "Ten Quick Ways to Analyze Books for Racism and Sexism"; also the McGraw-Hill "Guidelines for Equal Treatment of the Sexes." The author invites readers to disagree with her, and undoubtedly many will, over a few of the judgments that flow from her strongly felt commitments. It would be interesting for college students to compare her coverage and approach with Charlotte Huck's in *Children's Literature in the Elementary School.* In addition to Rudman's consideration of issues, she has a useful chapter on "Using Children's Books in a Reading Program." Book Award lists, publisher's addresses, and abundant bibliographies are included.

It would be a mistake to conclude this review without mentioning Nancy Larrick's vastly popular *A Parent's Guide to Children's Reading*. Addressed primarily to parents rather than to teachers and not conceived of as a "core text," still it is one of the most useful books on the market and indeed does appear as required reading in college courses. The new 4th edition (432 pp., paper 374 pp.) provides not only a very up-to-date coverage of books and an overview of children's reading interests through the grades, but also a new section on recordings, filmstrips, and films. There is something here for everyone who has an interest in children and reading and is looking for a lively book that reflects the wide knowledge of an expert.

NOTES

1. Bruno Bettelheim, *The Uses of Enchantment: The Meaning and Importance of Fairy Tales* (New York: Alfred A. Knopf, 1976).

The World of Children's Theatre

Nellie McCaslin

Children's Theatre and Creative Dramatics: An Annotated Bibliography of Critical Works, by Rachel Fordyce. Boston: G. K. Hall and Co., 1975. $21.00.

Children's Theatre and Creative Dramatics: An Annotated Bibliography of Critical Works is an important addition to this area of the theatre arts. Published in 1975 and including entries up to 1973, this book should be of particular interest to scholars and librarians. The

2269 titles make it a comprehensive work; it is hoped that the publisher will plan to have it up-dated regularly as the literature in the field increases. Although there are two other similar bibliographies available from the American Theatre Association, *Creative Drama* by Mary Klock and *Children's Theatre* by Wesley Van Tassell, each contains only one hundred titles, selected by the authors to meet the needs of students and children's theatre practitioners. The original works, like the Fordyce work, were also doctoral studies and, therefore, definitive.

Rachel Fordyce limits her bibliography to literature of a critical, instructural, and evaluative nature. She states in her preface that she has not included anthologies of plays unless they offer critical comment; nor has she included book reviews that do not go beyond the limitations of the review article. Her annotations are brief; indeed, one could wish for more information than she gives in many instances. The entries are categorized under "Children's Theatre and Creative Dramatics" (combined), "Children's Theatre," and "Creative Dramatics." Within each category she groups what she considers to be significant topics. In the first category she lists Bibliographies, Directories, and Reference Works; Theory and Evaluation of the Fields; Related Activities; Recreational Activities; and Outside the USA. In the other two categories she includes History, Pre-1950; Development, 1950-1973; Individual Plays and Playwriting for Children; Technical Aspects; and In Education and the Schools. The last topic is further divided into the specific areas of Literature and Language Arts; Sciences and Social Sciences; Special Education; and Religious Education.

This reviewer would like to have found a Subject Index in the book. Fordyce includes only an Author Index; this is useful to one who knows the field but it is not sufficient for the student trying to find material on a particular organization or place. This is a minor criticism, however, for the book is a monumental work and the author and publisher are to be commended for making it available at a time when the field is expanding so rapidly.

The Girl Sleuth

A Feminist Guide

Joan Joffe Hall

The Girl Sleuth: A Feminist Guide; by Bobbie Ann Mason. 144 pp. Illustrated. Old Westbury, New York: The Feminist Press. $3.75.

Like most nostalgia, *The Girl Sleuth,* a first-rate guide to series such as *Honey Bunch, The Bobbsey Twins, Nancy Drew, Judy Bolton,* and others, is profoundly ambivalent about its subject. And this is because Bobbie Ann Mason's own childhood was deeply influenced by her reading of this type of fiction. Only in books did she visit homes with central heating; only in books did she glimpse an escape from rural domesticity into a world of exciting and independent girlhood. Even while she deplores, then, she cherishes. A similar complexity lies at the heart of many good studies in popular culture.

Mason points out that although girl adventure stories began out of the "stirrings of liberation" before the turn of the century, and although the automobile and airplane soon came to represent, in the hands of these heroines, outdoorsiness and mechanical skill, much of what a child learns from such fiction contradicts mobility and nestles in the bosom of convention.

Nancy Drew first appeared in a book in 1929 and the series has been put out at the rate of about a book a year since then, regardless of Crash, Depression, War. Nancy is the ideal girl—smart, beautiful, poised, forever-young, financially independent. She has no mother to nag her but a wonderful daddy always ready to come to her rescue. She always knows how to act; when a leading lady falls ill, she can take her place after only one rehearsal. "Once!" Mason sighs, "I feel as if I have rehearsed my whole life." In her blue roadster Nancy is the embodiment of both real and illusory independence. "The books hold up one image of life and teach another." Nancy is trapped by the ideals she represents. Servants must know their place; undesirables and members of minority groups are likely to be villainous (except that's where the mystery is!); refinement and virtue are class determined; and the story's "job is to preserve class lines." Moreover, appearance and reality correspond perfectly in these mysteries with a regularity that would make a girl a "moral midget."

Sexually, too, Nancy's independence is a sham. She has a boyfriend, Nick, but whereas real girls giggle or worry about shaving their legs, Nancy is never either insecure or aroused. She is buffered by her two friends, silly Bess and tomboy George, female types "we are taught to loathe," who represent the extremes Nancy must shun. At her best Nancy "trespasses into male territory without giving up female advantages." Yet though she must not be silly it's seldom through intellect that she solves the mystery: coincidence does that. And so the typical Nancy Drew plot is like a "sonnet" with its variations, an enlarged dollhouse. Like *Honey Bunch* for little girls the Nancy Drew mystery provides the teenager with a "perfect playhouse," while luring her with the possibilities of adventure. The ultimate mystery to the adolescent girl is sex, of course, but from sex Nancy runs full speed, all the while chasing "substitute forms of evil." Ironically, at the solving of each mystery Nancy finds "the very world—the happy ending . . . the symbolic wedding—she seeks to escape."

For all Mason's disapproval, she loves Nancy Drew. Judy Bolton, whom she finds more individualized, more in contact with the real problems of girls, and more sympathetic to wrongdoers, gets only one-third Nancy's space. Nancy Drew is the female version of Tom Sawyer, especially if one remembers Leslie Fiedler's view of Tom as the Good Bad Boy, whose rebelliousness is real but superficial and who endorses the values—the slavery and violence—of his culture. Nancy is the conventional independent girl, the adolescent Honey Bunch (whose very name suggests both purity and sexuality). And if Tom Sawyer grows up to be Mark Twain, small wonder the avid reader of Nancy Drew grows up to be a sleuth, a scholar like Bobbie Ann Mason, whose first book was a study of *Lolita*.

At times Mason's style itself gives the reader the charming impression that she and we are together uncovering a mystery. She exemplifies one of the happiest results of feminist perception, that scholarly study is not disinterested—no more than reading is disinterested: it is personal. Her own rural southern childhood is as vital to this book as any exotic land the Bobbsey twins might visit.

Mason's book is delightful not only because of her method of "revelation," but also because of her evident love of this fiction—and for her insight into how it stimulates girls deprived of other and more admirable examples of female strength and independence even while it holds out conventional and impossibly idealized figures for girls to emulate.

Two Catalogs

Charity Chang

The Osborne Collection of Early Children's Books, 1476–1910, a Catalogue, Volume II. Ed. by Judith St. John. Toronto: Toronto Public Library, 1975. $25.00.
Early Children's Books and Their Illustration. Compiled by Gerald Gottleib. New York: Pierpont Morgan Library and Boston: David R. Godine, Publisher, 1975. $35.00.

Several publications of major importance in the field of children's literature have recently appeared. Outstanding among these are *The Osborne Collection of Early Children's Books, 1476–1910, a Catalogue,* Volume II and *Early Children's Books and Their Illustration.* Both catalogs are significant bibliographic works.

The first of these is a companion volume to *The Osborne Collection of Early Children's Books, 1566–1910, a Catalogue,* Volume I, published in 1958. Miss Judith St. John, curator of the Osborne Collection at the Boys and Girls House of Toronto Public Library and editor of both volumes of the Osborne catalogs, points out in her preface to Volume II that the Osborne collection has grown fivefold through gifts and purchases since Dr. Edgar Osborne presented his personal collection, described in Volume I of the catalogs, to the Toronto Public Library in 1949. Hence, the serious need for Volume II, which contains almost as many items as the first volume. Collectively the two volumes enumerate and bibliographically describe around four-fifths of the total Osborne collection of some 10,000 books.

Miss St. John was assisted in the preparation of Volume II by Miss Dana Tenny and Miss Hazel McTaggart. Volume II continues the pagination of the earlier volume and adheres to the same format, volume size, and cover design. Likewise it meets the high bibliographic standards characterizing Volume I. Regrettable, yet understandable in view of today's high cost of publishing, Volume II is void of color illustrations such as those appearing in Volume I, except for the colored frontispiece portrait of Dr. Osborne. The current volume, however, does contain a number of suitable and carefully chosen black-and-white illustrations. Two sections included in Volume I—"Periodicals and Annuals" and "Penny Dreadfuls"—have been purposefully omitted from Volume II.

These sections and other miscellanea such as holograph letters, original art, and the like, as well as a cumulative index and expanded appendices, are envisioned inclusions for a future Volume III, according to a recent article by Miss St. John. The proposed Volume III would indeed be a useful complement to the current two-volume set.

Among other distinctively useful features of the Osborne catalogs are the splendidly informative annotations provided for many items, the valuable indexes, and the illustrative matter. Outstanding among the inclusions in Volume II are the first edition, in two parts, of James Janeway's *Token for Children* (1672) ; the unique second edition of Maria Edgeworth's *The Parent's Assistant* (1796) ; an English translation (1707) of *Diverting Works* by Madame D'Aulnoy; the 1697 edition of Perrault's *Histoires ou Contes du Temps Passé*; and the incunabulum *Historia de Lionbruno* (1476?). The two Osborne catalogs cover the period 1476-1910. Collectively they constitute a veritable treasure house of information for the world of scholarship in children's literature; at the same time they furnish the more casual user a wealth of pleasurable reading.

Early Children's Books and Their Illustration is a handsome book prepared in advance of, and in conjunction with, a major exhibition of early children's books, original illustrations, manuscripts, and letters at the Pierpont Morgan Library in New York City, 2 September–30 November 1975. The book serves as a partial catalog to the exhibit and discusses 225 of the items exhibited. Mr. Gerald Gottlieb, curator of Early Children's Books at the Pierpont Morgan Library, was responsible for the compilation of the exhibit catalog. The items exhibited were, with few exceptions, taken from the library's own children's literature resources which have, as Mr. Gottlieb points out, been immeasurably enriched in recent years. The gift in the 1960s of an outstanding juvenile literature collection assembled by Elizabeth Ball and the acquisition, also through Miss Ball's generosity, of the Gillett G. Griffin Collection of American children's books—a collection formed, for the most part, by Wilbur Macey Stone—are notable. The various collections already at the Pierpont Morgan Library and others promised to it constitute, in the words of the director, Mr. Charles Ryskamp, "an imcomparable source for the study and enjoyment of children's books and their illustration." (Preface, xii-xiii)

The commentary provided by Mr. Gottlieb for each of the books listed and the stunning photographic illustrations done by the library's chief photographer, Mr. Charles V. Passela, alone make *Early Children's Books and Their Illustration* one of the most exciting publication events of 1975. It is indeed this, but much more. Like the Osborne volumes, *Early Children's Books and Their Illustration* is also a monumental research tool containing a useful bibliography and index as well as rich prefatory and introductory matter. To single out any particular item or section of the book as being the most outstanding would be difficult. Suffice it to say that all the inclusions are exciting: fables, bestiaries, courtesy books, old tales, ABC's, emblem books, school books, and fairy tales. Again, like both the Osborne volumes, Mr. Gottlieb's volume makes interesting and informative reading for pleasure as well as for scholarship.

Children's Literature

A Resource for Collection Development

Charity Chang

Building a Children's Literature Collection. Middletown, Conn.: Choice, 1975. $3.95.

For academic libraries, either those only beginning to develop a children's literature collection or for those needing to further develop and strengthen already existent collections, *Building a Children's Literature Collection* is a valuable and welcome publication. Included in its thirty-four pages are two brief but excellent bibliographic essays, each followed by listings of materials appropriate for consideration by those attempting to build basic working research collections for academic libraries.

The first section done by Harriet B. Quimby and Clara O. Jackson, "Building a Children's Literature Collection: A Suggested Basic Reference Collection for Academic Libraries," includes informative and perceptive comments upon the role played by twentieth-century America "in the development and promotion of quality literature for children." The authors have noted that efforts

to develop and promote quality literature for children have resulted
in the creation of awards designed to stimulate excellence in both
writing and illustrating. Library schools, departments of English,
and schools of education have developed courses which attract
students and stimulate faculty awareness. Concurrently textbooks,
bibliographic aids of various kinds, and literary criticism have appeared, all of which have resulted in emphasis on building more
adequate collections to support academic programs dealing with
literature for children.

Despite the growing emphasis on building better and more adequate collections, Miss Quimby and Miss Jackson correctly observe that many academic collections in children's literature have
been built "in a hit or miss fashion in response to student and faculty demands." In their commendable effort to help overcome this
situation, they have provided helpful discussions on texts, histories, authors and illustrators; readings on children's literature;
awards and prizes; international children's literature; storytelling;
anthologies; and general selection aids. They have also made useful
comments concerning annual lists, professional reviewing journals,
areas of special interest, and writing books for children and young
people. Within the text of each subject discussed, the authors have
called attention to and meaningfully illuminated 150 or more works,
in print in 1974, which they feel are the best reference sources
available in support of all facets of children's literature currently
studied in major academic institutions.

Following their essay, authors Quimby and Jackson have provided a convenient alphabetical listing, by author, of all titles mentioned within the essay. Each listing includes full title, publisher,
and date. The list will be particularly useful to those in academic
libraries charged with the responsibility of selection or service
whose knowledge of the children's literature field is limited. It will
also be reassuring to those with expertise in children's literature
and experience in the library selection and service processes, to
say nothing of its value to students and faculty who may discover it
in using a library's children's literature resources.

Complementing the "Suggested Basic Reference Collection for
Academic Libraries" is the companion piece by Rosemary Weber
entitled "Building a Children's Literature Collection: A Suggested
Basic Collection of Children's Books." Miss Weber's listing of
some 800 or more titles includes fiction, picture and easy books,

folk literature, biography, poetry, and nonfiction. Her suggested basic collection represents a synthesis of titles suggested in the text or listed in the bibliographies of the following works: *A New Look at Children's Literature* by William Anderson and Patrick Groff (1972); *Children and Books,* ed. by May Hill Arbuthnot and Zena Sutherland (4th ed., 1972); *Picture Books for Children* by Patricia Cianciolo (1973); *Literature of Children: History and Trends* by Margaret C. Gillespie (1970); *Children's Books of International Interest,* ed. by Virginia Haviland (1972); *The Child's First Books* by Donnarae MacCann and Olga Richard (1973); *The Elementary School Library Collection,* 7th ed., Phase 1 titles (Bro-Dart, 1972); the H. W. Wilson *Children's Catalog* (12th ed., 1971) and *First Supplement* (1972); and *Children's Books: Awards and Prizes,* 1973 edition (Children's Book Council).

Miss Weber points out in her essay that she found greatest difficulty in compiling the listing of general nonfiction works, but commendably she has attempted to include in her nonfiction listing titles "by authors whose work rises above the mere purveying of information." The area of nonfiction is indeed a difficult selection area. As an aside, it seems worth observing that there are often strong differences of opinion among those involved in academic libraries in the collections development process as to what properly constitutes children's literature. Such differences can be problematic in the absence of clearly stated collection development policy. For those libraries without clearly stated collection development guidelines, Miss Weber's nonfiction listing containing some "representative titles in areas of contemporary social concern" should prove particularly helpful. Miss Weber's selections for all categories of her suggested basic collection are worth consideration by those who are attempting to build collections which provide students opportunity to read as widely as possible.

Miss Weber's suggested basic collection of children's books reflects, appropriately, that children's literature encompasses far more than children's fiction—a fact which appears not yet to be fully recognized nor more than minimally reflected in academic library collections.

It is timely, therefore, and immensely helpful that *Building a Children's Literature Collection* should appear.[1] For, in the words of John Donovan from the preface to this highly significant and useful bibliographic tool: "As more courses in children's literature are being taught yearly, and taught in greater depth, as well, it has been clear that college and university libraries would find it useful to assemble a core of books in this discipline that students would find useful, and that would be honestly reflective of a part of our literature that has undergone vast changes in the last decade and that continues to attract gifted artists and writers.''

NOTES

1. Although the textual content and bibliographic listings of *Building a Children's Literature Collection* appeared in *Choice* in the November and December issues of 1974, its appearance again in 1975 as a separate publication is particularly helpful since the separate publication contains the extremely useful author and title indexes.

Varia

Dissertations of Note

Compiled by Rachel Fordyce

Armstrong, Dennis Lee. "E. Nesbit: An Entrance to *The Magic City.*"
DAI 35: 7897 A. Johns Hopkins University, 1974. 300 pp.
Armstrong focuses on *The Magic City* because of its emblematic representation of the "complex world of E. Nesbit's narrative, a world centered upon and integrated by the child. . . ." The author analyzes Nesbit's magic tales, their narrative form, her employment of fairy-tale plotting, "The Book of Beasts," dreams, religious encounters, utopian visions, and preeminently, "the alienation of the child and the adult in Nesbit." Chapter VII, the final one, is devoted to *The Enchanted Castle.*

Cornelison, Gayle Lynn. "Death and Childhood: Attitudes and Approaches in Society, Children's Literature and Children's Theatre and Drama." DAI 37: 37 A. University of Kansas, 1975. 245 pp.
The major issue of Cornelison's dissertation is "can and should the topic of death be openly and honestly presented to children in their drama?" Chapter I is an introduction to the methodology of the dissertation; Chapter II "explores the child's concept of death through a review of appropriate scientific writings and documents," Chapter III culls ideas from critical literature in education, psychology, psychiatry, theology, and medicine "to construct a societal view of death in relationship to the child." Chapter IV reviews critical works on the subject of death in children's literature; Chapter V analyzes the attitudes of children's theatre people; Chapter VI analyzes the topic in terms of typical children's plays; and Chapter VII "considers atypical approaches in children's drama." The author concludes that the topic of death can and should be "openly and honestly presented to children in their drama."

Gibson, Lois Rauch. "Attitudes toward Childhood in Eighteenth-Century British Fiction." DAI 36: 4508-09 A. University of Pittsburgh, 1975. 171 pp.
Although Gibson's dissertation is concerned primarily with the literature of Hobbes, Locke, Rousseau, Defoe, Smollet, Richardson, and Fielding, Chapter Five, the final one, is devoted exclusively to literature written for children in the eighteenth century—literature which had grown in popularity and importance during the century. "This chapter considers possible reasons for the development of the two genres [adult and child fiction] at this time, and it examines the similarities and differences between attitudes toward and depiction of children in literature written for them and those in literature written for adults."

Jones, Daryl Emrys. "The Dime Novel Westerns: The Evolution of a
Popular Formula." DAI 35: 274-75 A. Michigan State University, 1974.
375 pp.

Jones primarily discusses the simultaneous emergence of the dime-
novel western and the stereotyped western hero who "as the guardian
of the future, whether backwoodsman, plainsman, cowboy, or noble
outlaw. . . . , was a personification of the ideal world, a hybrid character who reconciled the popularly cherished values of the civilized East
with the equally cherished values of the wilderness West." Jones
analyzes the conventional plots, the traditional romances, the use of
quest themes, and the general popularity of dime-novel westerns for
both an adult and a child audience.

Kraus, Willis Keith. "A Critical Survey of the Contemporary
Adolescent-Girl Problem Novel." DAI 35: 7910 A. Southern Illinois
University, 1974. 118 pp.

Kraus' dissertation is a survey of the literature written for girls between
the ages of twelve and seventeen and published since 1969. He feels
that this contemporary body of literature contains more "sophisticated
subject matter and maturer themes," than the earlier works of authors
like Rosamond du Jardin and Betty Cavanna. For Kraus, "adolescent-
girl problem novels" contain· as heroine "a girl still in some stage of
physical growth and maturation who must cope with serious problems
such as sexual identity, pregnancy, racial conflict, mental illness or
physical handicaps, and drugs." Twenty-one representative novels
were selected for the survey, and the author concludes that "this transi-
tional period in adolescent fiction will be viewed [in later years] as a
truly revolutionary turning point in adolescent fiction."

Landford, William T., III. "Prisoners and Children: Forms and Growth in
Dickens' Novels." DAI 36: 4512-13 A. Emory University, 1975. 361 pp.

Landford's dissertation is a thorough analysis of *David Copperfield*,
Oliver Twist, and *Great Expectations*. He notes that in each, Dickens
"centers the narrative around the growth and progress toward maturity
of a single character," in these cases: a child. He is also concerned with
the intense morality of a Dickens novel, nowhere more apparent than
when the major character enters the novel as a child.

Linder, Lyle Dean. "Children in the Literary Works of Stephen Crane."
DAI 35: 5413-14 A. Duke University, 1974. 424 pp.

The major thesis of Linder's study is that "Before *Maggie*, [Crane's]
literary children were stock figures only, useful for panorama, irony,
and humor. While these functions continued to be refined, Crane began
to take careful stock of the child mind, of early social experiences, and
of the ways adults influence malleable young persons placed in their
care. The world of childhood from *Maggie* through *Whilomville Stories*
continues a nearly complete *comédie humaine* in miniature reflecting

generally on the short comings of adult behavior and upon the perils of the human condition. . . ." By analyzing Crane's child world, Linder "sorts out the range and relationships of Crane's literary uses of childhood." He concludes that Crane's "child fiction supports the same serious concerns as his purely adult fiction. . . ."

Mc Kenzie, Patricia Alice. "*The Last Battle:* Violence and Theology in the novels of C. S. Lewis." DAI 36: 907 A. University of Florida, 1974. 297 pp.

McKenzie traces the theme of the last battle through Lewis' *Till We Have Faces;* the Narnia series; the space trilogy, *That Hideous Strength, Out of the Silent Planet;* and his unfinished novel *After Ten Years.* "Topics considered are: issues underlying war, depiction of foes, emphasis on weaponry, use of martial imagery, presence of verbal violence, and participation of female characters in a traditionally male heroic ethic."

Mashiach, Sellina. "Allegory in Children's Theatre and Drama." DAI 37: 38 A. University of Kansas, 1975. 243 pp.

The midsection of Mashiach's dissertation is "an allegorical interpretation, a structural analysis of the literary sources . . . and a dramatic analysis that determines those dramatic means and those theatrical devices by which the secondary levels of meaning become accessible to both the child audience's intellect and imagination." She applies these analyses to *The Blue Bird, Punch and Judy, Androcles and the Lion, Little Red Ridinghood,* and *Hansel and Gretel.*

Neuleib, Janice Witherspoon. "The Concept of Evil in the Fiction of C. S. Lewis." DAI 35: 4539. University of Illinois-Champaign, 1974. 196 pp.

While Neuleib does not focus primarily on Lewis' fiction for children, she does map out his theories on evil based on his *Preface to Paradise Lost, Mere Christianity, The Screw Tape Letters, The Great Divorce,* and *Till We Have Faces.* And her conclusions are applicable to Lewis' science-fiction trilogy and to the Narnia books, both coming late in his career and both exhibiting his full mastery of a theory of evil. "As Lewis developed as creative artist, his evil characters became more vivid, as did his good characters, but never did the evil characters lose that particular quality of school boy nastiness that is Lewis' trademark. They are always wanting to possess and devour other characters out of a sort of spiritual starvation, growing from their own emptiness and their personal lack of worth."

O'Hare, Colman. "Charles Williams, C. S. Lewis and J. R. R. Tolkien: Three Approaches to Religion in Modern Fiction." DAI 36: 1532 A. University of Toronto, 1973. Obtainable directly from the National Library of Canada at Ottawa.

O'Hare shows the literary link between Williams, Lewis, and Tolkien and questions "whether dogma destroys art or whether art can transcend propaganda." He does not spend much time on Lewis Narnia books; however Chapter VI deals exclusively with Tolkien's *Lord of the Rings* trilogy. O'Hare concludes that art can circumvent propaganda and even triumph over it.

Parker, Patricia Anne Falstad. "Responses of Adolescents and Librarians to Selected Contemporary Fiction." DAI 35: 5357 A. University of Minnesota, 1974. 145 pp.

This analytical dissertation investigates "responses of early adolescents and of junior high school librarians to selected pieces of contemporary fiction written specifically for the adolescent, *i. e.,* Paula Fox's *Blowfish Live in the Sea* and Jill Paton Walsh's *Fireweed.* One-hundred-and-twenty-seven eighth graders and eighty-one librarians were tested.

Philips, Michael John. "Cultural Myths in Victorian Boys' Books by Marryat,. Hughes, Stevenson, and Kipling." DAI 36: 5325 A. Indiana University, 1975. 229 pp.

Philips notes that "Some Victorian boys' books present attitudes to culture and maturation that run counter to 'official' teaching. They attempt to salvage the 'natural' boy from the encroaching rigidity of the period. The ten books explored in the dissertation are Frederick Marryat's *Peter Simple* (1834); *Mr. Midshipman Easy* (1836), and *The Settlers in Canada* (1844); Thomas Hughes' *Tom Brown's Schooldays* (1857); Robert Louis Stevenson's *Treasure Island* (1883), *Kidnapped* (1886), and *David Balfour* (1893); and Rudyard Kipling's *The Jungle Book* (1894–95), *Captains Courageous* (1897), and *Kim* (1901).

Regan, Frederich Scott. "The History of the International Children's Theatre Association from Its Founding to 1975." DAI 37: 39 A. University of Minnesota, 1975. 299 pp.

Regan traces the history and impact of ASSITEJ from 1964 through 1974. He is particularly concerned with the ingredients which caused its foundation and the impact of the association on American and Canadian children's theatre. He acknowledges that the "progress made in easing the logistic, semantic, and philosophic differences that separate national approaches to children's theatre has been slow, but significant."

Taylor, Sally Thorne. "Children in Shakespeare's Dramaturgy." DAI 36: 2228 A. University of Utah, 1975. 131 pp.

Taylor is concerned with Shakespeare's treatment of children and childhood, specifically in *Titus Andronicus, Macbeth, The Merry Wives of Windsor, Love's Labours Lost, Henry V, Henry VI, Parts I and III, King John, King Lear,* and *A Midsummer-Night's Dream.*

Zeigler, Robert Earl. "Children and the Power of Imagination: A Study of the Child in the Works of Emile Zola, Alphonse Daudet, Jules Renard, Pierre Loti and Marcel Schwob." DAI 35: 5434-35 A. Cornell University, 1974. 353 pp.

Like Linder's study previously noted Ziegler's point of attack is on the distinct interest shown in children and childhood in otherwise adult literature. He notes that this interest, in French literature, was virtually nonexistent before the middle of the eighteenth century. He focuses on Zola's *La Faute de l'abbé Mouret*; autobiographical works by Daudet, Renard, and Loti; Daniel Eyssette's *Le Petit Chose*; Renard's *Poil de Carotte*; and other works primarily in the nineteenth century.

Index to Volumes 1-5

Compiled by Constance Gremore

This index consists of two sections, a general section and a book-review section. The general section includes authors, titles, and subjects. The names of reviewers can also be found in the general section with the letter "R" following the volume and page numbers on which the review appears. Passing references to subjects (whether they be the names of children's authors, titles, etc.) have not been included in the index. Only references to extended discussions are listed. In the book-review section, entries have been made for authors, titles, and illustrators of books reviewed.

Each entry is followed by an indication of volume number and page numbers. Page references are to all pages on which the item is discussed, whether or not by name on each page.

Pseudonyms, rather than the real names of children's authors, are used in the index.

Works discussed as series are entered under series, such as *Oz* books or *Pooh* books, not under individual titles.

Entries such as English literature, American literature, etc. are limited to general discussions. For discussions of specific works, see individual authors' names and titles.

Entries are filed in a straight word-by-word alphabetical sequence, without regard for punctuation.

GENERAL INDEX

folktales, 2:247; 3:61, 63
"For the Good of the Country:
Cultural Values in American
Juvenile Fiction, 1825-60,"
5:40-51
Foreman, Stephen Howard,
3:210-211 R
Fors Clavigera, 1:62, 67-68
French literature, Middle ages
4:51-58; 17th century 1:37-41;
20th century 1:162, 165-167,
170-171
French verse, 2:197, 202-205
"From Fantasy to Reality:
Ruskin's *King of the Golden
Rivers,* St. George's Guild, and
Ruskin, Tennessee," 1:62-73
"From Shakespeare to Brooklyn:
New Trends in Children's
Poetry," 5:273-285

Gagnon, Laurence, 1:98-103
"Philosophy and Fantasy";
2:61-66 "Webs of Concern: *The
Little Prince* and *Charlotte's
Web*"
Gandhi, Madame Indira, 4:3-9
Gardner, Martin, 2:110-118 "John
Dough and the Cherub"
Gassendi, Pierre, 1:37-41
gentleman, 1:58-61
George, Jean Graighead, 3:131-139
German literature, 20th century
2:173-191; 3:45-46; 5:162-180
Der gestiefulte Kater, 2:180, 187
Gibson, Donald B., 2:215-217 R;
2:230-234 R
gnomic expressions, 1:16-17, 19-20
The Governess, 3:108-109
Grahame, Kenneth, 4:80-90
Graves, Robert, 2:130-131
Great Expectations, 2:152-159
Greek literature, 3:56-60
Greene, David L., 3:173-176 "The
Concept of Oz"
Green, William H., 5:288-293 R
Greene, David L., 4:192-193 R
Greene, Graham, 2:130-131, 137

Grimm brothers, 1:31-35; see also:
fairy tales
Grips; see Reichskabarett
Griswold, Jerome, 3:103-106
"Sacrifice and Mercy in Wilde's
'The Happy Prince'"
Gruelle, Johnny, 3:140-146
Gruppe Spielumwelt, 2:185-186
Gueron, Jacqueline, 2:197-208
"Children's Verse and the
Halle-Keyser Theory of
Prosody"
Guiliano, Edward F., 4:186-191 R

The Half Sisters, 5:157-161
Hall, Joan Joffe, 2:235-236 R
Halle-Keyser theory, 2:197-208
"The Happy Prince," 3:103-106
Harriet the Spy, 4:120-126; 5:22
"Harriet the Spy: Milestone,
Masterpiece?" 4:120-126
Harris, Benjamin, 5:53-56
Haskins, Jim, "Racism and Sexism
in Children's Nonfiction,"
5:141-147
Havholm, Peter, 4:91-104 "Kipling
and Fantasy"
Heffernan, Tom, 4:203-209 R
Heidegger, Martin, 2:61
Heidi 5:163-167
Heisig, James W., 3:23-35
"Pinocchio: Archetype of the
Motherless Child"
Helbig, Alethea K., 4:30-35
"Manabozho of the North
Central Woodlands: Hero of
Folk Tale or Myth?"
Helson, Ravenna 3:66-75 "The
Psychological Origins of Fantasy
for Children in Mid-Victorian
England"; 5:22-39 "Change,
Tradition and Critical Styles in
the Contemporary World of
Children's Books"
Henke, James T., 5:130-140 "Six
Characters in Search of a
Family: the Novels of Paul
Zindel"

BOOK REVIEW INDEX

Contributors and Editors

PETER S. ANDERSON'S special interest is the Renaissance. He also is interested in children's literature.

MARILYN APSELOFF, an assistant professor of English at Kent State University, Kent, Ohio, teaches children's literature.

ELIZABETH ARNOLD is a Canadian illustrator whose children's book is being published by Tundra Press.

JAN BAKKER, Ph.D., University of Tennessee, 1976, writes on the nineteenth-century pastoral novel and in children's literature.

KATHLEEN BLAKE, assistant professor of English at the University of Washington, Seattle, is the author of *Play, Games, and Sport: The Literary Works of Lewis Carroll* (Ithaca: Cornell University Press).

BENNETT A. BROCKMAN has written on medieval literature in *MLQ, Speculum, Medievalia et Humanistica*, and *Medieval Studies*. He led the first permanent group on children's literature of the Modern Language Association and is also active in an advisory capacity with the Children's Literature Association. He is at work on a book which examines the consequences of the birth of children's literature as a distinct genre.

FRANCELIA BUTLER is the editor of *Sharing Literature with Children* (New York: Longman), and other books on children's literature and on the Renaissance, including *The Strange Critical Fortunes of Shakespeare's Timon of Athens* (Ames: Iowa State University Press).

JOSEPH CARY is the author of *Three Modern Italian Poets: Saba, Ungaretti, Montale* (New York: New York University Press, 1969).

CHARITY CHANG is reviewer of children's books for the *Hartford Courant* and coeditor of the forthcoming *Children's Literature in the Seventeenth Century*. (New York: Stonehill Publications). She has lectured widely on children's literature.

MARGARET P. ESMONDE is an associate professor of English at Villanova University. She is editor of the *Newsletter of the Children's Literature Association* and a member of the ChLA Board of Directors. She is also Children's Book Editor of the Fantasy Association.

JANE MERRILL FILSTRUP is Assistant Director of the Information Center on Children's Cultures, a service of the United States Committee for UNICEF, New York City.

EDWARD G. FISHER published the original volumes of *Children's Literature*. He has made a study of children's literature and the Bible.

RACHEL FORDYCE, who teaches English at Virginia Polytechnic and State University, Blacksburg, is Executive Secretary of the Children's Literature Association. She is the author of *Children's Theatre and Creative Dramatics: An Annotated Bibliography of Critical Works* (Boston: G. K. Hall).

JAMES A. FREEMAN is an Associate Professor of English at the University of Massachusetts, Amherst.

MARTIN GARDNER, author of over one hundred scientific and critical works, is best known to students of children's literature for his *Annotated Alice* and his introductions to several of L. Frank Baum's *Oz* books. He has also contributed some eighty short stories to *Humpty Dumpty*.

DAVID L. GREENE, Chairman, Department of English, Piedmont College, Demorest, Georgia, was editor of *The Baum Bugle*, 1968-73. He has published books and articles on children's literature and was a coeditor of *Bibliographica Oziana* (The International Wizard of Oz Club, 1976).

CONSTANCE GREMORE is a member of the reference staff of the Education Library at the University of Minnesota in Minneapolis. She is presently doing free-lance indexing and research consulting in education and the humanities.

JOAN JOFFE HALL is a prolific reviewer for various newspapers and journals and is active as a writer and teacher of Women's Literature.

MICHAEL PATRICK HEARN is the author of *The Annotated Wizard of Oz* and is a contributing editor of *Cricket*.

FATHER JAMES W. HEISIG, Ph.D., Cambridge University, teaches at Nanzan Institute for Religion and Culture, Nagoya, Japan.

ALETHEA K. HELBIG is an assistant professor of English at Eastern Michigan University, where she helped to develop a minor in children's literature and an interdepartmental major in drama and literature for the young. She has written articles on literature for children and coedited an anthology of poetry for children. She is a board member of the ChLA.

SAMUEL JOHNSON received an honorary doctorate from Cambridge.

CHRISTA KAMENETSKY is Associate Professor of English at Central Michigan University, Mt. Pleasant.

NARAYAN KUTTY teaches children's literature at Eastern Connecticut State College. A specialist in modern British literature, he is also interested in the comparative study of Eastern and Western literature for children.

CLAUDIA LEWIS has had a distinguished career at the Bank Street College of Education, New York City. She continues to write on children's literature and on poetry.

ALISON LURIE, novelist and critic, teaches children's literature among other subjects at Cornell University.

NELLIE MACCASLIN is a professor of Children's Theatre at New York University. She is the author of several books on the subject, including *Creative Dramatics in the Classroom* (New York: David McKay Company) and is President of the Children's Theatre Association.

RUTH K. MACDONALD teaches in the Department of Humanities and Communications, Cook College, Rutgers University, New Brunswick.

BETTY JO MCGRADE, Ph.D. Psychology, Yale University, is currently Clinical Director of the Parent-Child Resource Centers of Danielson and Williamantic, Connecticut, and Clinical Assistant Professor, Department of Pediatrics, University of Connecticut School of Medicine.

MERADITH TILBURY MCMUNN has written and lectured extensively on medieval children's literature. She heads the first seminar on medieval children in literature, Modern Language Association. She also is the author, with William Robert McMunn, of a forthcoming work on children and literature in the Middle Ages, to be published by Stonehill Publications.

LEONARD R. MENDELSOHN is an Associate Professor of English at Concordia University, Montreal. Besides children's literature, he has written on Renaissance drama, Milton, Kafka, and other subjects.

ROSS MILLER, Ph.D., Cornell University, has been an editor of *University Review* and the *Metropolitan Review*.

FRANCIS J. MOLSON, Ph.D. University of Notre Dame, teaches children's literature in the English Department of Central Michigan University, Mount Pleasant, where he is an Associate Professor. He is a Board member of the Children's Literature Association and has recently completed an annotated bibliography of juvenile science fiction.

PATRICIA MORLEY is the author of four books and several score articles on various aspects of Canadian and Commonwealth literature.

WILLIAM T. MOYNIHAN, author of a study of Dylan Thomas, is Chairman of the English Department at the Unversity of Connecticut.

PETER F. NEUMEYER is the author of *The Faithful Fish* and other books for children. He has taught English at Berkeley, Harvard, and Stony Brook, and is currently Chairman of the English Department at the University of West Virginia.

MARIAN PARRY lectures on the illustration of children's books at Radcliffe College. She has illustrated numerous children's books, including *The Ballad of the Long-Tailed Rat* and *The Space-Child's Mother-Goose*.

THOMAS J. ROBERTS is a Professor of English at the University of Connecticut who specializes in science fiction literature and literary critical theory.

WILLIAM ROSEN is the author of *Shakespeare and the Craft of Tragedy* and editor, with Barbara Rosen, of the Signet edition of Shakespeare's *Julius Caesar*.

GLENN E. SADLER teaches children's literature at Point Loma College, San Diego, California. His doctorate is from the University of Aberdeen, Scotland. He is the editor of the centennial edition of *George MacDonald's Fairytales and Stories, The Gifts of the Child Christ: Fairy Tales and Stories for All Ages* (Grand Rapids, Michigan: Eerdmans Publishing Company; 1973).

WILLIAM E. SHEIDLEY has written on Elizabethan poetry for several scholarly journals and is currently preparing a work on Barnabe Googe for the Twayne Series.

ISAAC BASHEVIS SINGER is a great contemporary Yiddish writer.

JON C. STOTT teaches children's literature at the University of Alberta, Edmonton. He is a pioneer in the scholarly study of children's literature.

C. H. TALBOT of the Wellcome Institute of the History of Medicine, London, England, is the author of more than thirty books and editions on all aspects of medievalia.

JENNIFER R. WALLER teaches in the department of English, Dalhousie University, Halifax, Nova Scotia.

RON WALTER teaches Russian literature and language at the University of California, Irvine, and translates contemporary poets.

WARREN WOODEN is Associate Professor in the English Department of Marshall University, Huntington, West Virginia.